In the Nick of Time

IN THE NICK OF TIME

Peter Kirsten's Life in Cricket

Telford Vice

VIKING

VIKING

Published by the Penguin Group
27 Wrights Lane, London W8 5TZ, England
Viking Penguin, a division of Penguin Books USA Inc, 375 Hudson Street, New York, New York
10014, USA
Penguin Books Australia Ltd, Ringwood, Victoria, Australia
Penguin Books Canada Ltd, 10 Alcorn Avenue, Toronto, Ontario, Canada
M4V 3B2
Penguin Books (NZ) Ltd, 182-190 Wairau Road, Auckland 10, New Zealand
Penguin Books, Amethyst Street, Theta Ext 1, Johannesburg, South Africa

Penguin Books Ltd, Registered Offices: Harmondsworth, Middlesex, England

First published 1996

Copyright © Telford Vice 1996

All rights reserved
The moral right of the author has been asserted

ISBN 0 670 86914 7

Typeset by Positive Proof cc in 11/13 pt Times
Printed and bound by National Book Printers, Drukkery Street, Goodwood, Cape Town
Cover photograph by courtesy of Allsport/Touchline
Cover design by Hadaway Illustration & Design

To
Lois Ruth

Contents

Foreword

Peter Kirsten is one of the 'three musketeers' that Western Province cricket produced in the 1970s. Each one of the 'musketeers' has had a distinguished career: Allan Lamb became one of England's greatest batsmen in the 1980s, Garth le Roux was one of South Africa's great fast bowlers, and Peter is one of the ten best batsmen South Africa has ever produced.

Peter's brilliance was obvious from a very early age – he scored 100 against Northern Transvaal for South African Schools in 1974. And his class was underlined in 1976 when he made six centuries in seven innings, four of them successive. But his stunning performances for Western Province in the early part of his career were unfortunately limited to first-class level because of South Africa's ban from international cricket.

The international restrictions meant that county cricket in England was the only way of competing with the greats of other countries – and this Peter did with distinction.

The Transvaal/Western Province clashes during the years of isolation were like Test matches for us. In the forefront of the Western Province team was P N Kirsten and he caused many a headache for Transvaal – not only with his batting but also with his fielding in the covers that must surely rank with the likes of Colin Bland and, currently, Jonty Rhodes. There was not a batsman in the country who did not take note of where Peter was standing on the field every over.

When the rebel series came along Peter showed his determination and the fact that he was an extremely gutsy player as well, even against the best that the West Indies, England and Australia could offer.

Happily, South Africa was readmitted to international cricket at the end of 1991 and, amid some drama, Peter Kirsten was included in the World Cup squad for Australia and New Zealand in 1992, where he was probably runner-up to Martin Crowe as Man of the Tournament. His brief career in Test cricket enabled him to post a Test century and Man of the Match honours at Headingley in 1994.

Naas Botha can thank his lucky stars that Peter decided to concentrate on cricket – his rugby talent early in his career was immense. All of us in cricket were extremely fortunate that he made this decision as we have been able to witness and enjoy his wonderful talent over all these years.

His story tells it all.

Clive Rice

Acknowledgements

The author and publishers express their appreciation to all those who gave permission for the use of their photographs.

Every effort has been made to trace photographers – not always easy over a period of some twenty years – and we apologise for any inadvertent infringement of copyright. We will be pleased to make appropriate amendments and acknowledgements in any future editions of *In the Nick of Time*.

Paradoxically, writing the story of Peter Kirsten's life in cricket, one man's adventure, has meant drawing on a range of other books and publications as well as on extensive interviews and conversations with him and those closest to him.

Among the sources utilised were the relevant volumes of *Protea Assurance Cricket Annual* and *Wisden's Cricketers' Almanack, The Cricketer* and newspaper cuttings from the *Argus, Cape Times* (both Cape Town), the *Sunday Times* (Johannesburg), the *Evening Telegraph* (Derby), the *Daily Telegraph* (London), and the *Daily Dispatch* (East London).

Naturally, the growing library of South African cricket books was an important well of reference. Among the titles that helped enrich this book were *Giants of South African Cricket* (Don Nelson), to which Michael Owen-Smith contributed the chapter on Kirsten; *Return of the Prodigal* (Jonathan Ball) by Colin Bryden; *Kepler: the Biography* (Pelham) by

Edward Griffiths, and *South Africa's Cricket Captains: from Melville to Wessels* (Southern) by Jackie McGlew and Trevor Chesterfield.

Thanks must go to Trevor Beling of East London for the extended use of his collection of Protea Annuals, as well as to Rob Abbott of Stutterheim for his help with information from *Wisden*.

Peter's wife Tuffy and his mother Lois have diligently kept comprehensive scrapbooks over the years and they proved invaluable in this project.

The encouragement of friends, colleagues and family – not to mention positively dangerous amounts of the strongest espresso, the odd Havana and a celebratory bottle of champagne in the aftermath of a particularly harrowing weekend – have all contributed to preserving the author's sanity.

Lastly, the stoic manner in which the author's wife Teresa accepted the invasion of this book and its untidy entourage into her home and marriage was the deciding factor in its completion.

Introduction

There were peaks, there were valleys. But it was always my way to try to scale mountains rather than merely stride the plains where the gradient is more gentle. The comfort zone is a pleasant place to be, but my perpetual pursuit of yet another sporting challenge has always disturbed that area.

I suppose the challenge started with beach cricket at Yellowsands, a beautiful stretch of beach and river along the East Cape coast, and with backyard battles with youthful friends Micky McClellan, Ian Greig, Deon Dreyer and, later, Peter and John Whitelaw, Warren Kruger and Mike Minnaar. Six and out over the neighbour's fence was always the most fruitful way to go. One hand, one bounce was like being run out off a no-ball, and you were never out caught behind off the wall. 'I missed the ball by miles!' always caused a moral dilemma.

Meaningful tuition came from father Noel, but there was never any pressure. Refreshments and attention were always available from mother Lois, and sister Cheryl was an able fielder and early confidante. The only real scoldings from administration in those days were from Lois after great shots had shattered window panes at number 67 Devereux Avenue, East London. Les Liss of Selborne Primary later refined the zeal. Watching Noel keep wicket for Border, Cheryl swim for Border and Lois participate in regular tennis sessions filled me with great pride, and there was much to live up to.

They were, without doubt, carefree, joyful hours of healthy development – even if I couldn't dribble a soccer ball as well as Micky McClellan or tackle like Deon Dreyer or play tennis like Roy Raffan. I certainly couldn't fish like my old man!

Professional cricket was something of a fantasy, but the lure of rugby and soccer was very real. Flyhalf Keith Oxlee of Natal and centre forward Bobby Chalmers of Durban City were my boyhood heroes. Buster Farrer of Border was a brilliant batsman, but he was far too good to try to emulate.

'Like father, like son,' they say. Noel built roads and airport runways. That was good enough for me – regardless of whether it was in Oklahoma, the middle of the Karoo, Pietermaritzburg, Mariental, Bedford or East London. A pity, then, that science, physics and geometry were to become my worst subjects at school!

A six-month stint in Mariental, Namibia (where Lois was stung by a scorpion) when I was eight years old proved to be a real tester. The Afrikaans-medium school I attended had an athletics track of fine gravel containing tiny thorns (*dubbeltjies*). This greatly improved my time in the 100-yard dash – it was like running on hot coals. I remember stabbing the girl who sat next to me in class just above the eye with a pencil in revenge for her putting chilli on the end of the pencil which I used to chew absent mindedly. I was punished for this vicious act and branded a *rooinek*. Cricket was non-existent in the desert, and I pleaded to return to Selborne.

Back in East London, John and Elaine Cowie were wonderful Sunday hosts. The roast beef was good, but the ice-cream and chocolate sauce was my weekly treat – far better than hostel food could ever be. Their sons Ian and Andrew, and later Neil, became good mates of mine and cricket on John's lawn was always entertaining. I scored many a ton and took some brilliant catches in the Cowie paddock!

Sandy and Joyce Greig fumed when their son Ian and I disturbed their afternoon nap with the sound of leather against willow and the occasional shattering of glass. Tony, of course, was a man of stature playing for Sussex and naturally we hero-worshipped him.

Apart from parents, family and friends, there were others involved in the development of character, that vital part of a young sportsman's growth: teachers. When I was nine years old, Les Liss spent many hours throwing cricket balls my way. Les was a cricket fanatic. David Rees and his wife Margie were pillars of strength while I was at boarding school. David was a rugby fundi, as was John Heather. John Heather was a rugby player himself – tough and disciplined. He was a great coach and one looked up to him as a kid. It is interesting that academically I had one of my most fruitful years with him as my standard three teacher. I'm not too sure what happened after that!

Bunny Stevens was headmaster of Selborne Primary at the time. Most of us feared him as he was strict and had quite a threatening presence. It was thanks to him that I learned never to be late for duties, especially if you were in a position of responsibility – which I was, as headboy, during my final year there. The school bell, a large one, hung from the main corridor ceiling and signalled punishment if one was seen standing under it for any length of time. One particular Monday was a bad one for me. I arrived late for an early morning duty called 'scholar patrol'. Bunny ordered me to his office, caned me three times on the backside, and made me stand 'under the bell' for two hours. I had to ring the bell at the end of each lesson. The corridor acted as the main thoroughfare for the whole school. Having a stream of boys on their way to classes passing their headboy under the bell was a terrible humiliation and embarrassment to me – although in a way I was rather pleased at having to stand for a while as my backside was pretty sore!

In the cricketing world being on time is a necessary discipline, and I have never forgotten my debt to Bunny Stevens.

The next comfort zone – at Selborne College – was disturbed by migration as a 13-year-old to another great school, the South African College (SACS) in Cape Town. In Newlands, with SACS above the railway line and Rondebosch Boys' High below it, it could have been quite easy to go off the rails. But I'm pleased to say that I managed not to.

There is no doubt that what kept me on track during my turbulent high school years was the superb circle of friends I built up during that time. Naturally, rugby and cricket and the Western Province sporting culture formed the basis of this closeness. How could I ever forget the Minnaars, Prices, Lloyds, Krugers, Tindales, Rabies, Whitelaws, Jacksons and Jenningses of this world.

There were more fantastic teachers at SACS. Andre Abrahams took over from Les Liss in the cricket department. Andre admired Australian cricket and waxed lyrical about Bobby Simpson, Keith Stackpole, Ian Redpath and Doug Walters. He had interesting theories, interesting technical advice and was always interesting to listen to. He was a dedicated cricket coach, unorthodox in many ways, and he provided me with a wonderful source of motivation. I remember one particular weekend when we lost badly. The following Tuesday was pouring with rain, but Andre made us field for an hour in shocking conditions because he was angry at the way we had lost.

From time to time I have contacted Andre for advice, in particular just before the World Cup in 1992. It is always good to see him standing behind a net studying a player intently.

From captain of the Selborne U13a rugby team to the SACS B team! That was my introduction to SACS sport. My first coach, for both rugby and cricket, was a wonderfully entertaining man named Johnny Ince. Eccentric in many ways, he had a great heart – and was also loyal to his incumbent flyhalf, Andrew Steyn, who also happened to be his team's vice-captain. Because my migration from East London to Cape Town occurred during mid-year, or mid-season if you like, I knew my transfer wasn't going to be smooth – it never is. Schoolboys can be cruel and the talk in the school corridors was, 'Hear there's a new guy arrived and he fancies himself a bit at rugby and cricket.' One of them actually came up to me and said, 'You'll never take Andrew Steyn's position!' (I learned later that he was the team's hooker.)

Because I had always been the captain and an A team player at Selborne, it was a shock to my system to have this B team tag in Johnny Ince's U13 domain – even if it was only to last for three games. Three weeks can seem like a lifetime to a 13-year-old and I turned practices into matches in my determination to regain my pedestal.

Johnny Ince could have suffocated a young man's spirit, but he never did. On the contrary, he coaxed and motivated. Andrew Steyn became a fine, attacking inside centre and the two of us became firm friends during our school rugby days.

Robin Whiteford ('The Boss') was headmaster of SACS. He was an academic genius and a born leader and he became a legend at this proud school. He possessed an intelligent wit and could either have you in stitches of laughter or destroy your ego with one simple sentence. The Boss also loved his cricket. When, as a rather tense 13-year-old, I arrived for my first day at my new school, he walked me to my new class saying, 'Laddie, keep your head, play straight and you'll be fine. If you have any problems or queries, appeal: you know where my office is.' And he then proceeded to introduce me to my new teacher and class mates. I understood Mr Whiteford's language and I appreciated it.

SACS has a very strong Old Boys' Union and this was apparent 21 years later when the Union sent me numerous faxes warmly congratulating me on scoring my first and only Test hundred for South Africa against England at Headingley in 1994.

My wife Tuffy, Lois, Cheryl, Don and Noel were my greatest supporters. So, too, was younger brother Andrew. It gave me tremendous pleasure to see Andrew go on to play many games of rugby for Western Province at scrumhalf. In many ways, when watching Andrew play for WP, I think I was seeing myself – as I would so dearly have loved to have played more games in the blue and white hooped jersey under the magnificent Morné du Plessis.

Andrew has a great sense of humour and I always loved his comment after each game when, battered and bruised, he would tell me, 'Another *koevertjie* (envelope), brother.' So much for amateurism! Yes, they used to get paid R800 'expenses' per game. That's a pretty high petrol bill from Newlands or Stellenbosch to Rondebosch!

Andrew, a talented sportsman, also represented Western Province B at cricket and, later, brothers Gary and Paul would excel for South Africa and Western Province with similar sporting prowess. It is such a tragedy that father, Noel, did not live to enjoy it all.

And all the while Lois was a quiet source of inspiration and steadiness.

Delving into the past has, perhaps, been a bit of self-indulgence on my part, but all these events and people were instrumental in my gradual inclination towards becoming a professional cricketer.

And so I left behind the early years and the people who had been such bastions of support, thinking I was ready to handle whatever peaks and valleys came my way. In many instances I have been below par, but I am happy that in general my intentions and actions in the cricket world have been honest and productive, if not impulsive.

'You only get out what you put in.' School, university, Western Province, Derbyshire, South Africa, Border. Naturally, international cricket is more suited to the younger man and, sure, I would like to have played more for South Africa with the likes of Allan Lamb, Eddie Barlow, Hylton Ackerman, Clive Rice, Garth le Roux, Denys Hobson, Ken McEwan, Kepler Wessels, Jimmy Cook, Henry Fotheringham, Barry Richards, Mike Procter, and Adrian Kuiper, among others.

But as time went by, one became more understanding and tolerant of the reasons for South Africa's isolation during those dark apartheid years. For me, the most humbling fact of all is represented by the person of Nelson Mandela. A man who had been jailed for 27 years and then becomes president of his country without showing bitterness towards the past is truly admirable. I am simply grateful for the opportunities that came my way. After all, we are only servants of the game.

Sport, we are taught at school should be an adventure, a healthy exercise to keep mind and soul together. And, as a 23-year-old, Derbyshire County Cricket Club in England offered me an adventure, a dream – and I was paid for it. It was a wonderful time, but it could last only five years.

The escape from the political infertility of South Africa at the time was thrilling, and being able to meet and play with different people from around the globe was in itself educational. I formed a close friendship with Derbyshire team-mate John Wright, later to become New Zealand captain. I simply loved batting with him and our left-hander/right-hander partnership flourished. He is still revered in Derbyshire. It is the South African cricket public's loss that they were not able to witness his batsmanship.

The Derbyshire folk treated me well and in many ways I am sorry that I didn't stay longer and score more hundreds and double hundreds for the Club. I know that one of my staunchest Derbyshire supporters, Brian Bowcock, would have loved that! Apart from the cricket, another great thing about returning to England with the South African team in 1994 was to see old English friends again.

After 17 years of marriage to Western Province cricket, I separated myself from this great cricketing province. I think I experienced all that one could hope for, or not hope for, in a cricket career and I will be forever grateful to the loyal Province supporters. Newlands is a great place and the traditions and culture of Western Province cricket made it an absolute wrench for me to decide to go to East London – but there was another challenge waiting. It was almost a 'calling' for me: something was unfinished in the Border. But I had toiled loyally for Western Province and still think of its cricket and rugby with passion.

The people of Border are a good sort and in cricketing spheres we have progressed amazingly over the last five years. Ian Howell has been a stoic on the playing front and, with his dedication to the Border cause, there is no doubt that he will become a respected administrator in the future. 'Boss' Lee Warren and Robbie Muzzell have set the standards and I enjoy being associated with the rising fortunes of Border cricket in this beleaguered part of South Africa. To lead Border to its first major trophy would make my cricket career as a player complete. After that ... well, I have much to offer, but only time will decide what it will be.

Why has this book been written? I'm not too sure myself as it has proved to be a lengthy process with much mental exertion involved. There was a lot of prompting from various sources and I finally succumbed to it and to my own 'gut' feelings that I should chronicle the events that have been a major part of my journey through life thus far.

Author Telford Vice, and Alison Lowry and Pam Thornley of Penguin South Africa have been my saviours and I thank them sincerely. But Tuffy has perhaps been the most creative of all: she saved us considerable mental strain by coming up with the title *In the Nick of Time*.

Peter Kirsten

1

Beginnings

The unshakeable triumph of youth shines from the faces of eleven of the twelve boys who square their shoulders and level their smooth, unblemished chins in the stuffily official photograph of the 1967 Selborne U12A cricket team. Their eyes knowing the joys of victories won and to come, their cheeks bursting with the promises of life, they are eternally 11 years old and more concerned about Chelsea buns and their next game of marbles than anything the real world might dare to set in their path. They are invincible.

To them, adolescence and all its turmoil is as much a mystery as the importance of schoolwork and not throwing socks under beds. Last week has long since evaporated into the cream soda, and tomorrow is another net practice. Today is what matters, and they can sit still just long enough for the photographer to push the button before rushing into their next adventure.

But one amongst this dozen is the unmistakable exception. Presiding in the centre of the black-and-white scene, the face of their captain, Peter Noel Kirsten, reflects not the carefree glow of his team-mates but an expression of ingrained discipline and an almost unsettling maturity. The crescent near his right eye, the legacy of a car accident, is but a metaphor for his wariness.

His lips are pulled into a thin smile, but the guarded eyes hold no glee. The hands from which will flow exquisite timing and craftsmanship are set, fingers interlocked, between lean thighs and vulnerable knees which poke, somehow embarrassed, out of short pants. His sleeves are rolled up with unnecessary precision; his socks are snug against his calves.

The picture is that of an older, wiser mind poured into the body of a mere sapling: even at the age of 10, Peter Kirsten surged ahead of his peers, most of whom were older than him.

Already he had bought respect with the valuable currency that would measure his worth for years to come: runs. A year earlier he had scored his first century, an undefeated 150 for Selborne U10A against sworn rivals Dale. Peter has little recollection of that innings, except that he fed off the wonder of it and was left brimming with exhilaration. But the boisterous reception given him by the rest of his adoring hostel that evening would linger as something to be cherished.

His father Noel Kirsten will be remembered for keeping wicket for Border from the mid-50s to 1960 and for producing two Test cricketers in Peter and Gary, provincial cricketers in Paul and Andrew – also a promising scrumhalf for Western Province – and a daughter, Cheryl, who swam for Border. Born in King William's Town in 1925, he was the quintessential Border man and the subsequent success of his sons turned him from a respected player in his own right into something of a folk hero among the cricket fraternity there and in Cape Town, where he died in 1986.

As a civil engineer, Noel travelled a great deal and Peter was put into boarding school, a time he recalls with both positive and negative memories. But the uncompromising life in the hostel did have its value. It was here that Peter's competitive instinct was sharpened and he has kept it keen throughout his career.

Whether it was being forced to pick up the dining-room bully's deliberately spilled peas, or to show what one was made of on the field, an unyielding image of toughness was what separated the best from the merely talented. And Peter was always going to be among the best.

Noel Kirsten's absence from Peter's formative years as a cricketer leaves a sad gulf of irony. It was, of course, Noel who was responsible for Peter's first explorations of the atmosphere and magic of cricket. While his father was on the field – in those days the drab Jan Smuts ground in East London – Peter was part of the legion of boys nearby, living out real and imagined episodes with oil drums and crudely hacked planks as props.

Scurrying around a cricket or rugby field is one of the bright memories Kirsten has of his childhood. And he found an escape of sorts with a bat in his hands or out on the rugby field, where he was noticed as a flyhalf with potential on both the physical and tactical battlefields. Fashioning runs or directing the orchestration of a try was in his blood. Importantly, Peter also discovered the acceptance that came with success on the sportsfield. Here was a world in which parents and background didn't seem to matter, and he wanted more of it and the friends he had made.

Peter's parents parted ways in 1967 and a year later came the most significant investment in his sporting future. Having already started his first year at Selborne College, after completing his time at the primary school as headboy, Peter moved to Cape Town, where his father had settled. The logic of the decision, prompted by his father after his mother, Lois, had moved to Amanzimtoti, could not be faulted.

Though the culture of competition was solidly anchored on the Border, sport there laboured under the Cinderella syndrome – more often than not, they weren't even invited to the provincial ball, let alone asked to dance. The mirror image that was Western Province glittered with proud tradition in both rugby and cricket. Not just that, but Newlands is home to the passionate spirit of South African rugby and cricket.

There are few sportsmen who approach a match in Cape Town without emotion cluttering their mental state. Those from up north detest the Newlands crowd, while the Province teams thrive on the rowdy, undying support. It was the place to be for a player of Peter's promise, and soon he was displaying his burgeoning talent in the colours of the South African College School, although Noel Kirsten had initially tried to enrol his son at Rondebosch Boys' High only to find there were no vacancies as the school year was already under way. Rondebosch, however, later netted the services of both Gary and Paul Kirsten.

As with almost all players of fine potential who go on to push the boundaries of their talent, Peter was able to tap into a constant source of astute, inspired coaching. At Selborne, Les Liss, David Rees and John Heather had shaped his budding game, while Andre Abrahams took over at SACS. He remembers endless hours facing Liss at Selborne. Their sessions, usually conducted with the morning's dew still untrampled by the urgent rush of schoolboy feet, played out the simple ritual of coach throwing to pupil, over and over and over …

Peter has adhered faithfully to Abrahams' lucid instruction in the fundamentals of batsmanship and has consulted him several times during his first-class career when he detected a technical flaw corrupting his efforts. Under such rare guidance, Peter rapidly reached the highest level: at age 13 he was included in the SACS First XI to play in the Cape Schools Week in Graaff-Reinet. It proved a memorable outing, with Peter batting third and scoring 98 not out against Grey High School with his side in trouble.

He was to play for the Western Province Nuffield team from 1971 to

1974, captaining the team in the last two years. At the age of 15 in his first Nuffield Week in Port Elizabeth, Peter blazed a trail of runs and wickets (in those days he competed for a spinning berth with Denys Hobson) but was not picked for the SA Schools team apparently because of his age.

In Johannesburg the next year he had, in his own words, 'a disaster', but he was back to form in Bulawayo in 1973 and was named twelfth man to the SA Schools team. It was no shame to find himself on the bench – the XI drew on the class of Allan Lamb, Ray Jennings, and a Grey College boy cast from much the same serious, smouldering mould as Peter himself: Kepler Wessels.

Less than a month before the start of the 1974 Nuffield Week, Peter made the headlines when he was selected to the Western Province team to play Eastern Province in a Currie Cup match at Newlands. Not only was he still at school, he had also not played any first league club cricket. But if the press and the cricketing fraternity thought that should have engendered respect in the cocky 18-year-old, they had their eyebrows lifted.

Peter remembers no great nervousness about his first Currie Cup innings, despite the fact that some of his cricketing heroes – notably Graeme Pollock and his captain Eddie Barlow – would be fellow gladiators in the match. Already an accomplished player, albeit at junior level, he took it all in his already confident stride. After all, SACS played in the 2A league – how difficult could it be?

As it turned out, it wasn't the most auspicious of début innings. Peter, batting fifth, made just five runs before falling to Dave Brickett but he didn't feel that bad – only four of his team-mates made it into double figures before Province were dismissed for 172, the first five wickets tumbling for 39 and Brickett and Rupert Hanley picking up three apiece. However, EP were reduced to 84 for four and eventually declared at 151 for nine. Graeme Pollock, their captain, rescued his side and dug himself out of something of a slump with an attractive 66 before becoming only the eighteenth player in the history of cricket to be given out handled the ball.

In the Province second innings there was a glimpse of what the wiry schoolboy had to offer. The first wicket fell at 11 and when Province bumbled along to 62 for three it seemed that Pollock's decision to declare 21 behind had been the right move. But Peter displayed the discipline and perseverance which were to become his hallmarks to add 75 for the sixth wicket with Peter Swart. He faced 177 deliveries and batted three and a half hours for his 50 before departing for 68.

Early in that innings he played forward and the ball popped up to the inimitable Lorrie Wilmot at short leg. Crusty, crafty cricketer that he was,

Wilmot bellowed an appeal. Not out, came the verdict. That gave Wilmot licence to verbally abuse the débutant whenever he was in earshot and for a while Peter was quite unsettled by what, for him, was a new cricketing tactic.

But he survived and, importantly, served notice: here was a player who seemed to have the discipline and self-belief to make it to the top. Province totalled 308 – a lead of 329 – but the match dwindled to a draw with EP six down for 296 and Pollock weighing in with 78.

Province's next match was also against EP, this time in Port Elizabeth. One solid innings does not a career make, Pollock's men might have said to themselves as they contemplated young Peter and how best to remove him. But Peter held the aces again, scoring 74 in another drawn match.

At the subsequent Nuffield Week there was no stopping the 18-year-old with the searching eyes of a poet, who celebrated passing matric with a flood of runs and was duly selected to the team proper and made vice-captain. Somehow Wessels was left out of the side and was not even given the consolation prize Peter had received a year earlier.

The tournament was held in Pretoria that year and the Northern Transvaal team which the SA Schools XI had to face contained the batting threats of Kevin Verdoorn and Alan Jordaan. But since Lee Barnard had won the toss and elected to put his schoolboys in, they had to contend with Peter first. And he was in no mood to go quietly. Instead, he hammered an undefeated 101, only the fifth century in SA Schools history, as his side totalled 225 for three on their way to a draw.

As Peter approached his first 50 the Northerns wicketkeeper Trevor Quirk, now a television commentator, felt he had illegally dislodged the bails and appealed for an apparently watertight case of hit wicket. But the umpires were unsighted, Peter survived, and went on to post his century. At the close, Northerns were hanging on at 180 for eight with Verdoorn's 57 and 42 from Jordaan keeping them in the match.

The arrival of Peter Kirsten as a player to watch on the domestic scene was thus completed. His languid timing, sound technique and, above all, his ability to make the best of the situation regardless of his own form, marked him as someone out of the ordinary.

But it might not have come together so neatly for this son of the Border who went on to bat his way to stardom under the protea of Western Province before coming home in 1990.

In 1972, as an impetuous 16-year-old, Peter yearned nostalgically for

East London and decided to return. His decision was the climax of two weeks of adolescent seething, a reckless period which resulted in him repeating standard nine at his own request. Noel Kirsten, who was working in Port Elizabeth at the time, was not to know his son had booked a plane ticket. However, when Peter alighted in PE en route to East London, he found a stern-faced Noel waiting for him. 'If you go back to East London, that's the end of your sporting career,' was the essence of Noel Kirsten's message to his son.

To someone with Peter's passion to play at the highest level, returning to East London at that stage would not have been a mere setback on the road to richer honours. It would indeed have been the end. Much as the Border had embedded its hooks in him, he could not deny that his father was right. Border sport was then a dead end for anyone with ambitions to play in the A section. The list of cricketers who learned to play and love the game in this small, parochial province before being forced to desert it in search of a higher challenge and a better living is depressingly long and includes such fine players as Ivor Foulkes, Kenny McEwan, Kenny Watson, Rodney Ontong, Chris Wilkins, Hylton Ackerman, Robbie Muzzell, Tony and Ian Greig, Daryll Cullinan, and rugby Springboks H O de Villiers, Andre de Wet and Ray Carlson.

Before Border were readmitted to the A section in 1991 there was no national exposure there, no chance of sports bursaries – only the depressing thought of unfulfilled potential.

The emotion of that episode at Port Elizabeth airport is still a raw gash in Peter's memory. He hadn't come that far to whimper back to Cape Town. But, listening to reason, he loaded his luggage into his father's car for a long, tense drive back to the Western Cape.

2

A Second Field of Dreams

Willow, leather and the rich smell of a summer's day have been part of Kirsten's life since the dawn of his sporting consciousness and his primary talents of discipline and perseverance have guided him to the highest peaks of batsmanship.

To the uninitiated it may seem he was born only to score runs, patrol the covers with the vigilance of an eagle, and make the important breakthrough with his significant, if not universally feared, off-spin bowling. But inside that 1,63m frame dwells not only a top class cricketer's heart and mind but also the physical and mental qualities of a man who knows how to uncoil the energy of a rugby backline.

Kirsten's first dabblings with football were on the soccer field. But there are few white South Africans who do not have a touch of rugby blood coursing through their veins. And it was to this code that Kirsten switched after his interest in soccer saw him labelled a sissy at Selborne. 'I didn't want that tag, so I changed to rugby,' was his logic.

That soccer should be regarded in any environment as a less manly pursuit than its cousin, rugby, does not make sense. In white South African schools, however, particularly in the era of segregated education, the only ball that mattered was oval shaped. In English-medium schools, especially those which imagined themselves as upholders of a peculiarly English way of South African life, cricket enjoyed a measure of parity.

But rugby bridged the chasm between two cultures and was at once a battlefield on which the English, or 'souties', and Afrikaners, or Dutchmen, carried on the festering conflicts sparked generations before.

On the Border it is different. Selborne, Dale and Queen's – all more than a century old and rooted in the English public school tradition – perennially vie for schools rugby supremacy in the region. Indeed, though there is no official national measure of the strength of schools rugby, all would feature prominently in a list of South Africa's top rugby-playing schools. Other schools challenge sporadically for the title of best on the Border but none can stay up there long enough to pose a serious threat to this trio.

A match between two of the three can draw crowds of up to 10 000. Far more people are interested enough to pay money to watch these schools play at grounds etched with character than to attend provincial games at the Basil Kenyon stadium. Much of the attraction is in the electric atmosphere. As each school fields at least 12 senior teams, pulling on a First XV jersey is in itself a notable achievement. Young as they are, these 15 players are elevated to hero status in the eyes of their fellow pupils as well as their teachers. The sea of black and white Selborne blazers – and their war cries and songs performed under the direction of a top-hatted cheerleader – is as chilling to the opposition as it is inspiring to those in the hallowed hooped jerseys of the First XV.

Although he was not in East London long enough to be one of these objects of adulation, barring one match for a nationally selected schoolboy invitation side which played against the Selborne first team to celebrate the school's centenary in 1972, Kirsten was repeatedly caught in the web of magic spun during school matches.

He and Noel were also regular spectators at Border matches, and the respect and love for the game flowed easily from father to son. And it was much the same when he moved to Cape Town and the traditions of SACS. Bishops, Rondebosch, Wynberg and SACS are the schools sport kings of the Western Cape and Kirsten's competitive spirit fed on the identity he embodied in the colours of his school. As Newlands cricket ground was to hold his heart for summers to come, so winter was the time for visits to its rugby counterpart.

Matches in the navy and white colours of SACS were followed by the weekly pilgrimage to Newlands, there to watch either a club match or Western Province themselves take on another of South Africa's provincial élite in the Currie Cup. Kirsten eagerly drank in the unique atmosphere and culture of Newlands and it left him intoxicated with just one supreme goal – to one day pull his own blue and white jersey over his head and sprint on to that lush green patch only heroes knew.

Others who had watched him play knew he had even higher honours lined up, and the fact that South Africa was still playing international rugby at that stage was further motivation to deliver perfection. Cricket would be his future and his fortune, but the young Kirsten had to admit that the feeling of taut leather in his hands excited him just a touch more than handling the hardness of willow. Whereas the competitiveness of cricket, though potent, often hid itself behind the laws and intricacies of the game, rugby left little room for doubt about either side's intentions.

And although there was no shortage of camaraderie in the company of his fellow cricketers, the undiluted passion the game of rugby unlocked in team-mates and opponents alike attracted Kirsten. His nimbleness and slight stature led his first coaches to put him into the number nine jersey. But it was soon clear that Kirsten had been born with the attacking instincts of a flyhalf. Not for him the life of a mere conduit between forwards and backs: Kirsten had ideas for slick line movements, incisive chips into vacant, unnoticed space and sudden stabs into enemy territory with the ball tucked under his own arm.

One inspired incident, still put forward as a measure of Kirsten's skill, seems to sum up his worth as a rugby player.

SACS and Wynberg were both unbeaten when they met midway through the 1973 season. The latter included the likes of Garth le Roux, later the feared fast bowler and hitter, and Rob Louw, on his way to assembling a vast and deserved fan club from his position on the side of the scrum. What SACS lacked up front they made up for with their quality backline. Kirsten was the captain and the kingpin.

The match, played at SACS, was watched by close on 6 000 spectators and the raw excitement of the day is still fresh in Kirsten's memory. SACS ran out 27-9 winners, but what stuck in the minds of the crowd who watched the match was the sheer audacity Kirsten employed in a few magic moments.

Wynberg had besieged the SACS tryline and only a sledge-hammer tackle, which resulted in a ruck, stopped them from scoring. SACS won possession and the ball was duly passed to Kirsten even as the Wynberg loose forwards loomed, bent on getting hold of him. Perhaps if he had been playing in France he would have had a choice of tactics, but this was South Africa and every coach would have insisted on the obvious – kicking it hard and far. But the ever-calculating Kirsten knew the Wynberg backline had been reduced to just three players: the rest had been pulled into the frantic loose scrum. So he ignored convention, put his head down and sprinted. A few sprinkled passes and an educated kick later, the SACS captain, his lungs burning with exhilaration rather than exertion, stooped to score under the crossbar.

He was indeed that rare being, the thinking rugby player, and his talents saw him selected to the Western Province Craven Week team in 1972 and 1973. A broken arm sustained on a tour by SACS to Rhodesia kept him out of action in 1972, but he was the Province vice-captain in Stellenbosch the following year and he impressed the man who mattered most in South African rugby, Dr Danie Craven.

Craven, among the giants of sport of any country or era, usually had a twinkle in his eye but for a young player to ignite it was almost unheard of. But in the SACS flyhalf he could see a second Bennie Osler, and he said as much.

As had happened with his cricket, Kirsten had not played a senior club match when the Quagga selectors nodded in his direction: time for his immense promise to start its inevitable metamorphosis into the confidence and reliability of a top class flyhalf.

Wednesday, 4 June 1974. Kirsten, 19 years old and nervous, took the field in front of 55 000 baying spectators at Ellis Park in Johannesburg on his first-class rugby début.

Kirsten's scrumhalf was Paul Bayvel and Gavin Cowley was at centre. Bayvel would go on to earn his Springbok colours and play ten Test matches, while Cowley became as much a household name for his rugby prowess as for his cricketing skill. Although Cowley was gifted and captained Eastern Province at cricket, he didn't rise above first-class level in either sport – despite an invitation to the Springbok rugby trials.

Kirsten and company's opponents on the day surged out of the tunnel in a menacing red flow – Willie-John McBride's all-conquering British Lions. It was to be the tour which brought home the sad state of decline in the once proud standard of Springbok rugby but the Quaggas, a side picked on potential, harnessed the arrogance of youth to good effect and only went down 16-20. Kirsten had a memorable début, scoring all but four of his team's points after taking over the place-kicking duties from the unsuccessful Cowley.

Ellis Park is a long way from Newlands, both geographically and culturally. A referee's disputed decision is somewhat more civilly received by the laid-back Cape Town crowd than by their demonstrably more aggressive Johannesburg counterparts. Kirsten recalls the naked hostility directed towards the referee, Ian Gourlay, because of a disallowed try and the shower of naartjies which greeted any development which didn't please the assembled masses.

Besides marking his entry into first-class rugby, 1974 was also the year Kirsten was conscripted into the South African Defence Force for his year of military service. And, by then accustomed to the rigid pecking order on which every army runs, he found it strange that officers who would normally eye him with studied contempt referred to him fondly as *mannetjie* or *Pietie* at the post-match function. So it seemed that the mercurial gifts of one of South Africa's finest natural sportsmen would endear him as much to the rugby fraternity as to cricket.

But there was to be no future in rugby for Kirsten. He had barely tasted the glory of it – and had been rewarded with a place on the Springbok selectors' shortlist for the tour of France in 1974 – when injury cut him down.

The match for the Quaggas was duly followed by selection to the Province team, led by Morné du Plessis, that took on Rhodesia in Salisbury, and then Kirsten played what turned out to be his only match at his beloved Newlands, against Natal.

In the days leading up to the match Kirsten, along with Hennie Bekker, had to go through the traditional initiation processes. This involved standing on a table, singing a song and telling a joke – all while stark naked. His song was simplicity itself: *Jou moer, jou moer, jou moer, jou moer …* (your arse, your arse …). And of course the joke, even if hilarious, didn't raise a titter from the assembled squad. This was followed by the downing of a pint of beer. To toughen the débutant, he had to run the gauntlet of the squad aiming their brawny hands at his bare backside. This was supposed to 'make you more of a man'. Boland Coetzee made a lasting impression on Kirsten, quite literally.

Though Natal were then buried in the B section, they had character beyond their talent and it was only after a comeback in the last 15 minutes that Province celebrated a 32-28 victory.

Kirsten remembers leaving the field with a sore head, not the result of any less than gentlemanly conduct by the opposition but rather the effects of John Gainsford's comments to him during the week before the match. There's more to this game than the glory of scoring points and buying applause with flashy play, the Springbok legend had said. 'You've got to tackle too, wonder boy,' was his message.

So Kirsten put more into his tackling that day – and came up with a painful head.

Kirsten's sixth first-class match and his third for Province was, tragically, his last and, with cynical irony, took him back to Ellis Park.

The north-south divide always added spice to Province's matches against Transvaal and this was no exception. Supplied with his preferred competitive environment, Kirsten got to work early via a penalty and a dropgoal. Province were still on top and in the lead midway through the opening spell when Kirsten spied another avenue of attack. He smuggled a grubber kick through the red and white defence and set after it, determined to profit. The Transvaal fullback waited, the ball bounced once, twice, and then ricocheted to the right. Kirsten, hot on the trail, instinctively propped on his left knee in order to veer right. But he was wearing new boots with shorter studs better suited to the hard Transvaal turf and he felt his knee collapse an instant before his feet disappeared from under him.

Pain shot through his body as he lay on the yellow-green grass, his face contorted with agony. The whistle brought the first-aid men and he was carried off. The damage was severe. Not only had he wrecked the medial cartilage in his knee, but he had also ripped the cruciate, or stabilising, ligament. Initially, however, Kirsten thought it was nothing a 'little operation' couldn't put right. But the Cape Town orthopaedic surgeon who repaired the damage, Dr Jan van der Merwe – the same doctor who had performed the procedure on Springbok captain Dawie de Villiers – had grave news. Unlike De Villiers, there would be no rugby comeback for Kirsten.

In fact, he should never venture on to the rugby field again, lest he endanger his cricket career.

The news hit Kirsten with all the impact of a flying flank forward. No more rugby? Surely not. But he had to concede that the doctors were right when, a few years later while studying at Stellenbosch University, he turned out in a trial match and felt his knee give again.

That should have been enough to frighten him off the field permanently, but his love for the game has defied common sense and lured him back for a handful of inevitably nostalgic SACS Old Boys affairs, as well as a sensibly aborted comeback at the age of 27.

Robbed of rugby, Kirsten had little choice but to immerse himself in cricket and he can now admit that besides the joys of playing the game, it also helped stave off the depression which could so easily have followed such an abrupt departure from what had become a winter way of life.

This meant that he would have to play elsewhere during the South African off-season. An English summer was the obvious choice.

3

Passport Denied

K irsten's first glimpse of England as a 20-year-old in June 1975 opened new avenues of consciousness for him. For two months, while he was on trial with Sussex, he delved into English culture with relish.

He found the people warm and appreciative of his, to them, entirely reported talent. Love of the game runs through the soul of many an Englishman and Kirsten snapped into place like the missing piece of a jigsaw puzzle. Off the field, the sometimes overly serious young man discovered a bright new world of fun, a place where people enjoyed themselves without letting race and other prejudices become hurdles to forming relationships.

And while the way of life was refreshingly different to what he had come to know in the Cape, there was reassuring commonality in the universal mannerisms of cricket and cricketers. Besides, he needed the distraction of a trip abroad: the after-shock of the abrupt end to his rugby career would be absorbed more easily and, coming as it did directly after the ubiquitous discipline of military life, the trip also served to focus his efforts on making good with Sussex.

However, there was no red carpet treatment for the young South African at Hove. The Sussex senior team was deemed too rarefied a side for him and he found himself on apprenticeship in the second XI. But that was perhaps a hidden blessing as Kirsten's knee had not fully recovered from surgery –

he describes it as being 70 per cent healed at that time – and the rigours of a county cricketer's playing schedule at that stage might have led to further damage.

Tony Greig, the Queenstown schoolboy who rose to the Sussex and then to the England captaincy, had engineered Kirsten's trial with Sussex. But the county, under the guidance of its skipper, planned to shop around for other young batsmen before offering contracts. The other candidate that year was an 18-year-old Pakistani who would become well known for his genius: Javed Miandad.

Although the two were as different as cricketers as they were in personality – the studious Kirsten grafting for his runs, Miandad notching his with outrageous strokeplay – they breached the divides of culture and race through their bond as cricketers. Miandad's favourite euphemism for a party was 'gigi-gigi', though Kirsten was never sure whether he understood the context of the term.

Kirsten remembers a particular match which might have helped the county decide which of the two to sign: 'We put on about 400. He got a double century and I threw it away at 128. And he ended up getting the contract.'

From 22 yards, Javed's innings was an education for Kirsten. Not only did the wonderfully talented Pakistani employ his considerable gifts to score his runs, he also tempered his ambition with remarkable discipline. Kirsten took careful note and applied the lessons he learned that day to his own batting. Indeed, ruthless accumulation of runs was to become a hallmark of his career.

In his only match for the Sussex first XI, Kirsten scored 31 against Ian Chappell's Australians. The tourists' side for the match included the fiery Dennis Lillee, whom Kirsten was secretly thankful he didn't have to face, and Allan Hurst, an underrated fast bowler who gave him something hard, red and sometimes lethal to think about.

Astute medium pace bowlers are the backbone of English cricket and South Africa has never been short of classy quicks, but the Australians were a step ahead. They loaded the pressure on batsmen in a way Kirsten had never experienced, drawing from a well to which South Africans had by now been denied access: Test cricket.

But Kirsten applied the most valuable of his skills, perseverance and concentration, and fought off his perennial weakness – impatience – to make a respectable contribution. Most importantly, he had passed something of a test, one most South African players could not even hope to undergo: he had survived and prospered, for a significant period, despite the efforts of internationally experienced opposition.

However, he returned empty-handed to Cape Town in August, having failed to reach an important cricket objective for the first time in his life. The shock of the realisation that, yes, there were more talented batsmen than he emerging into the higher echelons of the game rattled his previously unassailable confidence at first. But he soon turned the negative around: a challenge awaited across the seas.

The English sojourn also stirred Kirsten's notions of how the game should be run in South Africa. Even while he was being moulded as a player at SACS, he had felt that cricket needed a stimulus. The amateur and all he stood for was slowly ebbing away but it would be left to the likes of Kirsten to finish him off. It was to be a task which would gain him enemies within the game.

But, for now, his enhanced vision of how professional cricket should work would have to wait. The promise of his talent had opened a new door.

While in England, Kirsten had received a letter from the president of the Western Province Cricket Union, Boon Wallace, containing details of a sports bursary at Stellenbosch University starting in 1976. Eddie Barlow, sports officer for the Maties, had pulled the relevant strings and Kirsten, who felt he needed more direction in his life than that offered by a job in a Cape Town sports shop, opted for campus life.

What Kirsten remembers as 'jokkel' was officially called Physical Education and has now evolved into Human Movement Studies. He didn't see himself as a teacher – that pesky impatience all but precluded the notion – but he had found a rudder in rough seas. And although his Wednesday afternoons were taken up with catching and dissecting frogs in his physiology class, he was building a future of some kind.

The university, soaked through with the traditions of rugby, and the academic and spiritual home of Danie Craven, also had designs on nursing Kirsten's knee back to full fitness and then putting him in a maroon Matie jersey. But the ominous twinge Kirsten felt in a trial game in March finally buried his and the university's ambitions for him as a rugby player. Instead, he spent that winter immersed in his studies and in the long and difficult way back from the injury.

Fortunately, he found Stellenbosch the perfect environment both to heal his knee and to prepare for the coming cricket season. Well-meaning people, including such Stellenbosch stalwarts as Bokkie Blaauw and Justus Potgieter, created a fitness and strengthening programme for him.

Kirsten himself took care of the rest. He has not altogether fond memories of the Bergpad and the unyielding hill on the Stellenbosch campus up which he relentlessly trudged in the winter chill of 1976 and 1977 with Garth le Roux.

His rugby days might have been over, but there was nothing to stop him working on his body to make sure he went into the summer as fit as he could possibly be.

4

Promise Fulfilled

Ten innings do not a career carve, but those who saw Kirsten at the crease in that long-ago summer of 1973-74 could not deny that they had witnessed the entrance of a player of note, as evidenced by the ease with which he gathered his runs.

As W G Grace muttered while watching a young Jack Hobbs on his first-class début for Surrey in 1905, 'He's goin' to be a good un.'

Bolstered by his two half-centuries against Eastern Province, Kirsten scored 259 runs that first season. His average of 25,90 might not have lifted the eyebrows of the statistically minded, but the foundation was firm.

His second season followed a similar, if depressing, pattern. Cricket's scales of justice hold technique on the one side and personality, or temperament, on the other. And as it is essentially a game played by individuals who rarely forget they are individuals, the strengths and weaknesses of emerging cricketers, especially batsmen, are not immediately apparent. While it is not uncommon for a batsman of promise to make solid progress against older, more experienced opponents in his début season, extremely few are able to hide and prosper behind their cloaks of new flannel for a second summer.

Bowlers are, naturally, inclined to bowl away from a batsman's strengths if they can't attack his weaknesses directly. This makes the second season often a greater challenge to young players than the first, the word having spread that the new boy doesn't like it in the ribs, outside off, or wherever.

So it proved with Kirsten, who discovered in 1974-75 that the stream of off-side deliveries he thrived on a year before had dried up. In eight matches he scored 345 runs at 24,64 – perhaps not a significant decline from the previous campaign, but it was a summer in which he failed to break through barriers and make the big scores expected of a future top order batsman. The trial with Sussex followed and, despite the good times he had there, Kirsten's inability to secure a contract was a further knock.

A sliver of doubt pierced his already hardening psychological shield: could he indeed succeed at first-class level, or had it all been the stuff of schoolboy fantasy? No, he couldn't accept that. Kirsten has always been able to count on his mental toughness to pull him through the dark times, and he relied on it that season for perhaps the first time.

In that Province team he certainly had help in the positive thinking department. Eddie Barlow, his captain and the embodiment of ebullience, never encountered a cricket match he didn't think he could win, and Kirsten also came under the influence of Hylton Ackerman and Andre Bruyns, both of them eager, attacking batsmen who hadn't forgotten the difficulties they had encountered early in their careers. But still the uncertainty lingered. Kirsten knew he could establish himself in the first-class arena, but did he believe it?

The answer came early the following December. Rhodesia played Province at Newlands and despite the presence of pillars like Fletcher, Procter, Clift, Jackman and Traicos, the visitors were humbled. A first innings of 146 for nine declared – inspired by the bonus points system – led them straight into the wilderness and was a prelude to the second disaster: all out for 149 less than two hours into the third day's play to lose by an innings and 57 runs.

Between these two calamities, Kirsten came of age as a cricketer. With Bruyns, the Province number three added 162 runs in 175 minutes for the third wicket, and then 116 with Ackerman, while applying the lessons learned the previous season: to play as safely as he dared while scavenging runs off any stray delivery.

Given the flat pitch and the one-sidedness of the match, Kirsten couldn't have scripted a better scenario for his maiden first-class century. But he was careful with it, cradling his effort towards three figures, resisting the temptations which had led only to failure the previous summer.

After all of 339 minutes his first hundred was on the board, and it grew to an undefeated 128 and the total to 352 for three before Ackerman went for 60 and Barlow decided he had seen enough of his batsmen in action.

The taste of that innings of discovery was to linger with Kirsten. He savoured the challenge of finding the right stroke, of mentally outmanoeuvring the bowlers and fielders. Greater than that, however, was his achievement of surviving, hanging on when the bowlers drew strength from the new ball or a drinks interval, and having the energy and instinct to attack when they tired. But conquering his admitted impatience, even if it was only temporarily, was the lasting value of that innings.

Two months later, against much the same side but this time in Salisbury, Kirsten tuned into the same wavelength to score 123 in the second innings.

But this time the contest was far from benign. Rhodesia batted first and unearthed a seam of runs which ran to 328 for six on the first day, their captain, Brian Davison, making 74 and John Shepherd 65. They eventually declared 90 minutes into the second day at 410 for nine – and Province then stumbled to 170 for nine before Barlow declared with Shepherd and Jackie du Preez removing six batsmen between them. Kirsten and Ackerman had resisted with a fourth-wicket stand of 71, but there was little support for them.

The follow-on was duly enforced but there was no shifting Barlow on to the back foot. Out came that pugnacious bat and he was soon, and somewhat incongruously, dispatching his attackers' offerings to the boundary. The Rhodesians, who had thought they were in command, discovered that Barlow felt differently and his century, which was to be his only one of the season, came up in 145 minutes before Procter induced a catch.

Typically, Barlow's 104 banished the negative trend. Kirsten and Peter Swart were inspired enough to add 132 invaluable runs in 141 minutes for the sixth wicket and Province could see the edge of the woods. Kirsten, faced with the opposite scenario from that of two months before, showed the other side of his shiny new coin with a thinking innings that all but extricated Province from the dodgy position they had been forced into.

Both Barlow and Kirsten were dropped twice but had held their nerve, and Kirsten learned another important lesson: ride the wave while it is there; next week it might be gone.

Garth le Roux and Andre Nieuwoudt, who had made but one and nought respectively in the first innings, squeezed out a tenth-wicket stand of 28 before Province were dismissed for 374, leaving Rhodesia to score an unlikely 135 runs off 17 overs for victory. They didn't shrink from the task, falling just 16 runs short although their lust for runs cost them seven wickets with Denys Hobson taking three for 28 off six overs and Swart three for 46.

Kirsten found himself among the runs with telling regularity that summer. His average of 43,30 – the product of 655 runs scored in 15 innings – was second only to his captain's and, importantly, he now knew and believed that he could indeed keep company with the best.

As had been the case with Morné du Plessis, Kirsten was drawn to the image Barlow presented to both opponents and team-mates.

In terms of physical stature, the two could not have been more different. Du Plessis strode the rugby field with the presence and elegance of Zeus made mortal. Tall and imposing, with a reputation for hard but fair play, there was no doubting who was in charge of Western Province rugby and, in Test matches, South Africa. He directed operations from the back of the scrum and, naturally, much of his teams' tactics centred on his brawny savvy as a rangy, world class number eight.

An unsavoury on-field incident involving Naas Botha well into his career failed to damage Du Plessis' public persona of an intelligent, fair-minded man with much to offer the game of rugby. That he didn't involve himself in coaching or administration at the same levels he played until years after his retirement always surprised Kirsten. And so South African rugby was without one of its most celebrated men of action from his last match in 1981 until, having swapped his jersey for the manager's blazer and tie, Du Plessis became part of the Springboks' triumphant World Cup début in South Africa in 1995.

The comfortably portly Barlow, on the other hand, scurried about, apparently constantly on the verge of spontaneous combustion. Spouting energy as he went, the inimitable Bunter, as he is still known, rarely failed to light a competitive fire under his players.

Under his passionate leadership, Western Province emerged as a Currie Cup province in 1969 following a period in the B section doldrums. And such was his influence that they shared the trophy with Transvaal the following season. Derbyshire, whom he led from midway through the 1976 campaign to 1978, also felt the benefit of his presence and surged upwards from the nether regions of the county championship under his direction.

The way he played the game, Barlow was never going to be anything other than an all-rounder. Whether he was opening the batting, begging for the ball to bowl his aggressive medium pace, or willing a catch to come his way in the slips, a buzz of expectation followed him around. His Test career was cut short by South Africa's isolation from world cricket in 1970 but he made his mark in 30 matches, scoring 2516 runs at 45,74 and taking 40 wickets at 34,05. Of course, merely playing cricket was never going to be enough and he has since become a respected coach.

Now as passionate about his Cape wine farm as about the game, Barlow's latest cricketing caper has been to run the Western Province and Boland cricket academy.

But for all Du Plessis' and Barlow's considerable talents and subsequent accomplishments, perhaps their most intrinsic shared trait was a keen sense of adventure. Without resorting to outright recklessness, they would push the corners of the envelope in search of sweet victory. Even as professionalism, with all its safety-first mundanity, edged closer, they blazed the trail of the amateur's best intentions.

In their hands, Kirsten knew he had someone to rely on but he also breathed in the air of defiance and challenge.

Though there isn't much of either the Du Plessis or the Barlow blueprint in the cricketer and man Peter Kirsten became, he took to heart their approach to the game. Too guarded an individual to play the game with their legendary abandon, he nevertheless strove for the excellence that was their trademark.

As a young player Kirsten naturally had far more questions than answers, which often elicited a blunt response from his captain. But it was always an answer he could trust. And as he began to make waves in the bigger cricketing ponds, he learned that trust was at least as important as talent.

5

Golden Summer

K irsten's golden summer of 1976-77 was the culmination of what was bound to happen through the combined influences of SACS, Andre Abrahams, schoolmates such as Mike Minnaar, Gary Price, John Rabie, Roy Tindale, Warren (Percy) Kruger and Brian Jackson. Naturally the English trial the year before and the Stellenbosch experience with Garth le Roux had also bred confidence. And family support was always fanatical. To sister Cheryl, he was and always will be 'the boykie'.

Consequently, the Peter Kirsten who strode out to bat against Rhodesia on 6 November was a different man from the one who had made his mark on the Currie Cup scene the season before.

Rugby was gone – a brief, if blazing, moment in his senior sports career. But the work he and others had put into repairing the damage to his knee at Stellenbosch University was paying off: he emerged mentally and physically fitter than before. He had put the trials of his second season behind him and, with the support of Eddie Barlow, Andre Bruyns, Hylton Ackerman, Richard Morris and Peter Swart, had proved his promise in the third.

And there had been recognition of his talent the previous season with selection to the first South African Invitation XI to play the International Wanderers in March 1975. Captained by Greg Chappell and managed by Richie Benaud, the International Wanderers squad included the entire Australian attack, except for Jeff Thomson, and were to boot still savouring the satisfaction of having handed Clive Lloyd's West Indians a comprehensive 5-1 drubbing in Australia. However, the batting was thin and proved the tourists' undoing as they won one, drew two and lost one of the first-class matches they played.

Kirsten's selection to what amounted to a national team came as a result of the fall-out between Barry Richards, Graeme Pollock and Lee Irvine and the SA Cricket Union about the financial conditions of playing against the Wanderers.

Fine, said the suits. We'll pick the youngsters. And in came the likes of Kirsten, Henry Fotheringham, and Tiffy Barnes, a batsman from the Transvaal ranks of the non-racial SA Cricket Board of Control, for the four-day match in Cape Town.

Kirsten made 11 and two as the tourists won by 185 runs despite the virtual domination of proceedings by the South Africans.

The unhappy trio then resolved their differences with the administrators and were duly selected for the next match. Out went Kirsten, Fotheringham and, a match later, Barnes.

But the Kirsten of 1976-77 was indeed new and improved: in three seasons he had grown up, thanks largely to the university experience giving him some direction in life; he had tasted both triumph and failure and had put himself on the cricketing map. Importantly, he was single and his only responsibilities, apart from his studies (which always came second to sport anyway), were cricket and his family.

His performance for Western Province in 1975-76 had been heartening, though nothing the wise heads of Newlands had not seen before. Also, they nodded, he had discovered an enemy in the rising short delivery outside the off-stump. Good player, yes; great player, maybe; but there was a way to go yet.

Much of that path to greatness was about to be trodden, and in some style. At 21, he was fearless. His mind didn't need convincing of that and his body, save the knee, was eager to agree. Indeed, even as he reaches the end of his career, he finds it impossible to conjure a sense of wonder at his feat of making six centuries in seven first-class innings, four of them consecutive. Impressive though his form was, there were reasons for it and not just a sound, competitive body and mind.

'At night I used to tell myself there was no reason I shouldn't score another hundred. And it happened.'

Kirsten visualised himself succeeding against certain bowlers and their various tactics and he suspended the disbelief so often the downfall of promising players. The discipline and self-belief found unbeatable allies in timing and grooved strokes and he surged from one virtuoso performance to the next. He also thrived inside the cocoon of confidence spun by the consistent success of the Western Province team. His team-mates were inspiring and they played inspiring cricket.

As the season unfolded, Province would find themselves building a clear lead in the Currie Cup, only to be overtaken by Natal even as autumn nudged summer into hibernation.

In the Gillette Cup, the 60-overs-a-side competition, Province bowed out to Eastern Province by 58 runs in a lacklustre semi-final at Newlands. Four dropped catches – all during the sixth wicket stand of 113 between Dassie Biggs and Dave Brickett – and batting well below their usual standard were the chief reasons for Province's failure here.

But, generally, Barlow led a happy, eager team who were always more interested in winning matches than merely not losing them. It is no fluke that Kirsten regards that Western Province team, and that period of his career, as the most enjoyable of his years at the first-class crease. In that environment of hard, imaginative cricket on the field and the lively escapades of a daring collection of characters off it, how could he not succeed?

The summer dawned on an ominous note for any province with designs on getting the better of the men from the Western Cape. Rhodesia, far from the weakest team in the competition, were soundly thrashed in Bulawayo in a match which barely reached lunch on the last day, 8 November. Having been sent packing for a disastrous 136, the Rhodesians endured a Province effort of 361. Kirsten looked in touch but was bowled by Robin Jackman for 30, and the first three wickets were down with just 83 on the board. However, there were two batsmen behind him intent on staying longer. Hylton Ackerman and Allan Lamb, then an ambitious 23-year-old, added 164 for the fifth wicket to regain the initiative.

Rhodesia fared somewhat better in their second innings, scoring 238 with Brian Davison making 44 and Stuart Robertson 79, but still left Province with a token 13 runs to score for victory. These Barlow knocked off with relish in exactly two overs. His fellow opener, Kepler Wessels, left the field with his captain without having scored a run.

Five days short of a month later, EP captain Chris Wilkins won the toss at Newlands and, having noted the pitch's unusually grassy stubble, asked Barlow to bat. The decision must have haunted him with every rapidly passing milestone until 5 pm that afternoon, when Province declared at 399 for five.

Whatever the look of it, the pitch proved to be made for batting as both batsmen and bowlers discovered while the morning's dew was still hastening away. In just the second over, the normally circumspect Wessels hammered an unusually untidy Kenny Watson – renowned for the perennial glow of his figures as much as for his immaculate action – for 18 runs. But the paint was still damp on the 50, scored in 45 minutes, when Kenny McEwan in the gully conjured a magical catch to dismiss Barlow.

Kirsten rose from his chair in the Western Province Cricket Club, tucked his bat under his arm and collected his gloves and cap. Time to go to work. Fifteen minutes later he was still trying to get off the mark. So it wasn't that docile a pitch after all, and the EP bowlers had settled down considerably, the steady Brickett having taken over from Watson. Wessels made 38 solid runs before, soon after Barlow's departure, Watson returned to take his wicket.

Ackerman emerged, tall and well set, at 29 already the picture of the cool confidence that is the mark of all those born to bat. And who better than Ackerman, with his instinct for the romance and drama of cricket, to collaborate with his younger charge in something special.

Once Kirsten had opened his account, after 19 minutes, there was no stopping him. Anything wider than off-stump was cut and driven with a ruthlessness bordering on impunity. In Ackerman he found a partner willing to push the corners of the envelope, and left-handed to boot. Together, they mauled the bowling – but oh, so elegantly.

Three hours and 19 minutes after joining Kirsten, the satiated Ackerman launched an arching blow that was caught on the long-on boundary. His 114, punctuated by ten fours and five sixes, contributed to a third-wicket partnership of 242. Until it was matched by Terence Lazard and Daryll Cullinan in 1988-89, it stood alone as the Western Province record.

Kirsten, however, was not quite done when Ackerman left. Lamb hung about to add 77 for the fourth wicket and score 40 of his own, before Bossie Clark came and went without scoring.

Enough, said Barlow, and Kirsten tucked his bat again, this time with 173 undefeated runs behind his name. In five riveting hours he had shown that the serious young man who had learned the lessons of application and caution was beginning to add another important quality to his batsmanship – the knack of making the most of the scoring opportunities that came his way. Surviving at the crease was one thing and prospering there another, but turning good deliveries into mediocre offerings with deft, thinking footwork and refusing to be rattled when he was beaten, these were signs of greatness yet green but waiting to mature.

But there was a worthy EP team to deal with first. Simon Bezuidenhout and Wilkins, as fine a hitter ever to smack leather with willow, plucked 102 runs off the 23 overs that remained in the day. A total of 501 runs was scored off 114.5 overs that day and by the end of the second it had swelled to 864, with just 17 wickets falling.

EP, however, came off second best, being dismissed for 225 thanks to a collapse before lunch on the second day and being asked to follow on 174 runs in the red. Bezuidenhout and Wilkins, who put on 121 runs in 126 minutes in the first innings, were on song again in the second dig, adding 112 runs at a rollicking pace.

EP went into the third day 66 runs ahead with eight wickets standing, one of which belonged to Graeme Pollock. And he wasn't about to give it away. The finest left-hander South Africa has produced lashed a towering 180 not out, an innings overflowing with the power and sheer dominance that were the hallmarks of his career. Along with the efforts of the EP opening pair and lower-order help from Phil Carrick, Pollock's feat more than brought his side back into the match.

When Wilkins declared at 469 for eight, Province needed 296 in 115 minutes plus the compulsory final 20 overs – a stiff but not insurmountable task complicated by the threat of rain. It became harder when Watson bowled Barlow for four, but there was much drama to follow.

Enter Kirsten … enter fireworks. With Wessels, he rode a wave of adrenalin surging towards a simple but vital goal. The additional ten points Province would claim for an outright victory would put them almost out of reach of rivals Transvaal and Natal in the race for Currie Cup honours, and that after just two rounds.

Pulsating batting from both shoved the 100 partnership on to the scoreboard after an hour and a quarter. Slowly, the mountain was becoming a molehill. Then the pulses raced a tad too fast and Wessels was run out for 45, a victim of the growing tension. Tension which was building not just because of the match situation but because Kirsten, at 21, was on the verge of becoming the youngest player in South African cricket history to score centuries in both innings of a first-class match. In addition, no Province player had yet accomplished two hundreds in a match, and no cricketer had done it at Newlands.

Newlands held its breath as he threw his bat, with due regard for his wicket, into another drive. The team, of course, came first and any individual achievements would be a bonus. But he survived the odd reckless stroke and the century arrived. The crowd roared a salute, at once relieved that Kirsten had reached the milestone and glad to be able momentarily to divert their attention from the bitter struggle on the larger stage.

It was, however, to be the last Province celebration until stumps as

Hobson, Kirsten (who fell to Brickett for 103) and Ackerman trooped back to the pavilion in ominously quick succession. And when Lamb and Clark followed as the sixth and seventh wickets fell with fewer than 200 runs scored, the victory charge was rapidly reined in. Instead, EP smelled an extra ten points. But the eighth-wicket pair of Richard Morris and Gavin Pfuhl held out, and Province opened a ten-point lead on Transvaal at the top of the table.

Days after the glamour and glory of that match, Kirsten took the field with the rest of the Stellenbosch team in the comparatively lesser arena of the South African Universities Week in Bloemfontein. No time to catch his breath, to realise what was happening: another day, another game.

The Week would end with a three-day match between the Free State senior team and the South African Universities XI, to be selected after the inter-varsity matches. At that stage, Free State were a B section province but they did have first-class status and the match would be classified as such.

Kirsten couldn't help but bring his provincial form into the one-day matches played during the Week. He was duly selected to the SAU side. What followed added to the magic of what was steadily becoming Kirsten's golden summer.

The match was played at Schoeman Park on a pitch typical of South Africa's inland grounds – hard and true with little in the way of turn. SAU captain John Bristow won the toss and batted. And Kirsten scored his third consecutive first-class century.

That the students went on to win the match by an innings and 41 runs in two days was almost lost in the buzz around Kirsten's latest feat. South Africans in general have an obsession with records, and now Kirsten had claimed his third of the season. His 107 against Free State was perhaps not an achievement significant enough to rattle the flagpoles at Newlands and the Wanderers, but it was one sufficiently newsworthy to catch the eye of the casual cricket follower. Cape Town already knew they had a gem worth polishing, and now other corners of South Africa were beginning to discover the fact.

Among those suddenly interested in the cricketing fortunes of the diminutive number three was Stellenbosch Farmers Winery. They approached Kirsten with an offer to sponsor his run-making: R1-a-run for Province and 70 cents for Stellenbosch University in club games. It would be part of a promotion for Tassenberg wine. Kirsten thought this a fine idea. Though it was very cheap, very red, and very likely to bring on wrenching hangovers, Tassenberg was a South African institution. And students drank it by the bucket.

Yes, a fine idea. But what would the Western Province Cricket Union think of it? Individual sponsorships were regarded with undue suspicion in the 1970s. A few years previously Barry Richards had been offered, and had accepted, a similar proposition from an ice-cream company. 'He's a cricket mercenary,' fumed the committee men. But Kirsten, naively, thought times had changed. So he went to Boon Wallace, the president of the WPCU.

'Well, ch-ch-chummy, this hasn't happened before,' Wallace said, though he didn't veto the idea. 'I'll have to consult my executive.'

Wallace was an institution in South African cricket, a likeable man of positive disposition. Unusually, players liked as well as respected him because he looked after their interests first. However, whatever Wallace's feeling about the proposal, his committee would have none of it.

'We'd prefer it if you didn't, ch-ch-chummy. It might cause jealousy within the team,' Wallace reported back to Kirsten.

The suits had spoken, and although Tassenberg still disappears down many a throat in copious quantities and with ill-advised haste, no one can blame Kirsten for the mornings after.

Success at Newlands and the somewhat remote corners of the South African cricket empire, like Bloemfontein, wasn't enough for some. Away from his doting home crowd, and facing real opposition, not the likes of Free State, their cynical refrain went, Kirsten would prove to be human after all. 'Let's see him at the Wanderers,' they taunted.

The Wanderers – the bullring – scene of many massacres and usually at the expense of the visiting team. If Newlands captured the spirit of Cape Town – gracious, with an all too rare appreciation for the aesthetic dimension – the Wanderers told the day-tripper all he needed to know about Johannesburg.

Uncompromising face-brick and steel squatted on red dust. What it looked like was less important than whether it functioned. The brash quality of the place, especially when it was filled with 25 000 baying Transvalers, mirrored the realities of life in South Africa's engine room. Life here was about survival, both literally and economically. A few months earlier the Soweto Uprising had jolted South Africa into the era of mass political turmoil.

The mood was starkly Us and Them and shell-shocked whites were retreating into cultural laagers with terrified haste. The Wanderers made a neat laager and, along with Ellis Park, cajoled whites into ignoring the burning barricades beyond. Here the smoke smelled not of smouldering tyres but of barbecuing boerewors and the roar was for runs and wickets, not for fundamental political change.

When Kirsten and the rest of the Western Province team arrived in Johannesburg less than a week before Christmas, politics was far from his mind. Province topped the log with 31 points; Transvaal were second on 21.

The crunch was at hand. Transvaal captain David Dyer, who played the game with the passion of an amateur and the methods of the tempered professional, won the toss and batted. The Wanderers harboured the fastest pitch in the country, but it was also the truest and both batsmen and bowlers enjoyed the intensity invariably generated in matches there.

Aided by the dry highveld heat, Transvaal reached 100 for one at lunch. Dyer was going well and Clive Rice, at number three, was proving an able lieutenant. But after lunch Province inched back into it. Dyer and Rice added 104 runs in 134 minutes before left-arm fast bowler Stephen Jones had both caught by Barlow. The rest of the Transvaal order wasn't quite as solid and they floundered to 181 for six. Just four undistinguished wickets to take, but despite Garth le Roux's best efforts – he finished with five for 58 – they couldn't do it. The two catches Jones had dropped also didn't help and Dyer was able to declare at 285 for nine. Asked to face an awkward half-hour, Province advanced to 29 without loss.

The next day Kirsten alone stood between Transvaal and what would have been the springboard to a resounding win. And had a chance he offered on 37 been held, Province would have crashed to 104 for five. But Dyer found the sun in his eyes and the ball out of his grasp after Kirsten had launched a delivery skywards with what amounted to an undisciplined swipe of his bat.

It was that kind of innings. For once, Kirsten allowed the pace of the pitch and the frustration of the bowlers to exert undue control over his motives. Much of his five and a half hours at the crease was cameo Kirsten, all touch and restraint, applied knowledge and innovation. But there were moments when he stepped into another persona, embarking on desperate expeditions one minute, surviving the next thanks to a missing splinter of willow.

It wasn't perfect, but it helped Province reach 325 and banish thoughts of a Transvaal victory. His Jekyll and Hyde 165 also made him the twenty-sixth cricketer – and only the third South African – to reel off four consecutive centuries.

Transvaal resumed their second innings on 54 for one on the final day and, with Barlow and Le Roux sharing the top five wickets and Morris sorting out the middle order, they were dismissed for 260. This set Province a target of 221 in 85 minutes and the compulsory 20 overs. The Province top four all reached the twenties but none could build on the foundations and the partnerships were too brief to wear down the Transvaal attack.

Barlow, with 43, and Lamb, 52, ventured the furthest before Transvaal struck sharply in the final 20 overs to leave matters in the balance at 181 for seven at stumps.

The seven points Province garnered opened slightly their lead in the standings over Transvaal, who were awarded five.

Had Kirsten's glorious run been conclusively halted? Surely only the most superficial followers of the game could believe that.

Boxing Day dawned with Province in Durban. Kingsmead's is by far the quickest of the five coastal pitches on which regular first-class matches are played. It also has a reputation as something of a snakepit and over the years its groundsmen have at best not guarded against this and at worst encouraged it, particularly when the likes of Neil Adcock, Mike Procter and Vince van der Bijl were in the home side's attack.

Adcock had retired 14 summers before, but the latter two were definitely factors to be considered by any opposing batsman who had a notion to survive and prosper against Natal at Kingsmead in 1976-77.

However, any plan of action for dealing with the Natal pacemen was put on hold when Procter's side took first strike. And they threatened to expose any rumours about the pitch with a model display of top and middle order batting to declare at 361 for nine, Henry Fotheringham's 108 and Trevor Madsen's unbeaten 64 being their best efforts.

On a second day disrupted by rain, Province made a poor start in their reply, losing both openers with just 25 runs scored. With Kirsten in command, he and Bruyns began rebuilding and put on 64 runs before Bruyns departed. Ackerman helped add 41 before Lamb took guard, the total at 130 for four. A partnership of 86 runs later Kirsten, after a stay of more than three and a half hours, was dismissed for 111 despite a difficult chance offered to Neville Daniels in the gully off Van der Bijl when he was 84.

Another century?

Just think about it.

But there had to be more to it than that.

There was. Besides his advanced physical and mental fitness and the blessing of being in the kind of form that doesn't need thinking about – the eyes see, the brain decides and the body obeys, seamlessly, effortlessly – as well as the success of the Province team, which he had done much to generate, Kirsten had discovered a key principle: desire.

Merely to intend to do well, to want to score a century, was not enough. Desire it had to be – he wanted those runs, wished and willed them to come his way.

He desired them and soon they would be his: he knew it and believed it.

Lamb, more brutal than Kirsten at the crease, was in similar run-gathering mode and notched a century of his own, 105 in 169 minutes, while adding 111 runs for the sixth wicket with Morris, who ended up with 87 as Province batted into the third day for a total of 431.

A start delayed by 45 minutes because of rain and the slow progress of the Province tailenders, who ground out their innings into the mid-afternoon session with no declaration forthcoming, killed off whatever contest was left and play was abandoned with Natal at 151 for three in their second innings.

Going into the New Year match at Newlands, not only Kirsten but any South African with a vague interest in cricket was expecting him to reach three figures again.

Did the pressure build?

No. He was 21 and fearless.

He saw himself in the centre of a magical adventure and he was enjoying the role.

Pressure? Not a bit of it.

But as always when Transvaal were in town, there was extra needle in the match. Despite the north-south divide, the teams were captained by men with a similar approach to the game and both sides believed in positive, attacking cricket.

Culturally, there was a chasm between the teams. The Transvalers embellished their cricket with a trademark swagger, while the men from the Cape conducted themselves with what they perceived to be the superior intelligence considered a fringe benefit of being part of their supposedly more refined society.

It was arrogance versus snobbery and it still makes for wonderfully competitive cricket.

Moreover, Province and Transvaal were in the thick of a points duel at the top of the log and the result of this match was the crucial blow in placing Transvaal second and Province third at the end of the 1976-77 season.

Transvaal batted first, declaring at 334 for seven. By now, most of the country was watching Kirsten's every move and they knew another century would put him in the same bracket as Richards and Pollock as the only South

Africans to score six tons in a season.

Another century. Think about it.

Barlow and Bruyns scored 21 runs together before Doug Neilson flummoxed the Province captain and trapped him in front, calling up Kirsten. He spent 223 minutes at the crease and shared in three seemingly impregnable partnerships, putting on 94 for the second wicket with Bruyns, 62 for the third with Wessels, and 57 for the fourth with Ackerman.

Kirsten was not as fluent as he had been in some of the earlier innings that season and took all of 110 minutes to get his 50 on the board. Almost half an hour after he had passed three hours at the crease the left-hand column of the scoreboard cranked into action: P N Kirsten not out 100.

Swelling applause, the cap off, the bat raised, the public perception – valid or not – that he was a peer of the undisputed South African masters.

Twenty minutes later he was dismissed, caught Rice, bowled Barnes, for 128.

It had, in the words of a contemporary match report, been an innings 'not without blemish', but it was in the book for all to see. It also helped Province reach 366 and, at stumps on the second day, with Transvaal 45 without loss, the home side led the bonus points race 8-6.

The rest day passed with barely bearable formality. Monday dawned at last and Transvaal eased along at not quite three runs to the over to declare at 283 for seven. An innings of bits and pieces – 78 from Robbie Muzzell, 40-odd from each of Dyer, Rice, Jimmy Cook and Neilson – the Transvalers had none the less played themselves into a strong position. Only Hobson, who baffled and deceived his way to five for 79, had proved much of an obstacle to the batsmen. The only other wicket-taker was Kirsten himself who, the first time he was asked to bowl in a Currie Cup match, showed Barlow that he was more than a bowler to be turned to in desperation by getting rid of Muzzell, caught and bowled, and by bowling Irvine for a duck.

Given 85 minutes and 20 overs to score 252 and win the Currie Cup – an asking rate of around six to the over – Province advanced to 183 for three but then slumped badly as the quest for quick runs blotted out the basics of safe batting. Kirsten made 12 and the only worthwhile partnership was between Bruyns and Wessels, who scored 95 and 71 respectively in putting on 118 for the third wicket.

Somehow Province stayed in touch with the target and reached the last over with two wickets standing and needing eight runs to pull off a remarkable victory.

To bowl: Rice.

At the wicket: Stephen Jones and Rob Drummond.

Newlands scarcely dared to breathe.

Jones to face the first ball. Into the left-hander's pads and away for a precious leg-bye. The second, Drummond spars at it, misses … but gets bat on the third and takes a single. Six runs needed, three balls left. Maybe. The thought has barely registered when Rice leaps high – he has clean bowled Jones.

The blond mane and bevelled shoulders of the incoming batsman belong to Garth le Roux. He takes guard, trying not to think about the fact that his side needs six runs off two balls. Rice delivers, and the batsmen cross for a bye. Five off one. The chances of a win sink with the afternoon sun. But a draw would deny Transvaal ten points.

Rice walks back, rolling up his sleeves like he does after every delivery. He turns as if on parade and leans into that menacing run. Drummond waits, knowing the grim reaper now bearing down on him splayed his stumps in the first innings. Rice launches into his delivery, left arm high, head cocked to the side, and whips his right arm through.

Bowled him. Yes, bowled him.

Transvaal win by four runs and Rice finishes with the startling analysis of three for six off two overs.

And the visitors take home 16 points, putting them just two behind Province. So close …

But some of the damage was undone when Province collected 20 points from their next match, a four-wicket win over Rhodesia featuring the 19-year-old Wessels' maiden first-class century. Kirsten scored 44 and five, followed by 29 and 39 in the away match against EP, a game EP won by six wickets thanks to an inspired 82 not out by Pollock.

Had Kirsten finally mined it to dust, this rich seam of runs he had moulded into a trove of epic innings? Hardly. Rather, the record books had alchemised a nugget of fool's gold and it had captured his gaze.

To Kirsten, Barry Richards' record aggregate of 1285 runs glittered like some expensive jewel he had to have. And Richards' letter to Kirsten from Australia that season, where he was already involved, offering to assist him in a possible move Down Under spurred him on, coming as it did from one of South Africa's élite batsmen.

So, in the chase for the record, he took risks which sometimes didn't pay off.

But there was to be a last hurrah to what is still Kirsten's finest summer in more than 20 years of first-class cricket, though it did not involve another century. Province's last match was against the champions, Natal, at Newlands from 25 January, a clash billed as the Currie Cup decider.

Going into the match, log-leaders Province had 79 points and Natal 61, with two games in hand. Transvaal, a game in hand, were on 57 points. Both teams thus needed outright victory to stay in the race, but given the benign pitch the chances of daring declarations being made in a match of such importance were slim.

Province, who won the toss, were in no position to consider attacking tactics after they were forced to declare at 158 for nine to deny Natal their fifth bowling point. Procter and Vince van der Bijl had bowled with destructive fire, Procter profiting most with a haul of six for 28 thanks also to some indiscriminate wafting outside the off-stump by the Province batsmen. Amid the debris stood Kirsten and Lamb, who together scored all but 43 of Province's meagre total. Kirsten made 63, Lamb 52.

At the close of the first day, Natal had already reached 108 for two, both wickets falling to Le Roux's pace and swing rather than any unfair help from the pitch. With Fotheringham cooking, Natal looked set for a commanding reply. But they were all out for 240 – after being 220 for five – with Procter adding 56.

But the end of the second day's play came with Province reeling at 158 for five: just 76 runs ahead and with the undefeated Lamb and Barlow, batting an unlikely seventh, their last real hopes. As it turned out, the sixth-wicket partnership of 67 proved enough as Province totalled 252 and then sensationally dismissed Natal for 100.

Needing less than three runs an over, the potent Natal batting line-up plunged from one disaster to the next. Only Fotheringham and Tich Smith made it past 20. Though Hobson took four for 37 and Barlow three for 19, Jones took much of the credit for Province's resurrection. He bowled with rare hostility and variation and deserved much better than his two for 22.

Despite the Newlands heroics, Province were denied the Currie Cup when Natal went on to beat Rhodesia by an innings, negotiating a Bulawayo cloudburst in doing so. Procter took eight for 131 in the match to total 59 wickets for the season and claim the Currie Cup record for a season's work.

At the season's end, Natal had retained their title – and won the double by beating EP in the Gillette Cup final – with 99 points. Transvaal and Province each had 92. Transvaal were placed second because they had won more matches.

Kirsten's total of 1074 first-class runs saw him fall 211 short of Richards' record aggregate, a performance he never quite matched again in South Africa. It had, indeed, been a golden summer, a season that would open doors for him at home and across the seas.

After 1976-77, the question of who was the country's finest number three became irrelevant. There was only one answer.

6

The Three Musketeers

Much as they might be closer in character to their Australian counterparts, there is much that draws South African cricketers to England.

Until the 1990s, cricket in South Africa was cut from an indisputably English template. It was, after all, the game of the English-speaking South African, a remnant of the culture he had imported to the rugged plains of Africa in 1820.

And when white South Africa felt the grip of sports isolation, England, and the county circuit, took on even more importance. Their chance of Test honours gone, the South Africans who were in that league looked upon the shires as their international arena where they could take on the likes of Viv Richards, Ian Botham, Malcolm Marshall, Sylvester Clarke, Colin Croft, Joel Garner, Wayne Daniel ... the names, the legends that made it all so exciting.

It was far from the real thing, but the prospect of the depressingly endless travelling circus of familiar opponents, venues and challenges of the Currie Cup scene made it an attractive alternative. Having reached this plateau in the 1976-77 and 1977-78 seasons, Kirsten was ready to take another shot at landing a county contract.

Western Province had slipped at the crucial moments in trying to win the Currie Cup in 1976-77 but, despite having lost the inspiring Eddie Barlow to the marauding Kerry Packer's World Series Cricket circus, they got it right the next season to become outright holders of the championship for the eleventh time.

Without ever having led a team in a first-class match, Hylton Ackerman had taken over the captaincy from the inimitable Barlow and accomplished what many thought was out of his reach. Besides the loss of Barlow, Ackerman also had to do without Andre Bruyns who made a business move to the Transvaal, and Kepler Wessels who had been called up to the SA Defence Force and turned out for Northern Transvaal instead. Much of the batting responsibility thus fell to Kirsten and Allan Lamb.

For Kirsten to have branded his mark on this season as emphatically as he had in the previous summer would have been too much to ask, but his first-class contribution was still a valuable 579 runs at 41,35 with three centuries, one of which was the 102 not out which he scored for South African Universities against Eastern Province to become the only player to register two centuries in SAU history.

But for all his individual and team success, Kirsten was hungry for the fresh challenge county cricket would pose, as were Allan Lamb and Garth le Roux. It didn't take long for the press to label them 'The Three Musketeers', and together they made the trip to England in 1977 after the domestic season.

All three were to have successful trials which led to the offer and acceptance of contracts, Lamb signing with Northamptonshire and Le Roux with Sussex. Kirsten signed with Derbyshire, despite Northants courting his services beforehand. He remembers being whisked along the M1 between Northants and Derby in a red Jaguar as Northants, led by Ken Turner, tried to woo him.

This was heady stuff to the young Kirsten.

The trio had long and fruitful careers with these clubs. Le Roux remained in the county's employ until 1987 while Lamb, who has captained Northants since 1989, became an Englishman as well as by far the best attacking batsman in the country and the pillar of England's batting, especially against the West Indies.

A little South African blood and guts goes a long way, it seems. So it was more than mere irony that Kirsten, as talented as his mates, should end his glowing association with Derbyshire after just five years.

But he had his reasons, not that they were related to his performance as his 7722 runs at 49,50 testify.

Kirsten learned as much about himself as about cricket in the small industrial city of Derby, the midlands home of Rolls-Royce and many years of barren cricketing fortunes. He fitted in easily, sharing digs with John Wright, the New Zealander who was one of the county's other two professionals, and the pair soon became good friends. The memories of the years they spent together in the flat above Vic Cooper's butcher shop are undeniably happy. The meat downstairs was New Zealand lamb, of course.

The other Derbyshire pro was Eddie Barlow, who had helped pave the way for Kirsten in his quest to play in England. The 1978 season was to be Barlow's last in county cricket, his last summer inspiring a team perennially lacking in confidence. Kirsten captained Derbyshire occasionally and his presence provided the continuity of quality the county needed if Barlow's good work was not to be undone.

If he was happy on and off the field, and unarguably his team's most important and respected batsman, why did Kirsten abandon his seasonal sojourn in England after so brief a period?

Although he appreciated the opportunity to play for Derbyshire and its people, Kirsten says county cricket became stale for him and, naively, he didn't think of it as a business at the time. In addition, he was worried how his left knee would cope with the amount of cricket that had to be played. Would his impending marriage to Tuffy and the building of a family have been fair to all concerned?

In fact, it was Tuffy who urged Peter to stay with Derbyshire. 'Don't be crazy,' she said. 'You've done so well here, don't throw it away.'

But, for the reasons mentioned, it was his own stubborn decision to leave county cricket, no matter that he might want to return. In 1982, at 27, it was great to be paid for doing something he loved but he still wanted it to be an adventure, for Western Province and hopefully South Africa, although he had made many friends in Derbyshire.

Could it also have been that county cricket was not the international competition he was looking for? Locked out of the Test arena, Kirsten discovered he had stronger claims to play at the highest levels than some already doing so. This added to his frustration. Liberal-minded politically, he was being punished for the conservatism of others, and it hurt.

So Kirsten bade England farewell and had to be content with playing six months of the year in the sterile vacuum that was South African sport. But not before he had run up a string of county records and helped Derbyshire win the NatWest trophy in 1981.

When Kirsten opted off the circuit, he had made the highest score by a Derbyshire player against three counties. These were an undefeated 213 against Glamorgan at Derby in 1980; 209 not out versus Northamptonshire also at home in the same season; and the 228 Somerset suffered through in

1981.

His eight centuries in his final summer in England were the most in a season by a Derbyshire batsman, and his average of 64,70 in 1982 and 63,16 two years before were the two highest seasonal batting averages in the county's history.

In 1982, Kirsten joined William Storer and George Wright as the only Derbyshire players to score three consecutive centuries, and the first to do so in 77 years. With David Steele, he holds the county's third-wicket partnership record, a stand of 291 scored against Somerset at Taunton in 1981. John Wright and Kirsten twice – in consecutive matches in 1980 – also came close to breaking the second-wicket record of 349 with an unbroken 321 against Lancashire at Manchester and 253 playing Northants.

And – perhaps most famously – no one has bettered his career mark of six double centuries for the county nor the three he scored in the 1980 campaign, the record for a season.

But lists of records make boring reading, except for statisticians. Kirsten's most valuable contribution at Derbyshire was a class of batsmanship the county had failed to unearth from their own raw material.

To date, Derbyshire have won the championship once, in 1936, and have finished in the top five just 16 times since 1864. Their only other successes have been the NatWest triumph, winning the 55-overs-a-side Benson and Hedges Cup in 1993 (beating Lancashire by six runs to do so), and claiming the Sunday League title in 1990. They first reached the NatWest final in 1969 when they lost to Yorkshire by 69 runs, and were also involved in the B and H finals in 1978, in which Kirsten played, and ten years later, but bowed out to Kent and Hampshire, by six and seven wickets respectively.

So for the people of Derbyshire, as tuned in to cricket as every other county, winning consistently was a happy but all too rare exception to the more dreary rule. That it is one of the less affluent counties and has its headquarters at the rather inhospitable, almost invariably cold, County Ground in Derby doesn't help.

So the coming of Barlow in 1976, Wright the next year, and then Kirsten, who harvested runs almost from the beginning of his tenure, gave the members hope – hope which was at least partially fulfilled in 1981. And in return they welcomed the young Capetonian generously, and not just as a cricketer. Kirsten's list of friends made and kept in Derby is lengthy and close to his heart.

One of those was David Steele, as engaging an Englishman as Kirsten could hope to encounter and one whose self-deprecating sense of humour made him the almost willing butt of many of Wright and Kirsten's pranks.

But Steele used to get his own back, in a fashion, when the trio hit the road to travel to the next match venue. This journeyman county cricketer had a terrifying habit of nodding off while driving and, no matter how festive the celebration the night before, Kirsten and Wright had to be at their most alert when 'Steelie' was at the wheel.

Kirsten's time with the county may not have led to a dramatic upswing in their championship fortunes – they finished sixteenth in 1979 but fought back to ninth a year later – but there was no doubting they were getting their money's worth from their hired gun. And not only on the field. Kirsten well remembers the Derbyshire coach, Phil Russell, enlisting his help to erect fences around the ground as well as doing other duties which in South Africa have always been allocated to the groundsman and his staff. At first Kirsten was taken aback – going from sitting on something of a throne at Newlands to brushing up on his carpentry skills at Derby must have entailed a culture shock of sorts – but he soon accepted the extra work as part of a cricketer's apprenticeship and came to enjoy it as a diversion from the game itself.

It would be easy to paint Kirsten's time in England that first season as being all sweetness and light, but that was not the case.

There were frustrations, beginning with the trio of ducks he suffered in his first three innings for Derbyshire. But his by now ingrained perseverance and ability to conjure a clear picture of his objectives helped him strike back in fine style in the next match with an unbeaten 206 against Glamorgan at Chesterfield.

And although his New Zealander flatmate was a friend, being alternated with him in the Derbyshire team sometimes was not the best way to sustain batting form. 'He'd play and get a duck, then I'd play and get a duck,' Kirsten explains. However, Mark Burgess' New Zealand side arrived in June for a series of three Tests and Wright joined the tour, making way for Kirsten to play regularly.

Kirsten ended up pulling on his black Derbyshire cap in 20 first-class and 26 limited overs matches in 1978. The double century turned out to be his only three-figure effort of the season but, with the help of seven half-centuries, he managed a respectable 1133 first-class runs at 36,54. He was less successful in the one-day stuff, totalling 304 runs at 19,00.

Kirsten's ultimately lost battle to make a worthy contribution to his team's one-day totals that year generated in him a desire to improve his performance in the truncated game. Hitting wildly has never been his game. Indeed, Kirsten's subsequent spectacular success in limited overs cricket owes nothing to the 'hit the bloody ball' school of thought which has turned so many lovers of the game as it deserves to be played away from the vulgar spectacle one-day cricket is all too easily capable of becoming.

However high the required run-rate climbs, whatever Kirsten does with his bat is invariably recognisable as a cricket stroke. No corrupting cross bats nor, until rule changes demanded it, risky hoists over the top. The clean, cultured strokes which make his batting in first-class matches such a joy to witness have been smoothly carried over to his one-day innings, with due adjustments for the ubiquitously defensive field settings.

But that is not to say that his batting lacks innovation, as proven by his trademark one-day stroke: turning the wrists and running the ball down to third man for a single and, more importantly than many realise, enabling the strike to change hands.

Kirsten credits his limited overs batting prowess partly to lessons he learned in England, where the proliferation of one-day matches provides ample opportunity to analyse and improve. Though he played only one season before full covering of pitches came in, the surfaces he was faced with in subsequent summers were still varied enough to challenge his approach to the full range of batsmanship's attacking and defensive dimensions.

One-day cricket might demand pitches of a singularly bland character but adaptation is the key to every player's success. Kirsten changed his game sensibly but subtly, never resorting to exhibitions more suited to the baseball diamond. He showed it was possible to score rapidly without thrashing about like a wounded shark whenever quick runs were required. For this quality, he thanks Ackerman.

The genial left-hander might not have had the stature of Morné du Plessis or Barlow, but he still left an indelible impression on the young Kirsten. Batting together for Western Province in the Gillette Cup, Ackerman would curb Kirsten's understandable instinct to launch booming drives. No need, the astute Ackerman would say; far better to take the safer option of scavenging runs fine on both sides of the wicket.

More than his technical influence, Ackerman proved Kirsten's prime motivator; so much so that when he met with Northamptonshire officials in 1975, while on trial with Sussex, he told them it would be a good idea to re-secure Ackerman's services. The county however declined, despite the fact that he played 98 championship matches for Northants between 1967 and 1971.

Ackerman's influence over Kirsten went beyond the mere details and merits of one stroke or another. He is a character in touch with all the facets of the magic of cricket, and on both sides of the boundary. Whether at the crease or relating an anecdote in the dressingroom, Ackerman's style was polished and irresistible. The poet's touch shone through in his batting and the telling of it and a trove of other stories. Ackerman was the consummate entertainer professional cricket is often in danger of eradicating, consciously or not. Besides the expertise he brought to the Province team, Kirsten enjoyed his company on the field and off it.

Another great benefit to Kirsten of his time in England was the invaluable experience he picked up of succeeding against spin bowling. Perhaps it is not surprising that the majority of South African batsmen, at every level, are far from proficient against the turning, or supposedly turning delivery. On the quicker pitches here, spin bowling that is not overtly defensive is still seen as an expensive luxury by many captains. Pitches in South Africa, with a measure of exception at the coast, simply do not take any appreciable turn and it is no paradox that the country's most successful slow bowlers, among them off-spinner Hugh Tayfield and left-armer Alan Kourie, prospered through variations of pace and flight rather than the cultivation of prodigiously turning deliveries.

And, apart from the emergence of Denys Hobson in 1970, the last time South Africa produced wrist spinners of note was when matting pitches outnumbered the turf variety. One-day cricket, with its emphasis on containment rather than dismissal, did not create the problem but it certainly hasn't helped to alleviate it. The upshot is that today's captains have generally not been taught how to employ spin – and that South African batsmen have not had to deal consistently with quality slow bowling.

Kirsten had a similar deficiency in his game when he arrived at Derbyshire. But seamers and spinners are the backbone of English cricket and Kirsten soon realised that success in England was tied to mastering these forms of bowling. The key lay in his footwork: left leaden and unimaginative, it was fatal. Sensible forays up the pitch and deft movements back were essential if Kirsten was to be able to make use of his full range of strokes. Once he had managed to unlock those shackles, the world of spin became far less mysterious.

The confidence achieved in gaining his new-found skill also spilled over into other aspects of his game and he knew he was on his way to becoming a complete cricketer.

It didn't take long for Kirsten to be acknowledged as one of the better players of spin in South Africa, and he fully deserves the accolade. But the disturbing aspect was that he had to go half way round the world to earn it.

Conversely, Kirsten the off-spinner, a role he had last played with any seriousness in the Western Province Nuffield team, also came to the fore that first season in England. His 18 wickets might have come at the comparatively high cost of 32,27 but he had the makings of a canny bowler, although not one in the frontline.

Kirsten went to England in 1978 a gifted but obviously raw youth. He had that marvellous South African season behind him but the refined ways of the English game showed him he had much to learn. By early September that year, as he cheated the advancing northern winter and packed for Cape Town, he felt that his education had begun and that Derbyshire and England wicketkeeper Bob Taylor's comment 'quality not quantity' should be his watchword.

7

Lost Ground

The promise and eventual fruition of Western Province's efforts between October 1976 and March 1978 faltered in the summer of 1978-79.

Although they were runners-up to Transvaal in the Currie Cup, the gap of 38 points between Barlow's team and the champions told of a one-horse race. Province always seemed a step off the pace set by Transvaal that season, and Natal, Rhodesia and Eastern Province loomed large enough in their rearview mirror to cause distinct discomfort.

The bold cricket of the previous season, which saw them win the Cup under Hylton Ackerman's captaincy, mysteriously vanished to be replaced by a version still of high quality but perhaps lacking the drive that had taken Province all the way. Even allowing for Barlow's absence, the reasons were far from clear. To be sure, the loss of Garth le Roux's intimidating presence to World Series Cricket after three Currie Cup matches – at which stage Province were ten points clear of Transvaal with a game in hand – exacted a high toll.

As fiery a paceman ever to glare at a batsman, Le Roux – he of the wild blond mane and Herculean frame – had set a Province record of 53 Currie Cup wickets at 14,58 in 1977-78 and had emerged as one of the most feared fast bowlers in the game. He was in similar form the next season, with 14 wickets at 16,78 in the 79 overs he bowled, and his recruitment by Packer was a deal waiting to happen. Which impresario would not want to focus the spotlight on Le Roux's aggressive, highly marketable approach to the game?

But even Le Roux's departure, which took the edge off the Province attack despite the efforts of Peter Swart and Denys Hobson, should not have sent the team into the wilderness. After all, it was essentially the same combination which had unexpectedly provided the blueprint for success the season before.

This time, however, the batting held its own in one innings and then floundered in the next. Only Kirsten, Richard Morris, Allan Lamb and Stephen Bruce registered Currie Cup centuries for Province that season. Worse, only twice did a Province pair muster a century partnership.

By contrast, Transvaal notched seven centuries – five from the bat of Graeme Pollock – and enjoyed the benefits of the same number of stands over 100.

Kirsten and, less so, Lamb generally lived up to their joint tag as the Province batting kingpins, both averaging above 30, and Bruce's pugnacious approach injected some of the dynamism that had departed with Barlow.

But just three wins from their eight matches, not to mention an ignominious eight-wicket loss to Free State in the one-day competition, since renamed the Datsun Shield, punctuated a mediocre season made all the more ordinary by the shadow of the triumph that had come before.

Rhodesia, among the lower hurdles on the Currie Cup course, escaped from Newlands without being beaten for the first time since 1971-72, and Natal were twice victors over Ackerman's men: at Kingsmead by three wickets and at Newlands, with Procter back from WSC and terrifyingly rampant taking 11 for 90, by 127 runs.

The names of Adrian Kuiper, Omar Henry, Lawrence Seeff and Stephen Jefferies all appeared on Province scorecards that season but none made the impact they would, happily, do in future campaigns.

Kirsten's Currie Cup century came in the drawn New Year match against Transvaal at Newlands. It was his third successive ton at home against Province's perennial rivals, but even that feat was overshadowed by Pollock's 233. With just three and a half hours left in the match when Transvaal completed their first innings of 466 for eight declared, scored in reply to Province's 357 for nine declared, a result was all but unfeasible. Province reached 128 for three, a lead of 19, when play was abandoned.

Kirsten's other century that unmemorable season was scored, for a change, against SA Universities at Coetzenburg in Stellenbosch. A shirtfront pitch invited sparkling batting and Kirsten delivered it with 197 – then his highest score in South Africa – of the 460 runs Province scored in their first innings, a total amassed despite Kuiper's figures of six for 96. Lamb, Swart

Above: Under 12A cricket team, Selborne Primary. Captain Peter Kirsten is seated in the centre of the middle row.

Below: Border Cricket Union, 1960/61. Wicketkeeper Noel Kirsten is in the centre of the front row. (Fotopress)

Left: 14-year-old Peter Kirsten at SACS.

Below: SA Schools XI, Nuffield Cricket Week, 1974. Vice-captain Peter Kirsten is seated third from the left. (Fotoland, Pretoria)

Left: SACSY! – 1973. (Dana le Roux, The Argus)

Above: Knackered! Western Province U20, 1974.

Below: Ian McGeechan trying to block kick. Quaggas vs the British Lions, 1974.

Above: Quagga Invitation XV vs British Isles Touring Team, Ellis Park, 1974. The youthful Peter Kirsten is seated second from the left in the front row.

Below: The Bergpad, Stellenbosch, 1976. (Peter Stanford, The Argus)

Above left: Kirsten is congratulated by Hylton Ackerman after scoring his second ton of the match against EP at Newlands in 1976. Kirsten says of Ackerman, 'He was always a good partner to have alongside one.' (Die Burger)

Above right: 'Cute.' Natal captain Vince van der Bijl tousles Kirsten's hair during a Currie Cup match at Newlands in 1978. (Les Hammond, The Argus)

Below: Allan Lamb (left) and Kirsten in a match against Transvaal at the Wanderers in 1981. 'It was always great batting with Lamby for WP,' says Kirsten.

Above: 'Thanks, Ken. Thought you were my mate.' Kirsten is hit on the head by a Ken Watson delivery in the 1970s.

Below: Garth le Roux (left) and Kirsten were team-mates (and room-mates) for 10 years for Western Province. Le Roux is now a national selector and a fine golfer.

Peter Kirsten scored his first double century for Derbyshire in a match against Glamorgan at Chesterfield in 1978.

Above: Kirsten enjoyed many great partnerships with John Wright for Derbyshire: 'I loved batting with Wrighty.'

Below: Derbyshire County Cricket Club, winners of the NatWest Trophy in 1981. Kirsten is standing on the extreme left.

and Bruce all managed to climb halfway up the century tree before somehow crashing without completing the job. The students spiralled to 181 all out with fast bowler Evan Gordon taking six for 47 in his début match for the senior team, having shone with match figures of nine for 73 in his first-class blooding against Rhodesia B the match before.

Realising a similar disaster was unlikely to befall the SAU batsmen in their second innings, Ackerman declined to enforce the follow-on. Kirsten made 52 and Neville Daniels 100 not out as Province declared at 219 for three, leaving their inexperienced opponents the mind-boggling task of scoring 499 in less than five sessions.

What followed was one of the most determined run chases in the history of more than just South African cricket. The students went into the last day needing 424 runs – but with all their wickets intact. Lee Barnard, the captain, and Neville Wright put on 169 for the first wicket, an SAU record, before the former was run out and there were half-centuries from Eugene Muntingh and Noel Day. Even so, the target still seemed beyond the horizon. However, Kuiper wasn't quite finished.

In an innings which would see him elevated to the Province senior side for the rest of the season, Kuiper smashed a century off 93 deliveries and was undefeated on 110 runs when, with the help of Danie du Toit's 37 and Dave Alers' 12 not out, the students' five-hundredth run creaked on to the scoreboard for a remarkable three-wicket victory.

If Province's distant but probably worthy second place in the final Currie Cup standings didn't indicate too much was amiss on the field, events in the committee room said otherwise.

Barlow had returned to Cape Town towards the end of the season having done with WSC, which led to calls for him to be reinstated as captain. To have done so would hardly have been fair to Ackerman who, despite his team's lesser performance and his wretched personal form, could justifiably point to previous glory as enough to keep him at the helm. But Barlow's in-born leadership was not to be discarded lightly.

What to do, what to do …

No, Barlow would not return to the captaincy, said the selectors. A good decision, many agreed, and channelled by sound and admirable principles.

Of course, Barlow would be selected to help Province pick up the pieces in what remained of the season, would he not? No, came the somewhat disingenuous reply.

And so one of the greatest cricketers South Africa has produced watched a team which was patently in need of his all-round services from the safe side of the boundary.

There were also rumblings from within the Province ranks, unhappy hints that all was not well at the Cape.

Indeed, Kirsten, Le Roux and Lamb were on the look-out for greener South African pastures, such was their frustration at the way the game was being run in their backyard. But all three were secured for the 1979-80 season and Barlow came back, ironically, as captain and manager in one. Province stormed back to their championship form – but were still only good enough to take second place.

The Transvaal 'Mean Machine', as it was soon to be called, was geared for huge innings and destructive bowling performances. Province won four matches and lost just one, to Natal in the season opener, and finished with 103 points, their highest total yet. Incredibly, they still trailed Transvaal by 28 points. In terms of bonus points, the teams could hardly be separated but Transvaal had gained six outright victories and were deserved champions. Both matches between the only genuine Currie Cup contenders were drawn. In these matches, Province garnered 15 bonus points to Transvaal's 14.

Had Le Roux, undoubtedly Province's key strike bowler, taken a few more of his 36 wickets (at 17,25) in the matches that mattered, and had he been in the side which played at Kingsmead instead of nipping back to Australia for an eventually cancelled WSC bowling competition, the summer's sunset might have been far more picturesque for Province.

In the Datsun Shield, Province cruised past Griqualand West and Eastern Province to book a duel with – who else? – Transvaal in the final at the Wanderers. Inevitably Transvaal won, and by seven wickets with more than 13 overs remaining. Lamb, who won the batting prize for his 56, and Bruce, 33, made the biggest impact in a total of 224 for nine.

Alan Kourie seemingly could not avoid the ball and was involved in six dismissals, bowling Barlow and taking one catch at first slip, three at square leg and another at mid-off to become the first fielder other than a keeper to take five catches in an innings.

Barlow had won the toss and elected to bat on a shorn pitch. He and Seeff were out with just 30 runs scored, but Kirsten and Lamb shared a third-wicket partnership of 83 in 69 minutes despite an interruption of 20 minutes because of rain. Peter Swart and Bruce added 50 in 51 minutes for the fifth wicket but both departed just as Province were looking to mount their final assault and, on an unusually docile Wanderers pitch, the total was never going to be enough.

Just to emphasise the point, Jimmy Cook, dropped on 20 and 54, was elegance itself on his way to 113 not out. The fading light wasn't enough to stop Pollock scoring 58 and Clive Rice's unbeaten 33 wrapped it up for the home side.

Kirsten had passed the milestone of 5000 career first-class runs with Derbyshire in the preceding winter, in which he had scored by his standards a moderate 1148 runs at 31,88 with two centuries. That he failed to score a century for Province in 1979-80, despite reaching 50 four times and finishing with 551 runs at 45,91, was as much indicative of a grumbling hunger for a fresh challenge as of unsettled form.

That impatience, the very antithesis of which he knew was the key to success, began to seep into his batting as well as his public persona. He became known as a difficult player to deal with, perhaps not among team-mates but certainly as far as the press was concerned. Looking back, Kirsten says he was obsessed with a pervading sense of anger. Anger towards what, or whom? He still doesn't have a simple answer. His experiences in England had sparked his interest in the cricketer's lot, and how it could be improved in his own Western Province.

Today, he can see that an over-serious approach was probably to blame. And how could a talented but still maturing sportsman afford not to take things seriously? Then, as now, Kirsten was as forthright as a prominent sportsman could afford to be, sometimes crossing the boundaries of prudence. In contrast to his conduct when he was batting, he was easily put on the verbal defensive, an inevitable consequence of his not counting communication among a cricketer's more valuable attributes. He sometimes got the wrong end of a reporter's question, which led to accusations of his being over-sensitive.

But the truth was that Kirsten, as much as any top class player in South Africa, had stagnated. A bland diet of Currie Cup cricket, even if varied by what had become a pilgrimage to England, was far from satisfying.

Not for the last time in his career, he felt restless. The events of the winter of 1980 would go some way towards easing the gloom, but it would return.

8

Quality and Quantity

Pollock, Kirsten, Procter, Lamb, Le Roux, Wessels, Rice, Van der Bijl, McEwan: no follower of South African cricket could, or would, have avoided knowing the exploits of this magnificent band of sportsmen for much of the 1970s and '80s.

To say that they featured consistently and prominently would be akin to stating that W G Grace wore a beard. Rather, the contest often came down to which of these invincible eight cricketers stuck out above the others.

To the cricketing public of Johannesburg, Cape Town, Durban, Port Elizabeth and, up north, Bulawayo, they were as accessible as a beer on a hot afternoon. A ticket to the ground and a day off work were the only requirements for sitting in on their exhibitions of what could be accomplished with bat and ball.

The rest of the country had to be satisfied with scanning the newspapers or breathing the air so eloquently and passionately filled by Charles Fortune and, to a lesser degree, by his fellow commentators to keep up with the week-to-week happenings on the nation's Currie Cup cricket grounds.

Places like East London, Bloemfontein and Bedford, which counted some of those household names among their sons with pride, were as much centres of the game as Newlands and the Wanderers, except that they didn't have the economic influence – and consequently the cricket clout to lay claim to A section status. East London and Bloemfontein would eventually be added to the list of venues where the country's finest could be seen in glorious action, but the Eastern Cape village of Bedford remains farming country – and the birthplace of Kenny McEwan.

There were odd invitations to the most unlikely hamlets to play in friendlies, and the Datsun Shield offered an annual opportunity for some of the minnow provinces to host an A section team. But the media, including television which started beaming matches into countless homes and pubs in the 1975-76 season, was the primary source of cricket information for the geographic if not the demographic bulk of South Africa.

And the headlines seemed permanently occupied by Kirsten, Pollock, Procter et al. In the absence of Test cricket, the first-class arena became paramount and naturally the players were public property like never before.

Nor did it end when summer stole northwards to England. In 1980, 16 South Africans or Zimbabweans played county cricket, one of the few international openings left to a sporting culture which had had its growth severely retarded by the unbridled folly of politicians who were nevertheless voted back into power repeatedly, albeit by a minority electorate.

At the end of that English summer a South African in England, particularly one predisposed to cricket, would have felt strangely at home if he picked up a newspaper and turned to the sports pages. There, at the very top of the county batting averages, glowed the names of an immortal trio: A J Lamb, P N Kirsten, and K C Wessels. Lamb had scored 1797 runs at 66,55; Wessels – in ten fewer innings – 1562 at 65,08; and Kirsten 1895 at 63,16.

Another familiar, and unmistakably South African, set of initials and surname headed the bowling averages. A certain V A P van der Bijl had taken 85 wickets at 14,72 for Middlesex in what would be his only season of county cricket; and a chap called Procter, captain of Gloucestershire (or was that 'Proctershire'?), wasn't far behind with 51 scalps at 18,25.

And that was far from all. Clive Rice had taken 39 wickets, scored 1448 runs and led Nottinghamshire to an innings victory over the touring Australians as well as to third place in the championship; Big G, otherwise known as Garth le Roux, fired and brimstoned his way to 33 wickets and enhanced his growing reputation as a mighty wielder of the willow; Lamb's magic had helped Northamptonshire to a six-run victory over Essex in the final of the Benson and Hedges competition; McEwan's supreme batsmanship had helped him carve innings of 136 and 129 not out in the 40-overs-a-side Sunday League …

At home, South Africans fumed as well as celebrated. Clearly, some of the finest and most entertaining cricketers of that generation had risen from the shores of Africa. But they had no higher stage on which to perform. This was a crime, said white South Africa. No, it was a legitimate strategy to try to rid the world of apartheid, said many governments.

Kirsten had heard it all before, had said much of it himself. And he had managed to channel his frustration into a positive outlet. Mere centuries became just half of what he was after that season. To reach three figures meant only part of the job was done, Kirsten decided.

So he rode his luck, the troughs of uncertainty which have put an early end to many a budding innings and the peak of the wave of success which invariably followed, to score six hundreds – three of them double centuries, a record for a South African in a single cricket season. He managed to override the impatience which had tainted his batting the previous South African season, and the results staggered even the most jaded cricket followers.

But there were other underlying reasons for Kirsten's determination to set the county scene alight that summer. The endless cycle of travelling and playing, often for two weeks without a break, that was to drive him from England two years later irked Kirsten in 1980. But once again he converted negative energy into positive and he went out to bat with the express purpose of 'proving his worth', as he wrote in a letter to his mother Lois. It was the only way he would be able to increase his bargaining power, and exert some control over those so desperate to control him, come the following year.

Kirsten's amazing run of form was an unquenchable thirst for success. It started in the opening championship match against Lancashire at Old Trafford. He scored 162 not out, and John Wright made an unbeaten 166 as they shared a second-wicket partnership of 321 in a drawn match.

Another century: just think about it.

Kirsten did, and it came in cracking style.

That it was scored at Derby against Northants, which of course included Lamb, only added to the satisfaction. And there was plenty of that as Kirsten's 209 not out became the highest score of his career thus far.

Kirsten's effort and Wright's 117, which led to a stand of 253, helped Derbyshire declare at 372 for two and when stumps were drawn after ten overs of the visitors' first innings, they had already lost three wickets for the return of just 26 runs.

Kirsten's century took all of 190 minutes to arrive, but once it did Kirsten cut loose with rare aggression against a threadbare attack. When the 200 rolled up he had sent 22 deliveries crashing into the boundary and another three sailing over it. It didn't take the statisticians long to crunch the numbers: having been dismissed just once in three innings, a blushing Kirsten lugged the nonsensical average of 402.

At Bristol, not even Procter's inspiration was enough to stop Lamb hammering 113 not out to help Northants score 308 in the fourth innings and to beat Gloucestershire by the handsome margin of seven wickets.

A race of sorts was warming up between the two Capetonians. This might seem a shallow target to shoot for, but it must be remembered that the South Africans had little to aim at besides records and individual rivalries in those busy, but ultimately unfulfilling, years.

The legendary feat of scoring 1000 runs in the month of May, at that stage last achieved in 1928, loomed as an obvious goal. But it proved out of reach, although Kirsten did become the second batsman after Graham Gooch to breach four figures that season. The Essex opener passed the mark on 19 June, two days before Kirsten.

Ironically, it was against Essex, the reigning champions, that Kirsten scored his 1000th run of the campaign, during an acclaimed innings of 140 not out at Chesterfield on a day hampered by interruptions because of rain.

Eddie Barlow telephoned Kirsten that evening to discuss arrangements for the coming South African season. 'Looking forward to batting on tomorrow, Eddie,' Kirsten told his Province skipper. 'Reckon I can score another double.'

The next day Kirsten's score grew to 202 – not out, what else?

Before that, on 7 June, Kirsten had registered his second double ton of the season – and a new personal best – in taking 213 undefeated runs off Glamorgan at Derby. He had made his way to 200 in 226 minutes with the aid of 31 fours and five sixes. In this innings, Kirsten discarded what inhibitions he had left to thrash the bowling all round the ground with a magnificent display of seamless batting.

'I got the bit between my teeth,' he wrote later, 'and went crazy.'

Apart from the heap of runs Kirsten was constantly adding to, the trait of his batsmanship which caught the public's imagination was the way he clung to his wicket once given the chance to play himself in. Smashing a quick 40 is one thing; turning it into a century is another. Similarly, negotiating good times and bad to reach 200 was indeed a sign of rare talent welded with enviable determination.

And to do so three times in one season marked the player concerned as among the best.

But to prove undismissible in each of those three double centuries defied belief. Kirsten had his share of good fortune, and he expected it, as well as the bad luck.

However, his utter refusal to believe an innings could run dry was built on firmer foundations than those laid by the gods of chance. Virtually faultless technique combined with an unshakeable resolution to play bigger, longer, better innings every time he strapped on his pads made him as close to unstoppable as any batsman can come.

Three more centuries, not quite doubles, were to come Kirsten's way that season. In fact, he was on course for a fourth score over 200 against Lancashire at Old Trafford. But the Derbyshire captain, Geoff Miller, declared with Kirsten 162 not out and going strong. His other two centuries – 116 against Sussex at Derby and 101 against Somerset at Chesterfield – won back a little of the ground the law of averages had surrendered to the relentless number three. Perhaps he could not be stopped from making runs, but at least there was some happiness for opponents if they saw the back of him before he got the chance to turn one century into two.

Lamb scored 98 runs less than Kirsten that season, but he finished with the better average by virtue of a remarkable 19 undefeated trips to the crease. Although Lamb's contributions were not as big as Kirsten's – the highest of his five centuries was 152 against Leicestershire – they filled an important void for Northants and nudged him further in the direction of the England cap he would wear with such distinction in time to come.

Wessels, out of the Sussex line-up for six weeks after breaking his hand in a one-day match, stormed back to feature strongly in the race within the championship hunt which the South African batsmen had covertly run. Dismissed four times within ten runs of a century, he nevertheless scored an unbeaten 197 against Nottinghamshire, despite the presence of Rice and Richard Hadlee in their attack, and registered the highest score by a South African in England that year: 254 against Middlesex with compatriot Van der Bijl a proud, if frustrated, spectator.

It was impossible to ignore the South Africans' influence in England in 1980, and Wisden's announcement of their five Cricketers of the Year the following April amounted to official recognition of their superiority. The list included just one Englishman, Surrey fast bowler Robin Jackman, Australia's Kim Hughes – and all of Rice, Van der Bijl and Lamb. Even in this honour there was some bitterness as it was the last time Lamb chalked up a cricket accomplishment as a South African. From the beginning of the 1982 season he would be eligible for selection to the England team.

'When we come over here we have a point to prove,' Kirsten said in an interview with the Cape Town *Argus*' London bureau early that South African-swamped English season. 'We want to show the world what they are missing through the isolation of South African cricket. Certainly, that is the case as far as I am concerned. I am so much more determined. I concentrate much harder because I want to show what we can do.'

And there were few, whatever their politics, who didn't appreciate the show.

9

Captain Kirsten

If the public perception is that Eddie Barlow and Hylton Ackerman are giants of South African cricket, to Peter Kirsten they are the immortality just short of supping with the gods, cricketing and otherwise.

Each has coloured Kirsten's cricket with a broad brush, though not the same one. Barlow was the supreme mover and shaker; Ackerman the one capable of taking a step back and savouring the game's entire picture.

While he is of a different ilk to both, Kirsten acknowledges the influence they have had on his game. The debt he owes them will never be paid, nor do they expect it to be. It is, after all, the way of cricket for the mother hens to look after the chicks. Barlow and Ackerman might have employed different methods, but both took a keen interest in the cocky SACS prodigy when he was thrust under the spotlight.

Here was a player for the future, they realised. Better take care of him.

Both gave their all in the shadow of Table Mountain, as players, as teammates. And as captains.

Barlow's reign, stretching from the end of the doldrums that marked Province cricket near the end of the 1960s, was one of almost unmitigated triumph. A Currie Cup title shared with Transvaal in 1969-70 was followed by another championship in 1974-75, and in the other Barlow-led campaigns Province were invariably competitive.

Under Barlow, Province also won the inaugural Gillette Cup in 1969-70 and took one-day honours twice more, as well as qualifying for three additional finals. From the dark valleys of the B section to the very peak of the top flight: it was pure theatre, pure Barlow. Nevertheless, Province had slipped somewhat when Barlow headed east to Australia and the Packer circus before the 1977-78 season.

Ackerman was appointed to the captaincy and smoothed many an administrator's furrowed brow when he promptly steered Province to a deserved Currie Cup triumph. He did so without the fanfare entrenched in Barlow's game, employing instead an appreciation of the talents available to him and getting the best out of them through quiet motivation.

Province were distant runners-up to Transvaal in 1978-79 under Ackerman, and again the next season with Barlow back at the helm. Then, in the summer of 1980-81, they faltered. Province won just three matches, losing three and drawing two.

They sailed to victory in the first two rounds, thrashing Eastern Province by ten wickets and Northern Transvaal by five wickets. But then followed a ten-wicket loss to Natal and an innings thumping by Transvaal. And they had just regrouped somewhat with a draw against the mighty Transvalers at Newlands when Natal beat them by 141 runs – the two results which were to send the Currie Cup to Kingsmead.

They ended the campaign with a consolation 45-run win over Northerns at Berea Park.

In the Datsun Shield, Province easily overcame Free State's challenge before enduring ups and downs on their way to an eventual 1-2 defeat in the semi-finals against EP.

There was no blame slung between batsmen and bowlers to try to explain the events of Province's worst season since Barlow's arrival – both had let the side down. Province could muster just 16 batting bonus points, and while 32 points for bowling was respectable enough, they often battled to put a floundering innings out of its misery.

Among the batsmen, only Lamb and Seeff emerged with credit. Playing with his customary gusto whatever the match situation, Lamb had scored the only Currie Cup century by a Province batsman that season – 130 against Transvaal at Newlands – and finished with 578 runs, including five half-centuries, at 44,46.

The bowlers, apart from Denys Hobson (29 wickets at 21,89) and all-rounder Peter Swart (27 at 18,85), were in the same leaky boat.

Seeff, destined to become one of the most successful but least entertaining opening batsmen in the country, scored 549 runs at 36,60 and capped a fine second Currie Cup season by being selected to play for the

Rest of South Africa against Datsun Shield champions Transvaal, then an annual fixture involving the one-day title-holders.

Kirsten had been appointed Province vice-captain in July 1980 – an obvious nudge in the direction of the captaincy – but the added responsibility had done nothing for his batting. He finished fourth in the Province batting averages behind Barlow, with a mediocre 25,92. Despite solid form in the leagues, nothing seemed to come off when he took to the field for Province. Three half-centuries and a string of unmentionable innings were all he had to show for a long summer's work. It was also the second consecutive season he had failed to score a century for Province – a paucity only made worse by his heroics for Derbyshire.

And breaking the same finger twice – the second time preventing him from being part of one of the few highlights of the season, the second win over Northerns – didn't help matters.

Whatever the technical reasons for his poor form, a few perennial ghosts returned to haunt Kirsten that season.

Where was he going? What was the big picture? He didn't have any answers.

He could stomach one, perhaps two more winters in Derby, but even at home in his beloved Cape Town life as a professional cricketer had become strained. Was the game all his life consisted of, and could he accept that? Three years before, Graeme Pollock had urged him to 'do a course, get something behind you' and that had been half the idea behind going to Stellenbosch, but the county circuit had called him away.

Kirsten began to question the feasibility of making a living solely from playing cricket. The same uncertainty had clouded his elevation to the vice-captaincy before the season started.

'Look, I would be absolutely thrilled and honoured to be appointed vice-captain,' he told the *Sunday Times*, adding that he hoped a professional deal would be forthcoming. Wasn't it a fact of professional life? Kirsten asked.

The tone of a column penned by A C Parker, a South African sportswriting institution and always taken seriously in print, was distinctly icy.

'We do not see that Kirsten has much to complain about,' Parker opined in the *Argus* of 12 July 1980. And continued:

> His frustration over not being able to play Test cricket is understandable, and he has our own sympathies on this score. But, having some knowledge of his earnings as a professional cricketer, we

believe he is making a pretty good living.

Many a young man at Peter's age (25), a bachelor mind you, would be happy with half his earnings and savings.

We hope that those three double-centuries for Derbyshire this season aren't going to Peter Kirsten's head. He would do well to remember the loss of popularity (with all due respects) more famous and talented South African cricketer, Barry Richards, experienced when he denigrated county cricket which had given him an excellent living and a whopping benefit with Hampshire.

The column concluded: 'Peter should beware of putting too high a price on his head.'

Kirsten had the perfect riposte to this broadside in the form of the endless stream of runs he was scoring for Derbyshire. And he was still putting his bat where his mouth was that December, but this time his sights had shifted from salaries to the Province captaincy.

'KIRSTEN MAY MOVE NORTH', blared the banner headline in the *Sunday Times*, under which Ted Partridge had written a story hinting that Kirsten, who then had two years of his contract with Province left, was considering cutting off his Cape Town roots to settle in the Northern Transvaal.

'Obviously I love every second I am at Newlands but my commitment to cricket is total and having seen what a success Eddie has made of organising Newlands, I would like to try to do the same,' Kirsten threatened.

In fact, had Barlow won a parliamentary by-election earlier that year, Kirsten would already have been Province captain. Barlow had stood for the left-of-centre Progressive Federal Party, then the Official Opposition, against Nationalist John Wiley, a former Province cricketer, for the vacant Simonstown seat. He lost, and so returned to cricket. If Barlow had won the election, he would have had to break his contract with Province for the second time, the first being when he had followed the Packer trail.

As the season spiralled into a nightmare for Province, stories of another, more cynical, flavour began to hit the headlines.

'Champs or are they chumps', the *Sunday Times* wanted to know, adding 'It's time we hopped off cloud nine and took a long hard look at our kings of the willow.'

'TALENTED WASTRELS!' the same newspaper yelled in January 1981 above photographs of Lamb, Kirsten and Henry Fotheringham. The caption under Kirsten's picture was less than profound: 'Should be scoring more runs for Province.'

But the point it made was none the less valid.

It was happening. The sports isolation the South African government said, with typical arrogance, would never work was proving more effective than even its supporters had hoped. Not only was South Africa deprived of international competition, but the enviable standard it had built up in its domestic cricket over the years was declining at a depressing rate.

The players knew it too, and playing the county circuit was an option open to a privileged, talented few. It also had its limitations.

Kirsten was in the wilderness as much as any South African cricketer. But then came something to take his mind off such depressing matters – a fresh challenge of daunting proportions.

Despite his philanderings with Packer and politics, Barlow had seemed as secure as ever in the Province captaincy seat before the 1980-81 season. Contemporary Province cricket history could, after all, be neatly divided into BB and AB periods: Before Barlow and After Barlow. But there was a murmur of displeasure concerning his actions, especially as he had turned down the prospect of a benefit year in order to go to Australia, and the problems of 1980-81 had left a cloud hanging over Newlands. They had finished third in the Currie Cup – not a disaster, it may seem, but the knives were nevertheless unsheathed. There was also a growing feeling that what had worked for Province in the 1970s had outlasted its usefulness and that a new approach and new ideas were called for.

The two obvious candidates to lead Province into the future were Kirsten and Allan Lamb. Both had the character to do the job. But Lamb had already mapped out a future in England, so the shortlist was halved. Besides, Kirsten had been identified as the Western Province Cricket Union's successor of choice when he was made vice-captain.

Kirsten remembers being asked to speak at various functions as a representative of Province cricket: he was being tested, he realised, though he didn't necessarily enjoy the question paper.

On 22 April 1981, the murky waters parted. Edgar John Barlow, then 40, 'severed his connection with the Union – player, captain and Promotions Manager', as the *Argus* put it. Before the end of the month he would sign with the Stellenbosch-based Boland Cricket Union, closer to his pig farm at Klapmuts, and take on much the same role he had filled at Newlands in an attempt to inject into the then B section province's cricket the same brand of adrenalin that had made Province such a force.

The way was thus cleared for Kirsten to lead Province from the 1981-82 season, to follow the likes of Barlow and Ackerman, to recapture the glory they had won and lost.

He was officially appointed on 6 June 1981 and the ideas and innovations he wanted to pour into Western Province cricket were immediately evident.

One of Kirsten's suggestions was the appointment of a full-time professional coach – a first for Western Province. A former Kent professional and sometime centre forward for Charlton Athletic and Queen's Park Rangers, Stuart Leary, was named to the position the same day Kirsten got the captaincy. Public relations and promotion were also handed over to the professionals: the Kirsten touch again. He would be free to play and captain, as he thought it should be.

It was a big enough job on its own, a huge challenge.

10

English Honours

Kirsten arrived in England in the first fresh days of April 1981 imbued with a driving enthusiasm to get going on his fourth county season.

He already knew he would be leading Western Province in six months' time and the thought, far from causing him anxiety, excited him. Yes, much hard work awaited him, but the restlessness which had seeped into his cricket had been swept away.

He was in the nets soon after touching down, and the reporters gathered. Bit of a dry South African season, eh, Peter?

'I am out to redeem myself after my worst season in South Africa,' Kirsten replied. Then, showing a glimpse of the man behind the sometimes prickly exterior, he said: 'I have buckled down to hard work and am enjoying it. A disastrous season here will shatter me.'

And there was no doubt it would have. Western Province captaincy or not, Kirsten needed a good season in England to make up for the agony of 1980-81. He was indeed working hard in the form of a month's pre-season training with the rest of the Derbyshire squad. Something else he could introduce to Western Province, Kirsten noted.

As it turned out, Kirsten was a vital part of one of the most successful seasons in Derbyshire's history. They might have finished twelfth in the championship, but there was much to celebrate when they won the NatWest competition. Before this epic triumph, the last time Derbyshire had had cause to chill the champagne was in 1936 when they won the championship, to date their only success in England's premier competition.

It was the summer of Ian Botham's Ashes heroics, and nothing less than a pulsating NatWest final would do. Pulsating it certainly was, with the scores ending up tied and Derbyshire claiming the trophy on the strength of losing six wickets to Northamptonshire's nine.

'Derbyshire la-la-la, Derbyshire la-la-la,' sang their jubilant fans as they took over the greensward, Lord's or not.

When Barry Wood, the transplanted Lancastrian captaining Derbyshire, won the toss and put Northants in, Lord's was painted in the mellow tones of late summer. But the backdrop to the desperate run-chase by the Derbyshire numbers seven and eight, Geoff Miller and Colin Tunnicliffe, was decidedly gloomy. Fortunately the umpires, David Constant and Ken Palmer, had to do without lightmeters or the trophy might well have ended up in Northampton.

Wood's plan was to bowl Northants out for less than 250 but when Geoff Cook (who earned a trip to India as his man-of-the-match prize after scoring 111) and Wayne Larkins put on 99 for the first wicket, it seemed that groundsman Jim Fairbrother's prediction that he had prepared a 500-run pitch was not far wrong.

But three dazzling run-outs removing Lamb, Peter Willey and Tim Yardley, ensured Northants were kept in check and they could total only 235 for nine off their 60 overs.

Derbyshire opener Alan Hill went early and John Wright and Kirsten got going, content to take runs as they came. Then, 123 runs into the partnership, Neil Mallender struck from the Nursery End. Not once, but twice in the same over to remove Wright for 76 and Kirsten for 63, both lbw.

Twelve overs left. All of 71 runs required.

David Steele, all snowy-topped experience, he should be able to do something here … Bowled! For a duck. Five wickets down, 191 on the board. Only the light hurried from the scene as Cook steered fielders hither and thither. Thirty-four needed off four overs. Derbyshire hearts sank with the sun. A six, by Miller, and they rose again. But then Kim Barnett was run out, swinging the pendulum decidedly in Northants' favour. Not quite. Tunnicliffe hit two fours with lusty intent, and Nawaz Sarfraz's last over cost Northants 12 runs.

The final over. Seven runs needed to pass Northants' total but all who were present and correct knew a tie would be enough to win it for Derbyshire if they didn't somehow contrive to lose three wickets in the six balls remaining. Miller found three runs from the first two balls and

Tunnicliffe a single off the third. Four left, four to score.

A dot ball. A bloody dot ball! But then two singles off the next two, leaving Derbyshire on 234 for six with a ball to come. A single would tie it in terms of runs which Miller, at the non-striker's end, knew full well. He set off as early as good sportsmanship would allow – perhaps a mite earlier – and arrived at the opposite crease, belly down, not long after the ball. Tunnicliffe pinned his ears back and embarked on a mad dash for the bowler's end – and made it.

Derbyshire la-la-la …

Unbelievably, Derbyshire had won the trophy in similar circumstances to those in which they had beaten Essex at Derby on 19 August. Having dismissed Essex for a lowly 149, Derbyshire had stumbled to 145 for eight and needed at least five off the last two balls. Paul Newman hit a four off the penultimate delivery, and it all came down to that final ball.

Norbett Phillip, the Leeward Islander, bowled it and was so surprised to have it played straight back at him that he lost his head and, instead of calmly removing the bails at the vacant non-striker's end, he took a wild shy at the stumps, missed, and watched in horror as the ball scooted across the boundary.

The scores were left tied but, as in the final, Derbyshire won because of fewer wickets lost.

Kirsten's 1981 season contained other nuggets of the luck that befriends every on-form cricketer. He hit three centuries – including two more double-centuries – and seven fifties and was dismissed in the 90s in both innings against Essex.

He wasn't quite as consistent in the three one-day competitions, hitting seven half-centuries but averaging 29,00 with an aggregate of 725 runs, but he batted at his fluent best in the championship. He averaged 55,34 in first-class competition that year and he deserved it. And those were just the statistics.

The real story was the way Kirsten had rediscovered his zest for cricket, the desire which had deserted him so cruelly in South Africa.

The kind of rain that can only fall in an English summer at first threatened to prolong the drought, but then he hammered 300 runs in ten days, including a 90 against Essex and 41 not out against the touring Australians.

Then, on 23 June, the floodgates were opened. Kirsten scored his first century of the season – 114 in the second innings against Northamptonshire at Derby.

Not for the first or last time, Derbyshire, who declared their first innings closed at 252 for two and their second at 257 for five, were well beaten. Northants, with scores of 234 for nine declared and 279 for one – courtesy of 126 from Larkins and Cook's 120 not out – were nine-wicket winners.

Three days short of a month and several weighty scores later, Kirsten cracked a big one. Despite the unhelpful weather, it was turning out to be a season of only dreamed of opulence for the batsmen and Kirsten and Lamb headed the run harvest.

Both were in the second 500 of the 1000-run mark when Kirsten took strike against Somerset at Taunton on 20 July. Joel Garner – Big Bird, big aggro, big ego, big bouncer – was in the home side's attack, and Viv Richards also skulked under the Somerset dragon. But it wasn't to be their day – or any other bowler's – as Derbyshire racked up 459 for five declared in reply to Somerset's 335 for eight declared.

Twenty minutes short of three hours after his arrival at the wicket Kirsten's century was on the board. A shade under two hours later he had scored the fifth double-century of his career, and when he was eventually dismissed for 228, having stroked a six and 29 fours, he had hit his then highest score in first-class cricket.

With him for much of the way was the affable Steele, who didn't do too badly himself with 124 not out. During that innings, 'Steelie' came down the pitch and said to Kirsten, 'Don (as in Bradman), you take Joel and I'll take the others. I just can't fathom the Big Bird – he's far too tall for me.' Together they set a new Derbyshire record of 291 for the third wicket, wiping out the mark of 246 which had stood for 24 years.

Steele was the batsman who, on his Test début at Lord's, a ground he didn't know well, went down one flight of stairs too many on his way out of the pavilion to bat. Instead of walking out to face the Australians, he found himself in the toilets downstairs. When he eventually emerged on to the field, looking somewhat bemused, the Aussie wicketkeeper, Rod Marsh, asked: 'What have we here? Groucho Marx?'

Kirsten mounted one other championship extravaganza that season. And in the unusual setting of Blackpool, the seaside resort which serves as a venue for some of Lancashire's matches. By the time Derbyshire got to Blackpool, the championship had long been out of their grasp – as it usually was – but that did not stop Kirsten turning on the talent to score an undefeated 204.

Michael Holding and Paul Allott were not in the Lancashire side for the match, but that didn't detract from a performance that included two sixes and 23 fours and helped Derbyshire run up a first-day total of 406 for seven.

Kirsten finished sixth in the national averages that season, behind the third-placed Lamb and Clive Rice at number five. The Northants star, who was to earn his first Test cap in India the following northern winter, had a magnificent season scoring 2049 runs at 60,26 with five centuries and a remarkable 14 half-centuries. Rice had also had a solid season with Nottinghamshire, scoring 1462 runs at 56,23 and taking 65 wickets at 19,20.

Garth le Roux had taken the eighth spot in the bowling averages with a haul of 81 wickets at 19,53, including a career best analysis of eight for 107, against Somerset at Taunton, and a hat-trick against Warwickshire at Hove. Two places above him was Ian Greig, brother to Tony and at that stage still a South African. Greig boasted 76 wickets at 19,32 and a batting average of 30,36 having scored 911 runs.

It had been another memorable season for South Africans in England, but not as memorable as the next six months were to prove.

11

Double Delight

F ar from lying low for six months, the Western Province Cricket Union couldn't stay out of the news in the winter of 1981.

First came the shock of Barlow's departure, followed by the less surprising news that Kirsten would be his successor. But then Peter Swart, along with Barlow the top all-rounder available to Western Province, and left-arm fast bowler Stephen Jones announced that they would also be playing their cricket in the Boland the following season.

Kirsten issued periodic reassurances from England. Not to worry, he told various newspapers. We can win both trophies and we can do it largely with the existing personnel. But he would need to do some shopping. 'I have had several chats with players. I know exactly what I'm looking for and you could say negotiations are in progress,' he told the *Argus* in June. 'The chaps I have spoken to are not necessarily Derbyshire men. I cannot say more at this stage. There is still a lot to be arranged.'

The 'chaps' included the Eastern Province and Essex batsman Kenny McEwan, and the young Transvaal B batsman, Roy Pienaar, who had already enrolled at the University of Cape Town for the following year.

But while the pool of players Western Province drew from that 1981-82 season showed minimal, though significant, changes from that of the previous summer, there was a new administrative broom in use.

Out went the WPCU president Selwyn Myers in favour of Ronnie

Delport, whose vice-president's seat was filled by Fritz Bing. Bing had also been convener of selectors, a post taken over by Ken Funston, and, of course, Stuart Leary became Director of Coaching.

Kirsten also made a significant move by changing clubs from Cape Town Cricket Club to Avendale, a club with a predominantly 'coloured' membership ably led by Bert Erikson and financially assisted by Mike Stakol. Kirsten was to find the way of life in Athlone interesting – a far cry from the cosy southern suburbs of Cape Town.

Predictions of the great Western Province revival came from all quarters. 'We're going to win both trophies' didn't take long to become a cliché. Delport said his piece, along the lines of 'We'll miss Barlow and Swart but we have a few plans of our own up our sleeves'.

Kirsten, at 26 still gauche in public, was more direct in his column in the *Argus*:

> The loss of several experienced players to Western Province cricket has created a golden opportunity for several talented young players to make their mark in the South African first-class game.
>
> We have certainly been left with a gap in our bowling resources with the departure of two of our frontline attackers from last season.
>
> However, I am not worried about filling these places as there are plenty of talented, young players coming through.
>
> Players such as John During, Stephen Jefferies, Danie du Toit, Adrian Kuiper, Bossie Clark and others have all been around for several seasons.
>
> And it is high time they came through the test of first-class cricket.

Thus was the gauntlet thrown. It was time to produce.

Kirsten arrived in Cape Town, via a holiday in the Greek islands, on 28 September accompanied by McEwan who had been appointed to Barlow's former coaching position at Stellenbosch University. Early the next morning Kirsten was out running. Another challenge to his players: you've got to be fit to play in this team.

'We have got to get back to enjoying our cricket,' he told cricket writer Michael Owen-Smith. 'This is a top priority with so many young guys likely to make the side.'

The 12-man squad for the annual limited overs triangular tournament featuring Western Province, Transvaal and Natal was announced on 1 October and included both McEwan and Pienaar.

Clive Rice's Transvaal squad contained Graeme Pollock, Alan Kourie and Alvin Kallicharran, the West Indies and Warwickshire left-hander who was to spend the next seven seasons playing for Transvaal and later for Free State.

Natal, led by Barry Richards, boasted Vince van der Bijl and Chris Wilkins, though they missed Mike Procter who was in the throes of recovery from his knee injury.

Transvaal were the favourites to win the event, but it was Natal who scraped home on a superior overall run-rate after each team had registered a win and a loss.

The first game, between Western Province and Transvaal (which Transvaal won by three runs) was remarkable if only for the fact that Kirsten, Pollock and Kallicharran were all dismissed without scoring. Western Province then beat Natal by seven wickets in a match reduced by rain from 50 to 30 overs a side, but the winners' cheque of R3 000 was not to be theirs.

No one took the result of the Computer Sciences competition too seriously and Kirsten, now taking everything in through a captain's eyes, returned to Cape Town confident he had the raw material to beat his rivals that season. It wouldn't be easy to come back from the tribulations of 1980-81 but it certainly wasn't out of reach.

Such scant match practice, not added to by a surprising two-wicket loss to Eastern Province in the annual Hunt's Challenge Cup at Newlands on 17 October, was perhaps not the ideal way to prepare for the Currie Cup. But Leary, the consummate old pro, had done a good job of ensuring Kirsten would have a squad of raring cricketers on his hands for the first fixture of the season proper, against Eastern Province at Newlands. Kirsten was already feeling the benefits of having Leary on board. A highly respected coach, he dealt with various players' technical flaws, problems his eye was trained to spot and irritations Kirsten would otherwise have had to try and sort out himself.

In terms of players, Kirsten was also about to get what he needed to put Western Province back on top. During this season, Garth le Roux and Stephen Jefferies would emerge as the most successful new ball attack in the country and with himself, Lamb and McEwan forming the heart of the batting order, only the worst of form could prevent the kind of totals which win matches.

In fact, their batsmen failed Western Province just twice the entire season, and perhaps fortunately in the same match – against Natal at Kingsmead when they were bowled out for 155 and 144 on their way to a five-wicket loss, their only defeat of the campaign.

As far as spin bowling was concerned, Denys Hobson was in his prime and the promising Omar Henry provided left-arm variation. Kirsten did have reservations about the depth of spin in the province, but at the top the situation was healthy.

If there was a weakness, it was at the top of the order where Western Province battled to find a reliable partner for the consistent Seeff. John Nel and During each had a turn and Pienaar was preferred for the other six matches even though he had virtually no success, finishing with a highest score of 25 not out and averaging a measly 8,80 from ten completed innings.

But even such an important deficiency could not stop Western Province that season. Kirsten had noted that Transvaal and Natal, the champion provinces of the previous two seasons, had won six of their eight matches. The Wanderers was the quickest, bounciest strip in the country and, with Procter in the line-up, Kingsmead was invariably green and hostile. Without stooping to the level of preparing result pitches, Western Province had to ensure a better chance of a result being reached at Newlands.

The clean-shaven Newlands pitches of the 1980-81 season, when Western Province won just one of their four home matches, had to go, Kirsten decided. More grass, please, Mr Groundsman.

That wasn't difficult to organise. The chief groundsman was Noel Kirsten.

Kirsten had thus arranged his pieces on the Western Province chessboard, and the tactics had long since been discussed.

Enter Eastern Province.

The toss went to Kirsten. It's Newlands, we'll bat, generations of captains before and after would have decided.

'We'll field,' said the Western Province skipper. Winning matches, instead of not losing them, has always been Kirsten's first priority as a captain. This has earned him the reputation in some defensive quarters of not knowing when to call off the hounds, when it would be prudent to dispense with the three-slips-and-a-gully barrage and opt to save runs.

On 11 November 1981, however, his attacking instincts were exactly what was required. Four and a half hours after Kirsten put them in, EP were a spent force, bowled out for 172 with the ninth-wicket stand between the captain, Dave Brickett, and Kenny Watson as valuable for the 80 minutes it used up as for the 66 runs it realised.

Le Roux, with five for 30, and Jefferies had blown a hole through the EP top and middle orders and Henry, two for 40, had helped lop off the tail.

At the close, Western Province had advanced to 120 for two. Kirsten was 52 not out.

It had been a taxing but thrilling first day in charge. The feeling of steering his own ship appealed to Kirsten, described by A C Parker as perhaps young but 'having a wise head on his young shoulders' for an inherently difficult job.

Playing under the protea involves more than on-field prowess. The people of Western Province never leave a match at the ground: it goes home with them, stays for supper, and often till the next morning with relentless discussion swirling about incessantly. The players who call Newlands home get a ready-made family with it – and you can pick your friends but never your family.

As captain, Kirsten came in for special attention. His examination started that November day, and he passed the first part of it well. Not only had he efficiently managed his forces to clinically dispose of his opponents, but he had stayed in the game with a swooping run-out to remove Watson and scuttle the only remaining chance EP had of mounting a respectable score. And then he grafted his way to an unbeaten half-century, an innings with important implications for both Kirsten and his team. Should he continue and reach a century, it would be his first in South Africa since his 105 against Transvaal in the 1979 New Year match and what better way for a young captain to lay his foundation.

Kirsten had scored his first 50 off 78 deliveries, but he would battle through a further 166 to see his twenty-sixth first-class century registered. His timing was not what it should have been in South African conditions and he managed just two boundaries in the second half of his innings before falling to Watson and the new ball for 114.

Magically, his twelfth century for Western Province was a provincial record, as was the fact that 11 of them had been scored in Currie Cup matches. Kirsten shared in partnerships of 94 for the second wicket with Lawrence Seeff and 73 for the fourth with Lamb. He had laboured for five hours for his century and a further 45 minutes thereafter. Watson had added to the difficulties Kirsten faced with his timing by peppering him with short deliveries, no doubt intent on exploiting any chink he might have opened in the batsman's armour when he hit him on the head with a bouncer during the Hunt's Challenge match.

But Kirsten stood firm, and although it was far from his fastest or most attractive ton – the press dubbed it a creepy crawly century – it showed that the impregnable determination and calmness which had brought him so much success in previous seasons had not been affected by his dry 1980-81 season. Moreover, these would be important qualities in a team which pinned much of its chances on overtly attacking players.

'I'm happy,' proclaimed Kirsten, despite the fact that the morning session had yielded just 31 runs and, with McEwan making 21 against his former team-mates, the rest of the batting order crumbled to limit Western Province to a total of 284 – a lead of 112.

Bad light and rain forced an early end to the day with EP 15 for one in their second innings. The Sunday papers flew at Kirsten the next day, charging him with engineering slow play. But it all blew up in their faces on the Tuesday, following Monday's rest day, when Jefferies and Hobson ripped through the visitors' batting on a pitch that wasn't kind to batsmen to begin with. The paceman took four for 51 and the spinner four for 65, with Le Roux also making two important breakthroughs as EP were shunted for 158, leaving Western Province to make 47 for victory.

At 4.42 pm, Nel stroked a delivery from James Carse through the covers for four and Western Province were home by ten wickets, earning 17 points to EP's two and taking an early lead in the standings.

Having strolled to an eight-wicket win over Northern Transvaal in a Datsun Shield match at Newlands on 21 November – the visiting captain, Norman Featherstone, won the toss and batted despite heavy cloud and humidity, leading to an embarrassing total of 98 – it followed that Western Province would be odds-on to perform similarly in their Currie Cup encounter at Berea Park in Pretoria starting six days later.

The victory which followed, by an innings and 31 runs, had most of the hallmarks of champions at work. There were no centuries but Kirsten made 86, McEwan 53, and Jefferies 63 in a total of 368, scored in reply to Northerns' meagre 129.

Kirsten had won the toss and, without hesitation, put Northerns in. Giving up first crack at the pitch once, as he had done against EP, was encouragingly adventurous. Doing it twice in succession invited enquiries. His argument was logical. Pretoria had had rain leading up to the match, leaving moisture below the surface. Also, Kirsten had decided that there was excess grass on the pitch, an opinion shared by selection convener Funston who had made the trip with the team. Given his devastating new ball pair, these were grounds enough for bowling first, the best course of action for the only goal he had in mind – winning.

Jefferies ensured the Northern Transvalers wouldn't forget him in a hurry by following up his batting performance with a haul of five for 46, and Le Roux was no less devastating in taking three for 22 off 14.4 overs.

In Northerns' second innings, openers Brian Whitfield and Allan Barrow stayed together for almost two and a half hours, putting on 105 runs, but by the close of the second day they had lost Barrow and nightwatchman Bruce McBride for the addition of just one run.

Hobson came into his own on the last day, taking four wickets before lunch and ending with five for 82 off 30 overs. The rest, except for Featherstone who fought to the end for his unbeaten 36, followed meekly and less than half an hour after lunch Western Province had notched up another 14 points.

Already a pattern was emerging. Le Roux and Jefferies would do most of the damage in the first innings when the pitch had more grass and bounce, and Hobson was lethal on the wearing surfaces of the second innings. With a line-up of confident but not arrogant batsmen – which meant that they performed just as well in partnerships as in solo efforts – the attack almost always had runs to play with, not that they needed much leeway to dismiss most of their opponents.

Bowling first also became part of Western Province's success. They batted first only three times, in both the drawn matches against Transvaal and in the loss to Natal at Kingsmead.

Perhaps the player most disadvantaged by this trend was Hobson. What he could have accomplished had he been let loose in the fourth innings of a few more matches will always be a matter for conjecture, especially as Transvaal batted only once at the Wanderers and he didn't play against them at Newlands, while he had the opportunity to bowl just three overs in the second innings against Natal before they wrapped up their win.

Against Transvaal, Kirsten admitted that his first priority was not to lose, and this led to accusations of negative tactics by, among others, Transvaal captain Rice. But Western Province could hardly be expected to play attacking cricket after they totalled 269 in the first innings, though they were careful not to be dismissed within 88 overs and thus give Transvaal a full house of five bowling bonus points.

Transvaal had also helped take the needle out of the contest by being unable to beat Northern Transvaal at Berea Park in the opening round. Western Province's need for an outright victory against Transvaal was thus diminished and they could afford to play it safe.

With a draw the most likely result on the evidence of even the first day's play, Transvaal were anxious to get runs on the board, a task Pollock and Kallicharran warmed to with a third-wicket stand of 155 in 174 minutes. Kallicharran went on to make 129 – marking his feat of having scored a century in every major cricket-playing country – while Pollock went for 70, just 20 runs short of 10 000 runs in Currie Cup cricket.

Rice took up where they left off, hitting two sixes and nine fours in his 70, 52 of which came in a fourth-wicket partnership of 90. However, had Le Roux not been rendered unable to bowl by a chest muscle injury which took him out of the attack for an entire session, Transvaal might have found this somewhat harder to come by. Lunch brought the declaration at 397 for six, a lead of 128 with two sessions left in the match.

Any thoughts Transvaal might have entertained of a Western Province collapse following the early capture of Pienaar's wicket ebbed away in the 110 minutes Seeff and Kirsten consumed in adding 80 runs for the third wicket. Seeff, who batted more than three hours for his 57 not out, and Lamb, on nine, convinced Rice it was hopeless. Transvaal garnered four points and Western Province three.

Not the best result, but good enough, thought Kirsten. Western Province led Northern Transvaal by 12 points at the top of the table with a match in hand, followed by Natal and Transvaal, by far their strongest rivals. And it was the first time in five seasons that Western Province had emerged from the Wanderers with a share of the spoils.

Rice was unhappy with the pitch he was given – not the average green, seaming Wanderers screamer but instead a decidedly more friendly strip. 'I can promise we won't be getting another one like it,' he bristled, cursing the top-dressing of compost that had been applied during the rugby season.

The Transvaal captain was surely even more grumpy when Transvaal bombed out of the Datsun Shield in a three-leg semi-final against Natal, in the process ending a run of consecutive titles at three. But the hype surrounding the other semi-final, between Western Province and Boland, devoured far more newsprint in Cape Town than the happenings at the Wanderers and Kingsmead.

It was, of course, the Young Turk taking on the Old Stager: Kirsten versus Barlow. And, for that matter, versus Swart and Jones.

'If I were in Peter Kirsten's shoes I would be as worried as all hell,' Barlow blustered in inimitable fashion to the *Sunday Times* a week before the first match. 'They have a lot more to lose than a match and let's face it they haven't been the most sparkling team in one-day cricket this year. I, for one, am not unduly worried at the prospect of meeting Province. But if the shoe were on the other foot – if I were captain of Province – I would most certainly be a worried man. Terribly worried. All the pressure would be on me. I would know that I would be expected to win, that there would be a lot more at stake than victory or defeat in a single match and that wouldn't be the best way to go into this game – particularly if I had the same one-day record as Province this season.'

Good old Bunter, always ready with a quote. But this time he had something to shout about. Whether Western Province one-day form was as lamentable as he made out was closer to hype than truth, but Boland had beaten Eastern Province by all of 66 runs in the second round of the Datsun Shield, at St George's Park no less, and celebrated an innings victory over Border – with Barlow scoring his forty-first century – earlier that month.

They would go on to win the Bowl at their second attempt that season, registering outright victory in four of their six matches and losing the other two. Already Barlow's presence was having the required effect.

Kirsten, in contrast, spent most of the week before the match wondering whether Le Roux was going to play. His ribs felt better – but was there much point in risking further injury in a match Western Province should be able to win without him, a match that meant nothing in terms of the Currie Cup campaign?

So Le Roux sat it out, leaving the new ball to Jefferies and Kuiper. First, however, Western Province had some batting to do. The weather contributed splendidly to the occasion and Newlands was packed to the rafters with 10 000 devotees, for once not all shouting for the home side.

The first duel: the toss. Kirsten won it and defied what had become that summer's convention by electing to bat.

Pienaar's unhappy season thus far evaporated in the festive heat and he weathered the unaccustomed relatively early loss of Seeff, with whom he put on 45, and McEwan's cheap dismissal, to add 62 runs for the third wicket with Lamb. After scoring 67 immaculate runs in two and a quarter hours, Pienaar tried to force the pace and paid the price. But all his dismissal accomplished, from Boland's point of view, was to bring Kirsten into action. Lamb and his captain, best of friends off the field, showed just how well they could get on together on the field as the momentum which had been brewing all morning reached boiling point.

In terms of runs, the partnership netted 105 in just over an hour. But it also spelled the effective end of Boland's challenge. Besides opening the bowling, Barlow cajoled, encouraged and willed his eager players to the greatest heights. They responded like soldiers on a battlefield, throwing themselves at virtually every batted ball not within easy reach. The clatter of ball against stumps was heard more than once but each time the inspired fielder's throaty plea was turned down.

However, when Lamb and Kirsten defied their courage and began punching the ball through and over them, and ran them ragged between the wickets, the pace began to show. More than once the stumps and bails were launched by an inspired throw but each time the batsmen were home. Suddenly they were indeed minnows and the pond was rather big.

There was contrast: Kirsten clinical, Lamb decidedly more bloody. But the runs flowed from both with equal inevitability. Kirsten, 57 not out in an hour, saw out the 55 overs with Kuiper. Lamb faced 89 balls and hit three sixes and six fours in his 90 before hoisting one off-drive too many and falling to a remarkable catch by Jacques de Villiers just a metre inside the rope.

The applause that greeted Barlow as he strode out to open the Boland innings with Andre du Toit would have done any home side skipper proud. And for a while it did seem as if Bunter was back home as his side faced the uphill task of bettering Western Province's 258 for four.

With Barlow directing operations, Boland had to get somewhere and after an opening stand of 30 he and Andre Odendaal added 40 for the second. Barlow ended up with 43 and Odendaal with 42, but the only other worthy score was Swart's 51. On three, Swart had a life at long-on off Hobson, but he survived to knock up 48 runs for the seventh wicket with Carl Schultz, who was 19 not out.

As a contest, the match had long been over but Newlands wasn't ready to lower the curtain. Seeff held a remarkable catch at short mid-wicket off Pienaar to dispose of De Villiers, while During held a difficult chance at backward square leg and Jones departed second ball, also off Pienaar.

However, the final over was the scene of the real drama. Having opened the bowling in Le Roux's absence, Kuiper stood ready to deliver the last six balls of the match. He immediately smuggled a delivery through Pine Anker's guard, bringing Charl Coetzee to the crease. Kuiper's next delivery was a touch quicker than usual and the inswing on it nipped past Coetzee's bat and bowled him.

Kirsten responded by bringing in the field for the Boland number 11, Howie Bergins, who came limping to the wicket as a result of the leg injury he had sustained while fielding. Kuiper, adrenalin pumping, charged in, bowled quicker still. Thud. The ball had too much on it for the stricken Bergins, who could only get his pad in its path.

'HOWAZAAT?' came the predictable, howling appeal from the entire Western Province team. But umpire George Hawkins would have none of it and shook his head slowly in disagreement.

Western Province won the match by 76 runs, though the Bolanders, who totalled 184 for nine, probably deserved to go down by a lesser margin if only on the strength of their enthusiasm. But they were somewhat less competitive in the second leg at Oude Libertas in Stellenbosch on 9 January, a match Western Province won by 118 runs despite the absence of Lamb who had contracted viral meningitis towards the end of the New Year match. (He recovered in time to take the field against Northern Transvaal at the end of January.)

In that second semi, Western Province totalled 236 for nine with a more controlled batting performance than in the first leg. Pienaar made another noteworthy contribution with his 42, and McEwan hit 32. But the most valuable batting came lower down the order via Bruce's 47, an unbeaten 42 from Henry, and a similar score, though out, by the then fully fit Le Roux.

Barlow had dropped himself to fifth in the order, ostensibly to take advantage of the less lethal bowling, but the tactic failed when he was caught off Jefferies for a duck having faced just four deliveries. Swart, who faced three balls, also failed to score as Boland slumped to 118 all out in 41.1 overs.

While Le Roux was economy itself in conceding 13 runs and taking two wickets off his 11 overs, Jefferies let fly to take four for 34. During was of a less fiery pace but almost as effective with his three for 20.

Boxing Day in Durban. They might just as well have called it Big Vince Day. Only Seeff, Lamb, Hobson and the not-out man, Jefferies, escaped the clutches of the outlandishly tall, balding seamer on a pitch better suited to billiards than first-class cricket.

Leary called it the greenest pitch he had ever seen and claimed that the umpires had had to ask the groundsman to cut a line into the turf to enable them to see where the pitch ended and the outfield started!

Van der Bijl, who finished with seven for 31 off 23.5 explosive overs, and the Kingsmead green mamba made for powerful cricketing chemistry. Less than 56 overs after they took to the crease, Western Province were back in the hut for 157.

Only Kuiper and Jefferies made it into double figures. Kuiper, showing the first signs of what would become a wonderfully entertaining disregard for the shackles of convention, hammered boundaries almost as frequently as he greeted new batting partners. Unperturbed at being dropped on 12 and 35 and feeding off the surfeit of legside deliveries he received, Kuiper hit three sixes and 11 fours on his way to a memorable 89.

Jefferies, of similar intent but lacking the technique, made 17 not out – but at a price. He took a delivery on his right hand that fractured a metacarpal bone, although he was still able to bowl.

After Van der Bijl's success it was reasonable to expect Le Roux and

Jefferies to prosper. But after the openers had opened the initial crack it was the far less hostile Pienaar, bowling nothing more than line and length, who ran through the order to finish with five for 24 off 12 overs. Hobson hadn't been handed the ball when Natal were dismissed for 143. Only the left-handers Rob Bentley and Daryll Bestall, as well as Paddy Clift, made themselves heard, and none reached 40.

But Western Province fared just one run better in their second innings, Van der Bijl picking up four for 33 and Les Taylor four for 47. Mercifully, they were spared the wrath of the still recovering Procter, although his off-spin, with which he took two for 15 off 17, proved lethal enough.

Natal were left to make 159 on what had hardened into a decidedly more trustworthy pitch, but lost openers Richards and Wilkins for 10 runs. Both fell to Jefferies, who had received pain-killing injections in his hand, and both were caught not far from the bat by Kuiper. However, Bentley and Bestall sorted matters out with a third-wicket stand of 99, making 48 and 57 respectively, and Procter's 24 helped Natal to a win in 43.5 overs. Fittingly, the ailing Jefferies took four for 50.

Back to Cape Town for the New Year match against Transvaal, and this time it would be an even bigger occasion than usual. With Western Province and Transvaal shaping up as the top contenders for the trophy, and the fact that the Wanderers match had ended in stalemate, all who were interested knew that the Currie Cup's destination could well be determined by the events of 1, 2 and 4 January at Newlands.

Clive Rice understood this all too well. 'I have a feeling Peter Kirsten will have enough self-confidence at Newlands to take Transvaal on,' he sneered to the press. 'And that's what I'm looking forward to. We want to thrash Western Province.'

Any friction there was between Rice and Kirsten stayed strictly on the field – off it they have the utmost respect for each other's achievements and talents – but it didn't come across that way from the comfy side of the boundary.

Perhaps Rice didn't consciously portray himself as a boorish Transvaler, but his comments didn't do much to shatter the myth in Cape Town. Kirsten, by contrast, argued with measured logic and the subdued confidence his public knew and had come to expect of him. Besides, Kirsten didn't have much to say. All three of his strike bowlers – Le Roux, Jefferies and Hobson – were doubtful for the match. The pacemen were still struggling with their injuries and Hobson was battling – of all things – chicken pox. Kirsten knew that if he wanted to beat Transvaal outright his bowlers would have to take almost as many wickets in this match as Transvaal had lost all season.

In fact, Rice's team had yet to be dismissed that summer and averaged 367 for six in the first innings. In addition, they had scored 19 batting points while the rest of the A section teams had mustered only 17 between them. Western Province knew that the key to improving this tally was to score more quickly, but against an attack that included Rice, future England fast bowler Neal Radford and the treacherous Alan Kourie, runs would have to be earned.

With the quest for a faster scoring rate uppermost, Stephen Bruce, the beefy wicketkeeper who batted with murderous intent, was called up for his first senior Western Province match. Richie Ryall, indisputably the better gloveman, carried the lighter bat and had to make way.

The home side had mixed results from the fitness tests on the morning of the first day: Le Roux and Jefferies were fit, but Hobson was unable to play. Transvaal had a significant injury problem of their own, with Kallicharran ruled unfit.

As they had done so many times before, north and south were about to collide on the cricket field. And the southerners didn't make the best of starts.

Rice made the early grab, trapping Pienaar in front for seven. But it would be Kourie who would strike the hammer blows. He bowled Seeff, caught and bowled both Kirsten and Lamb before removing Le Roux and the impressive Henry after having broken their eighth-wicket partnership eight runs before it reached three figures. After 12 overs, Kourie had figures of four for 12.

He stepped up to bowl his thirteenth just as nonchalantly as in the rest of his spell. But Bruce was waiting in ambush, looking for an opening to make his mark. Twelve deliveries later Kourie's previously shining figures were somewhat tarnished. Eighteen runs came off the first six, and 14 off the second. Incredibly, Bruce claimed all 32 of those runs by launching three sixes, three fours and an incongruous couple.

The rotund left-armer would suffer more punishment before the day was out, but of the 153 balls he bowled, only 31 had runs taken off them. Bruce hit one of his deliveries clean through the scoreboard's tiled roof. He smashed 89 runs but needed only 35 scoring shots to get them, employing five sixes and eight fours as his most efficient weapons. With the equally aggressive Kuiper he shared a sixth-wicket partnership of 157 to dig Western Province out of the hole they had fallen into after being reduced to 90 for five.

Seeff had guarded his wicket admirably through the crisis but it was left to the sixth-wicket pair, and to Le Roux and Henry, to nudge Western Province past 350. Three runs after the target was reached Kirsten declared, leaving Kourie polishing figures of six for 88. Kirsten wondered just what Hobson, a genuine leggie, would have got up to if Kourie, a master of flight and pace rather than spin, could wreak such havoc on the first day.

Just three batsmen featured in Transvaal's reply: the elegant Jimmy Cook with 72, the dashing Kevin McKenzie with 78, and Rice himself with 35. Only two others reached double figures as the visitors stumbled to 251 all out. Cook and McKenzie batted responsibly for their third-wicket contribution of 151, as did Rice. But the second day belonged to the Western Province pace pair: Le Roux and Jefferies, between them, accounted for eight of the wickets.

Le Roux took five for 63 and Jefferies three for 73. Kirsten had mixed feelings: he didn't doubt his quicks had it in them to kill off most floundering batting performances, but he couldn't help thinking of Hobson ...

Kourie was at it again in the second innings, sending five batsmen on their way at a cost of 102 runs. With Radford, he helped send Western Province spiralling from 53 for one to 55 for four – removing Kirsten, Lamb and Seeff – and chased the home side into a defensive corner from which they decided to play safe. But Henry proved that arms and legs not much thicker than stumps are no deterrent to hitting a cricket ball a long way by lashing four of Kourie's last five deliveries over the sightscreen at the Kelvin Grove end.

Earlier, McEwan and Kuiper had added 71 valuable runs for the fifth wicket. Henry's final fling convinced Kirsten he couldn't lose the match. He declared at 186 for seven, leaving his Currie Cup rivals to make 289 in 110 minutes and 20 overs to win. Batting at six runs an over to win a crucial first-class match is not a simple matter, and Rice again had plenty to say about Kirsten's tactics.

But the fact that Transvaal could only manage 118 for three, with Pollock and Rice putting on 56 for the unbroken fourth wicket, was as much a product of Kirsten's cautious approach as miserly bowling, particularly by Henry, who took two for 28 off 15 tight overs.

That the captains called it off with nine overs remaining didn't detract from an enthralling contest that had attracted more than 36 000 spectators over the three days.

Had Kirsten been able to tie up one end with Henry and attack from the other with Hobson, the result might have been different. But the nine points Western Province earned inched open the gap between them and Transvaal, who went away with six points.

The six-wicket defeat Western Province inflicted on their guests in the Protea Assurance Challenge one-day match at Newlands two days after the Currie Cup match might have been irrelevant in the greater context, but it served to intensify Kirsten's ambitions of winning at least one trophy that season.

So much so that he surged back to personal form with his second century of the season in the first innings against Northern Transvaal at Newlands. His 130 was the only century of the match – Northerns captain Norman Featherstone was unfortunate to be trapped in front on 99 by Jefferies in the first over with the new ball – but Western Province delivered a consummate batting performance to answer Northerns' mediocre 251 with 422 for nine declared.

Kirsten created special interest by twice taking the part of a left-handed batsman and playing a pull of sorts when facing gangly left-arm spinner Willie Morris. It was better to play with the spin, he would explain later, but the impression created was one of supreme confidence in his own and his team's ability.

With Seeff, who made 50, Kirsten put on 108 for the second wicket and he had enough left to add 133 for the fourth with McEwan, who scored a solid 61. Kuiper could not play because of university examinations, but Western Province were in such firm control throughout that his valuable presence was hardly missed. Hobson had returned to the team but found himself with little to do as the unstoppable Le Roux and Jefferies gobbled seven wickets between them in each innings. Le Roux took six for 44 and three for 23, and Jefferies one for 41 and four for 25.

It was all over before lunch on the last day. Western Province were a full 21 points richer, having won by an innings and 96 runs.

Kirsten knew it wouldn't be quite so easy in Western Province's next match, against Natal at Newlands, starting on 12 February. Both teams knew outright victory was important to their Currie Cup hopes, virtually guaranteeing attacking cricket.

That Western Province had not beaten Natal in their five previous first-class encounters didn't bother Kirsten unduly. He knew their attack would have the added burden of having to adjust from bowling on the green monster at Kingsmead to the more sedate pace of Newlands – and he knew he had the best attack in the country in his dressingroom.

He also thought their batting vulnerable – though he didn't think they would tumble to 169 all out off 67.5 overs. Le Roux and Jefferies used the new ball well and Henry got stuck into the middle order to take four for 22.

The pitch was atypical for a Newlands strip, the bounce being unreliable, and Natal battled to build worthwhile partnerships. At first, Western Province fared no better. Natal had seen the back of Seeff, Kirsten and During, who opened after Pienaar was dropped, at a cost of just 36 runs before Lamb and McEwan did an admirable repair job to take Western Province to stumps at 96 for three.

The fourth-wicket pair continued their fine work the next day, completing a partnership of 152 in 192 minutes. Finally given the chance to play a measured innings instead of chasing bonus points, McEwan's batting blossomed into his first century for Western Province, while Lamb's 89 represented an improvement on his recent form.

McEwan, who was in complete command during the five and a half hours he was at the crease for his 117, also put on 115 with the adventurous Kuiper, who scored a round 50. A handy 22 not out from Henry and 12 from Jefferies, who both hit sixes over long-on, helped Western Province total 363 – a lead of 194.

The Natal attack, even with Procter back to pace bowling, had indeed failed to fire on a pitch that turned out to be more helpful to their cause than they would have thought.

It had not been a pleasant day for the visitors. Not only had their main strike bowler, Van der Bijl, toiled for 30 overs without success – not to mention dropped a catch – but they lost the services of first change bowler Les Taylor and at one stage also had three substitutes on the field. By the close Natal were 64 for two, having endured some fine fast bowling by Le Roux and Jefferies. But it was Hobson who profited, taking both wickets for 13 off nine overs.

Natal seemed to be on their way to saving the match when they reached lunch on the last day at 176 for four. But they advanced just 67 runs from that score, with Procter's 63 the best of their efforts, before the Western Province openers padded up with the easy target of 50 well within their sights. The powerful alchemy of Le Roux, Jefferies and the second new ball had undone the morning's diligent work: each took three wickets with the new cherry finally to deny Natal the chance of notching two consecutive championships.

Kirsten pulled the penultimate ball of Robin Smith's only over to the railway stand boundary just after 4 pm as Western Province won by seven wickets and collected 18 points.

This put Western Province on 93 points, three ahead of Transvaal with a match to play. After initially leading the log, Western Province had spent much of the campaign playing catch-up-to-Transvaal, who were invariably a match ahead of them, but the slender lead couldn't have come at a better time for Kirsten's team. Natal were third on 62 and out of the running.

So it would all come down to Eastern Province at St George's Park for Kirsten and his team. Transvaal would face Natal at the Wanderers. There was no denying it, not at the Wanderers or anywhere else: Western Province were favourites to win the Currie Cup.

Those matches would start on 1 March. On 20 February, the focus was on the Datsun Shield final to be played, with cynical irony, at the Wanderers by virtue of its being South Africa's biggest and most well-equipped cricket venue.

Tickets were sold out eight days before the match and the South African Broadcasting Corporation announced that much of the day's proceedings would be covered live on television. South African cricket was on the brink of the media goldfish bowl and it would be an occasion to be remembered, though as it transpired not entirely for positive reasons.

Kirsten had finished on the losing side in his three previous Shield finals but he felt this one could be different. The neutral venue was an important factor because it would deprive the Natal bowlers of their beloved Kingsmead snakepit, one-day match or not. Kirsten also thought Western Province had found a viable formula for winning limited overs matches.

A crowd of 28 137, who spent R147 973 on their seats, jammed the cavernous Wanderers stadium as match day finally dawned on a clear late summer Saturday. Like all cricket crowds, they had come to be entertained, and they would not leave disappointed though it was not to be the classic one-day match based on runs galore.

Procter called correctly and sent Western Province in to bat. Their total of 178 for eight off 55 overs looked puny next to a batting line-up that included Wilkins, Bestall, Procter and, in particular, Richards. Kirsten's men had not got the start they wanted and were reduced to 69 for four. The captain himself played responsibly after coming to the crease in the second over after Seeff was caught behind with but a single on the board.

But when the shine left the ball Kirsten took it as a licence to hit out and chased the runs a little too eagerly. Still, his 35 was second only to Kuiper's 38. McEwan and Kuiper also fell to rash shots but Lamb, the other big gun, became the victim of the first of two controversies that would cast a pall over the match.

Van der Bijl bowled to Kuiper with Lamb awaiting developments at the non-striker's end. An unhealthy 'plock' issued from Kuiper's bat as he drove the ball back to the bowler and he immediately walked to the side of the crease, motioning to the dressingroom for a new bat.

Big Vince, the epitome of sportsmanship, picked up the ball, turned round to see Lamb out of his ground but by no means attempting a run. He feigned a throw at the stumps, at which Lamb, himself one of the more jovial players in the game, waved his bat at the bowler in mock retaliation.

And then Van der Bijl threw down the stumps with Lamb stranded in the middle of the pitch. Unbelievably, an appeal followed. And up came the finger. Lamb left, patently furious, as the Natal players yelled in jubilation.

Was the ball not dead? the television commentators and millions more asked one another as the replays rolled by. No, said umpire Perry Hurwitz. And in terms of Law 23 the ball only becomes dead 'when the umpire considers it so'.

Kirsten had seen what happened from the dressingroom. Upset by his own form and the mess his batsmen were making of things, his ire rose. Fine. They've also got to bat today.

Natal were shocked out of their pleasant daydream of ambling to a third national limited overs title in the opening over of their innings. Jefferies came flying in, let loose his lethal left arm and bowled Tich Smith for a duck. Still shocked at being one for nought, Natal gulped again when Wilkins was run out, also without scoring.

But Rob Bentley and Bestall weathered the storm and made 73 runs together before the former was caught behind off Pienaar. Bestall and Richards, in sublime form, then shared a fourth-wicket stand of 43 in 50 minutes, both eventually falling to fine catches at mid-off by Kirsten and Jefferies respectively.

But even at 118 for five it seemed a not unreasonable task for Natal, who were originally asked to bat at just 3,25 runs an over to win. Procter had only just arrived at the crease and had Neville Daniels with him. And Paddy Clift was padded up and waiting, and Van der Bijl wasn't the worst hitter in the business. Sixty-one runs required and 15 overs: time enough, surely, to get them.

A doddle? Maybe not. But if someone had started clearing a space in the Kingsmead trophy cabinet just then he wouldn't have been accused of premature celebration.

And when Procter and Daniels put on 49 at a cracking pace for the sixth wicket, Natal could smell the polish on the trophy. Procter then fell to a blinder of a catch by Seeff. Indeed, quite besides the several outstanding catches that were held, Western Province had kept the pressure on the batsmen all day with tenacious, attacking fielding, begrudging Natal even the most obvious run.

Then Daniels was bowled by Jefferies, bringing Van der Bijl to join Clift. Going into the second last over, Natal had mustered 172 for seven and still looked to be on their way to if not a comfortable then a fairly unhurried victory. Seven runs off 12 balls, three wickets standing. Translation: easy does it.

Jefferies tore in to deliver the fourth ball of the over. The ball screamed past in the vicinity of Van der Bijl's bat and Bruce gloved it. The Western Province fielders were convinced that the batsman had got an edge and the cry went up. But umpire Hurwitz said not out on the grounds that he was unsighted.

The usual mutters about walking were aired, and Kirsten went up to Van der Bijl. 'Did you hit that?' he asked in unnervingly calm tones as the appeal roared on in the stands. 'No, I think it must have clipped a stump without dislodging a bail,' came Van der Bijl's equally unflustered reply.

What happened next was still blaring from the headlines – and not just of the sports pages – more than a week later. Kirsten was fielding near the bowler's end stumps and, via the slips, received the ball as it made its way back to Jefferies. Noticing that Clift had gone to confer with Van der Bijl, Kirsten broke the wicket at the bowler's end and appealed for a run-out. Again, Hurwitz's finger came up.

This did not go down well with the crowd, who were expecting the by now stereotyped one-day finish, and Kirsten was roundly booed. Not many realised that Jefferies had bowled a maiden over and that Natal still needed seven to win, now with two wickets in hand and just one over left.

The precarious job of bowling those last six balls fell to Pienaar. His first delivery veered to the legside and Kenny Cooper, who had replaced Clift, pulled it well but it yielded only a single. Van der Bijl, renowned for his bludgeoning, had his familiar full-blooded go at the second, missed and then came perilously close to being dismissed when the ball, after thumping into his body, landed centimetres from his wicket.

But he swiped successfully at the third, sending it to deep mid-on, and the batsmen took a single. Three to go, five to get. Cooper pulled lustily again, managing to avoid the clutches of two fielders and running two.

Pienaar kept his head and pitched it up. Cooper swung, missed, and survived as the ball whistled past his off-stump. One delivery thus stood between what the masses would regard as the rehabilitation of Western Province cricket and just another season. One ball to make or break it all.

Pienaar, no more than a respectable medium pacer but a bowler of exceptional accuracy, trundled up to deliver the ball of his life. Cooper waited to play the ball of his life.

Short, straight, rising. Cooper made an awkward attempt to get something on it, but failed. Instead, it thwacked sweetly into Bruce's gloves and Western Province had won by two runs, the smallest victory margin in the history of the competition, to be crowned champions once more.

The prize-giving that followed was distinctly icy. 'We don't mind losing. But there is a way of losing and a way of winning,' Procter mouthed off. 'It's a black day for South African cricket. If that's the way to win, I'd rather lose.'

And it didn't help when Kirsten was awarded the fielding prize by the match adjudicator, Hugh Tayfield.

There was no case or two of beer in the winners' dressingroom for both teams to share in celebration of the cessation of hostilities. Just the handing over of cheques. In some cricket quarters, people thought they had identified a disturbing phenomenon on that dramatic but ultimately sad afternoon – the pursuit of money at the expense of good, honest cricket, of winning above all else, no matter what the methods employed.

It smelled of greed. It smelled bad.

Kirsten still has no rational explanation for his actions. He and Clift were the best of opponents, if not friends, and Kirsten's respect for him is evident from his embarrassment when he discusses what the cricketing world came to call the 'Paddy Clift incident'.

When pressed, he falls back on the anger which smouldered marginally below the Kirsten surface throughout the 1970s and '80s. The way Lamb, one of Kirsten's closest friends both on and off the field, had been dismissed and Van der Bijl's let-off at the crease proved the outlet for an ugly spurt of that anger. Clift happened to be in the wrong place at the right time.

Kirsten is adamant money did not play a role: 'The last thing on my mind, or indeed on the mind of any cricketer – pro or not – when he is out there in a match, is how much money he can make by his actions.

'And certainly that was the last thing on my mind when I threw down Paddy Clift's wicket. And it sickens me to think that some people have made suggestions that money was my motive.

'As it is, I still do not know what the difference in cash would have been between winning and losing.

'But what I do know is that I play cricket to win.

'If I didn't play to win, I wouldn't practise so hard at the nets and I wouldn't graft as much as I do out there on the field. I have a strong competitive temperament and nothing will kill that spirit in my game.

'But by the same token, I admit that what I did to Paddy Clift went against my grain. I have never run a man out like that before in my life and I will never do it again.'

Few writers on the game will succeed in summing Kirsten up as succinctly as he himself did in the above six paragraphs which appeared in the *Sunday Times* under Ted Partridge's by-line the week after the final.

On the positive side, Jefferies, whose fiery performance saw him take three for 17 off 11 overs, left no doubt that he was the most dangerous opening bowler in the country. However, his effort on the day wasn't enough to win him the bowling prize, which went to Natal's Les Taylor for his figures of four for 26.

Predictably, Van der Bijl took flak in the Cape Town press and even contacted Leary, who had managed the South African Universities XI which the fast bowler had captained in 1971, to discuss the incident. Van der Bijl was concerned that the controversy would make future trips by Natal to Newlands – which he told Leary he enjoyed – less than pleasant.

Van der Bijl also spoke to former Transvaal captain David Dyer about the matter. Dyer, whom Van der Bijl held in high regard, pointed out diplomatically that he might have acted rashly in running out Lamb in such unorthodox fashion.

At least Kirsten saw the lighter side of the whole business. In his *Argus* column dealing with the match, he made one aloof reference to the run-outs before adding his regular coaching tip: 'Stay in your crease until you have ascertained from the umpire that the ball is dead.'

The wake of the drama of 20 February 1982 did trouble the waters between Western Province and Natal – or perhaps there was more unhappiness in the stands – but it was sensibly put to rest before their relationship drowned in acrimony.

It took much of Kirsten's considerable discipline to divert his attention from the aftermath of the Datsun Shield to the single challenge he had left that season, and unquestionably the one which mattered most. Eastern Province might not have been the strongest of teams, but they had to be beaten comprehensively if Western Province were to take the Currie Cup.

But before the spotlight could fall on Port Elizabeth the sensational news broke that a squad of English rebel cricketers was on its way to South Africa

– not on a mission to break the isolation that had kept the pariah state out of international cricket since 1970; rather, they came in search of padding for their wallets.

Kirsten, along with Western Province team-mates Lamb, Le Roux and Jefferies, was selected to the first South African cricket team chosen to meet international opponents in 12 years. Lamb, who had qualified for selection to England at the beginning of the year, withdrew from the side.

So for a month Western Province didn't play any matches together, though their national representatives undoubtedly benefited from the higher level they were suddenly playing at. The last of three four-day internationals, a series South Africa won 1-0, ended two days before Western Province and EP clashed swords one last time that season.

Kirsten won the toss and, looking for all five bowling points despite the sound pitch, sent EP in. Fifty-one overs later Le Roux had his fourth five-wicket innings haul of the season, taking four for 20 in his last ten overs and finishing with five for 28. Jefferies was similarly menacing, ending with four for 48.

EP had been shot out for 120 and at stumps on the first day Western Province were already 60 runs ahead with nine wickets standing. Kirsten was not out and one run away from his twenty-ninth first-class century, and Seeff was on 65. It all went according to Western Province's plans the next day with Kirsten completing a masterful 151 and sharing 189 runs for the second wicket with Seeff, who made 79, before Lamb dominated an unbroken stand of 105 with Kenny McEwan.

McEwan was unbeaten on 28 when Kirsten declared at 384 for three, but Lamb, in what would prove his first-class farewell to his team-mates, had hit an undefeated 106 off 100 balls with the help of four arching sixes and six fours.

Lining the EP batsmen up 264 runs in arrears and with a day and a half to go, it seemed all too easy for Western Province. But for once the pace express went off the rails and opening batsman Simon Bezuidenhout, at a steadily ripening 36, took up the cudgels with relish, hooking and cutting wonderfully to post a 110 overflowing with guts and flair.

He and Robbie Armitage put on 120 for the second wicket and Dave Richardson, Rob White and Russell Fensham all contributed useful scores. But meaningful partnerships were rare down the order, a consequence of Le Roux having regained his control as well as his composure. Showing he had as much brain as brawn, Le Roux came back from a shaky opening spell to take five for 51, giving him ten for 79 in the match. Jefferies finished with three for 88 as EP were dismissed for 307, leaving Western Province to make just 44.

It took Seeff and Pienaar 11 overs and one ball to reach the target, which they did shortly after lunch on the final day. It wasn't the most cheerful news to crackle over the tannoy at the Wanderers, where Transvaal were on their way to a three-wicket win over Natal, a match clouded by Barry Richards' unhappiness over a pitch he considered below first-class standard.

Western Province's ten-wicket win earned them 23 points, while Transvaal's less comprehensive victory could garner just 17. Western Province totalled 116 points and Transvaal 107. Natal mustered 85, followed by Northern Transvaal on 52 and Eastern Province on 37. Eddie Barlow's Boland won the B section, beating Western Province B by 149 runs in the final at Stellenbosch.

The St George's Park dressingroom was a scene of unbridled celebration that evening but amid the mirth Kirsten had to ask himself if what he thought had happened had indeed happened. Western Province, battling to keep pace with their rivals a season ago, had won the double. Not one trophy, as he had hoped, not in three seasons, as he had said he might need, but two trophies. In one season.

The double! And under his captaincy – the man who dared to follow Barlow. It had been an exhilarating first season in charge for Kirsten, who added successful captaincy to his other recognised talents as a world class batsman and fielder.

He was back to his best in his primary role, scoring 624 first-class runs at 56,72 with three centuries and just one unconverted half-century. Kirsten, who scored his highest aggregate in South African domestic cricket that season, was undoubtedly the star but the supporting cast was any captain's dream.

Seeff, perhaps dour but highly effective, scored 426 runs at 38,72, despite losing his opening partner early on in virtually every innings. McEwan was unlucky at the start of the season but came on well to total 364 runs at 40,44, while there was always something happening when the gallant Kuiper – 338 at 42,25 with four half-centuries – unleashed his broadsword of a bat. Lamb had also been solid enough in scoring 393 runs at 43,66.

However, most of the praise for Western Province's success in 1981-82 must go to Le Roux and Jefferies. On their day they would have given any Test line-up problems, and the fact that they took 64 per cent of all the wickets Western Province captured was no exaggeration of their contribution.

Though aggression was an important part of their approach, they managed to bowl 156 maidens between them – more than a quarter of their total overs. Le Roux, often used in short, sharp spells, took 43 wickets at 12,18, while Jefferies took 41 at 20,48. Each also shouldered his fair share of the workload, Jefferies sending down 322.4 overs and Le Roux 239.3.

The senior spinner, Hobson, would no doubt have had more impressive figures had his pacier team-mates not snapped up most of the wickets, but his 19 scalps at 28,26 was still evidence of a solid season, while Henry showed real promise with 11 wickets at 22,63.

Of the frontline bowlers, only Henry and During didn't experience the satisfaction of taking five wickets in an innings, and they were just one short.

Kirsten could justifiably look back on a virtually faultless season, the only blemish worth mentioning being his team's inability to get into the running for the honours in the inaugural Benson and Hedges night series. But the first attempt at what was to become South Africa's premier limited overs competition was an experimental affair that season with the last three matches being played in four days because of the rebel tour.

On 6 April, Transvaal won the first domestic night series title with Natal runners-up, as the lights finally dimmed on one of the longest seasons in South African cricket history.

12

English Enterprise

'Will passengers Boycott, Knott, Underwood, Amiss, Lever, Emburey and Gooch please disembark and spark consternation in world cricket.'

Of course, no such words to that effect were uttered on the jumbo jet which touched down at Jan Smuts airport on Sunday, 28 February 1982.

But they might just as well have been.

The seven England cricketers, each one a household name wherever the game is played, arrived on the supposedly isolated southern tip of the dark continent that day and turned upside down the then International Cricket Conference's policy on contact with South Africa.

None by representative teams, the ICC said, until democracy came to that troubled land. Democracy was still 12 years away and those seven Englishmen were joined the next day by three more and two others, who had been playing and coaching in South Africa as individuals, also threw in their lot. Another three were not far behind.

Just when South Africans thought the umpteenth season of sterile, if entertaining, domestic competition was winding down, there were 15 compelling reasons to crack open another beer in front of the television set.

Under Graham Gooch's captaincy, Geoff Boycott, Alan Knott, Derek Underwood, Dennis Amiss, John Lever, John Emburey, Wayne Larkins, Peter Willey, Mike Hendrick, Chris Old, Les Taylor, Bob Woolmer, Geoff

Humpage and Arnie Sidebottom were ready to undertake the first of nine rebel tours organised to help white South Africa lick its sporting wounds.

But while the rebels were being hailed as boycott-busting heroes in establishment South African cricket circles, they were generally painted in less flattering colours at home. Accused of 'going in search of the Krugerrand', they were seen as mercenaries of the most thoughtless kind.

The story of the tour's organisation reads like a spy novel. It had taken a year to put together and included clandestine negotiations with players on official duty in India and Sri Lanka as well as the Caribbean. The masterminds included Peter Cooke, born in Lancashire but relocated to Johannesburg where he was an executive with a record company, and former Zimbabwean Martin Locke, a familiar face to many South Africans who still appears on television as an all-round sports summariser with a special interest in horse racing.

It seems ludicrous that South African Breweries lent financial support and their name to the venture as 80 per cent of the products they sell are consumed by blacks, whom the sports boycott was ostensibly helping in their struggle to defeat apartheid. But this was the old South Africa, where facing reality was asking to be labelled a communist and cricket was a white man's game.

The itinerary of the 'SAB XI' was short but wide ranging. They would begin with a two-day match against a South African Colts XI in Pretoria, play three limited overs internationals in Port Elizabeth, Johannesburg and Durban, take on Western Province at Newlands over three days, and play three four-day matches against the full South African side in Johannesburg, Cape Town and Durban.

The latter were billed as Tests in all South African newspapers, sometimes with the guilty addition of quotation marks around the word, sometimes not. But when the tour got going it was clear to the players on both sides that the standard was well below Test level. Whatever their waffling about wanting to 'encourage multi-racial sport in South Africa', Gooch and his rebels came for the money, nothing else.

After attempting to persuade the tourists to return to England without playing a match, the Test and County Cricket Board took a tougher stance, threatening to prevent them from playing against India and Pakistan, who were to tour that northern summer.

So what. OK – no Test cricket for you lot for three years. That hurt, but a fat bank balance wasn't a bad consolation.

However singular the rebels' motives, the tour was anything but a simple issue for any South African with even the most tentative connection to the game. There could be no political or moral justification for a rebel tour, but South African cricket was decaying from within and had already lost Lamb to England and Kepler Wessels to Australia. Before them, Tony and Ian Greig had chosen to play with three lions rampant on their chests, despite their rural South African upbringing. Robin and Chris Smith were also to become honorary Englishmen solely to play Test cricket.

The very heart of the game in South Africa, the once high standard of first-class cricket, was close to petering out or, at best, shrivelling drastically and, from SACU's perspective, the tour was nothing short of emergency treatment to an ailing patient.

Black cricketers pointed to the immense resources being, as they saw it, squandered on a month-long illusion that South Africa was back in international cricket. Why, they asked, was that money not being spent on developing all the country's cricket and its cricketers? Why not, indeed?

Keep politics out of sport, the whites wailed. Who put it there in the first place, came the retort. Touché.

The cricket itself was bland, lacking the unmistakable aura of a contest played at the highest level. That the tourists failed to win a match was almost expected, given the storm and its consequences which they knew they had created in England and elsewhere.

Procter was chosen to lead the South African team – called, of course, the Springboks – in the three-match first-class series. Kirsten played in all three, as well as in the match against Western Province and the three one-dayers.

Batting third behind Jimmy Cook and Richards, he finished with the highest aggregate and average – 247 at 61,75 – and scored a fighting 114 in the first innings of the second four-day match at Newlands.

Kirsten was also responsible for upsetting the balance of the tourists' attack when, playing for Western Province, he drove hard and the ball fractured Emburey's thumb, putting him out of the tour.

Though he was thrilled to be playing international cricket of a sort, Kirsten remembers the uneasy vibe in the stands during that tour and subsequent rebel ventures, as if a public starved of international competition felt duty bound to support whatever came their way – even if they knew it wasn't the real thing.

But it was over soon enough and Kirsten had time to savour something palpably real – winning the Currie Cup – before, once again, turning his attention to Derbyshire. He was feeling good, in form, and ready to score runs – big runs.

13

The Last Dance

Any Derbyshire member watching Kirsten's exploits in the 1982 English season would not have wanted to believe it would be his last campaign in England.

Surely no team would let a batsman of his calibre, temperament and form out of their clutches. But there wasn't much the county could do to change his mind.

He had burnt out and that was that. Had Kirsten agreed to another contract there was every chance of his being asked to assume the captaincy, especially following his stunning success at the helm of Western Province.

Although Kirsten did not add to his tally of five by then trademark double centuries in 1982, the magical run of centuries he embarked on enthralled all who watched him. Starting with 143 at Gloucester and ending with an unbeaten 140 against Yorkshire at Scarborough, it was vintage Kirsten. He totalled eight centuries that season, a Derbyshire record, as well as six half-centuries, and all the attributes which had made him one of the top number three batsmen in the world were to the fore.

His determination saw to it that there was almost no getting rid of him once he had played himself in. As proof, five of those eight centuries were unbeaten.

The intensity Kirsten brought to the crease meant he was always going to gather runs at a steady pace, as evidenced by his aggregate of 1941 scored at 64,70 – both the highest of the 13 South Africans who took to county cricket that year.

There is nothing like competition to stir Kirsten's soul and when John Wright matched him with seven centuries, which also broke the old record of six in a season, he promptly went out and took that ton off Yorkshire.

Kirsten in that kind of form is a disconcerting opponent. Though his off-side game still dominates, it is difficult to close the gaps because of the variety of shots he commands even on one side of the wicket. And the calm acceptance with which he lives through close calls – as if he deserves his good luck – is calculated to make most bowlers declare him cold-blooded.

For Derbyshire in 1982, he began without fanfare, but near the end of July it all came together as Kirsten hit four hundreds in five innings, three of them in succession. It was undoubtedly Kirsten's best year in England.

'At age 27, you reckon you can conquer the world. Anything is possible,' was his rationale. Years later, he would remark: 'I probably quit the county scene too early, but that was my psyche.' The desire to return to rugby was also surfacing again.

The second county to feel the full length and breadth of Kirsten's bat that season was Leicestershire at Derby. In a match in which almost half the playing time was lost to rain, Kirsten scored 121 not out to help Derbyshire win by eight wickets.

When the last day dawned, Derbyshire were 34 for one in their first innings in reply to Leicestershire's 126. A result would ordinarily have been improbable, but the captains got together and Derbyshire declared at 73 for one. The 43.4 overs of largely chummy bowling ended with Roger Tolchard declaring Leicestershire's second innings closed at 175.

Down to business at last – Derbyshire were left to score 229 in one and a half hours and 20 overs on a sluggish pitch. Tolchard should really have known better.

Just more than two hours of chanceless, immaculate batting later, Kirsten hammered a no-ball from Jonathan Agnew for six and raised his bat as his second century of the season went into the scorebook. John Hampshire had joined him at the fall of the second wicket, at 50, and the pair confidently picked clean the Leicestershire spin attack at close to five runs an over in adding 179 for the unbroken third wicket.

Derbyshire registered their second victory in nine matches with 3.4 overs remaining, to settle into seventh place in the championship standings.

Less than a month later, on 13 July, Kirsten hit his third century. The victims were again Leicestershire, but this time at the stupendously named North Leicestershire Miners' Welfare Ground in Coalville.

The weather was kinder this time and there was no need for contrived cricket. Leicestershire made 234 and 222, and Derbyshire needed 207 in just less than three and a half hours, having totalled 250 in their first innings to which Kirsten contributed 84.

But this time the pitch was breaking up and the Leicestershire bowlers, who included Les Taylor and Gordon Parsons, fancied their chances. When Wright launched Parsons' first ball over the square leg boundary, however, they knew they had a match on their hands.

The New Zealander, driving and pulling with gusto, and Kirsten, who played all manner of strokes, then took control with a second-wicket stand of 102 scored in 21 overs. The 50 was up in the ninth over as the imported pair raced each other to respective half-centuries.

Wright reached 60 before departing via a lofted pull to square leg, and Hampshire didn't stay long. Number five, Geoff Miller, who had been rampant in the Leicestershire first innings, taking eight for 70, also came and went.

But there was no dislodging Kirsten – though there were certainly opportunities to do so. Parsons couldn't quite get to a catch at long-off and, on 76, a ball from John Steele was hammered heavenwards only to fall safely even as Nigel Briers, at deep extra cover, made a despairing effort to reach it.

Just for variation, Kirsten was then dropped at slip and duly went on to his century in ten minutes short of three hours before surviving another chance, this time off the hapless Steele's bowling. He was finally bowled by Agnew for 102, 52 of which were scored in boundaries, and put all but the finishing touches to a deserved five-wicket win for Derbyshire.

Although the trail of chances he left might indicate otherwise, Kirsten's innings was far from an exhibition of reckless hitting. Several batsmen lost their wickets on the whim of the pitch that day and Kirsten's effort was better described as a master-class in coping with difficult conditions.

And it helped to hoist Derbyshire to an unfamiliar third place on the log.

Another century …

Derbyshire's defence of the NatWest trophy they had won in 1981 lasted exactly one game. The six-wicket loss to Hampshire in the first round at Southampton the day after their victory at Coalville marked the beginning of a slide that would see them finish eleventh out of 17 counties.

Losing the toss and being asked to bat in high humidity and on a pitch dampened by morning showers wasn't the best start for the champions. The Hampshire batsmen had by far the better of the conditions.

But Barry Wood and Wright made the best of it with an opening stand of 59 before Wood was caught off a mis-timed pull, summoning Kirsten to the wicket. Wright, who made 56, stayed long enough to add 46 runs for the second wicket. From then on, however, Kirsten was virtually on his own as his team-mates arrived and departed with the ominous regularity of traffic at a busy airport.

Dropped on 25 after Norman Cowley spilled a return catch, it was the only chance he offered before going on to an undefeated 110 and the honour of being the first Derbyshire player to make a century in a Gillette Cup or NatWest trophy match.

There were 20 overs left in the Derbyshire innings at the lunch break, which arrived with Kirsten on 28. His sustained assault on the bowling after the resumption (which included one of his audacious left-handed swipes and netted 60 runs off the last 13 overs) was all that stood between Derbyshire and ignominy. Their total of 239 for five off 60 overs was competitive under the circumstances.

But the contest was stillborn. Gordon Greenidge and John Rice, both dropped early on, made sure it didn't breathe its first with an opening stand of 137, and though Derbyshire struck back to make it 172 for four in the forty-seventh over, Hampshire were unperturbed by pressure from bowlers and fielders and knocked off the last 70 runs with 20 balls to spare.

Derbyshire slipped to fourth place in the championship when they lost to Essex by 85 runs at Southend on 20 July, their first loss of the season. However, none of the blame for the result, which flattered Essex somewhat, could stick to Kirsten.

An Essex first innings of 262 was followed by Derbyshire's meagre reply of 130 with John Lever taking six for 48. Essex declared at 261 for four in their second dig, leaving the visitors to make 394 at a run a minute.

At stumps on the second day, Derbyshire were 33 for two with both openers dismissed and a long final day ahead of them. Kirsten and the number four, Bernard Maher, were soon parted and it was down to the South African and John Hampshire to make a fight of it.

They did more than that. For the next two and a half hours Derbyshire looked like winners as the fourth-wicket pair refused to believe they should be on the defensive, opting instead for expansive strokeplay all round the wicket. Kirsten, by then as familiar with his fine form as with a favourite bat, revelled in his own confidence, while Hampshire celebrated the end of a run drought with a veritable flood, hitting three fours and a six off consecutive balls delivered by the marauding Lever, no less.

When Kirsten reached 28 he had scored his thousandth run of the season, the second Derbyshire player to do so after Wright, and both had passed 50 at lunch, taken with Derbyshire still 225 runs in arrears. When Kirsten's fourth first-class century of the season – not to mention his third in all cricket in eight days – rolled up, the Essex faithful shifted uneasily in their seats.

But on 113 he tried unsuccessfully to avoid a delivery from Lever for wicketkeeper David East to dive and take a stunning catch, ending a partnership of 158. Hampshire didn't stay much longer and was also caught behind, just five runs short of what would have been his first century for the county.

But there wasn't enough left in the Derbyshire batting line-up to complete the job and they were dismissed for 308, the last four wickets falling for 50 runs.

It had been a particularly gruelling period for Derbyshire, with a Sunday League game against Middlesex at Lord's coming bang in the middle of the three-day match, as is the curious but thoughtless English wont; and another first-class outing, against the touring Pakistanis, starting in four days' time.

For all his success, Kirsten was exhausted. He and Wright managed to escape the Pakistan game and Kirsten flew to the island of Jersey for a week's break. And then he decided: enough of playing year in and year out, seven years without a break.

The bombshell duly dropped in Derby. Kirsten, in the second year of a three-year contract, asked the county if he could miss the 1983 season, and they agreed. He needed the time to establish a business outside of cricket and, in the words of Derbyshire chief executive Roger Pearman, 'If it is suitable to both parties, he will be back in 1984.'

Kirsten said he would 'think very seriously' about returning to Derbyshire in 1984 'if they want me back'. The county would be without both their star batsmen in 1983, as Wright would be playing in the World Cup. But there was a notion to acquire a fast bowler as Derbyshire had a good crop of promising young batsmen coming up, including Kim Barnett, Iain Anderson and John Morris.

Stephen Jefferies was recommended by Kirsten as a willing replacement and, in fact, he played in the match against Pakistan, taking five for 109. However, Jefferies was to turn out under the red rose of Lancashire from 1983 to 1985, and for Hampshire in 1988 and 1989, largely in limited overs matches.

Refreshed by his brief change of scenery and motivated by the fact that he would be in South Africa same time next year, Kirsten went into the championship match against title contenders Surrey in an even more positive frame of mind than usual.

Never mind next year. There was plenty of cricket to be played before that. The routine suddenly seemed less dull now there was some light – far away but unmistakable – at the end of his own dark tunnel.

Wood won the toss and, as Derbyshire had won three matches via a run chase, asked Surrey to bat. This time, however, the tactic backfired badly.

At the close they were 401 for nine and had picked up maximum batting points with the help of 121 from New Zealand Test captain Geoff Howarth, 94 from one of the two West Indians in the side, Monte Lynch, and two century partnerships. The only news to break the gloom was the announcement of Bob Taylor's half-century in the Edgbaston Test.

On top of that, Surrey ended Derbyshire's slim hopes of featuring in the Sunday League by beating them by 56 runs the next day. Kirsten top scored with 43 in a total of 149.

The grey skies under which the championship match resumed on the Monday were thus indicative of more than Derby's prevailing weather. Surrey had declared overnight and when Wood was caught in the slips for a duck in the second over, the first lines of prayers for rain were already being composed.

Indeed, the rain did come, and with some force. But it waited until 20 minutes before tea to flood the County Ground, and that was that for the day. Derbyshire had progressed to 221 for four at a steady rate. And Kirsten was 145 and definitely not out. Facing a virtually new ball and the considerable talents of Sylvester Clarke and Robin Jackman, Kirsten welded all the elements of his batsmanship into a sword of excellence. His timing was superb and the ball sped from his bat between fielders as if on a string.

His intent was made plain in his first over at the wicket. A quicker ball from Jackman, no doubt fired up by his early disposal of Wood, rose above Kirsten's pad and thumped him hard on the thigh. Padded or not, he felt it.

Jackman sped in and delivered his next ball – and watched it disappear to the cover boundary by way of a sumptuous drive. It was the first of the 16 fours Kirsten would stroke on his way to three figures, the century coming up with a deft pull off Jackman in just less than three hours.

The only time it looked as though he wouldn't reach his twenty-sixth first-class hundred that day was when, on 79, he edged Clarke to Howarth at third slip. For once the fiery West Indian, whose action has been politely described as suspect, did not profit from the extra zip he seemed able to extract from even the most benign pitches and the catch was grassed.

By the time the rain came, Kirsten had outlived two batting partners. John Hampshire scored 40 of the 119 he helped realise for the third wicket in 35 overs before Barnett, who made 21, shared 76 runs for the fourth. The hoped-for rain, no doubt hurried on by a few Surrey prayers, then washed out what was left of the day's play, much to the disappointment of its original summoners.

The next day Wood declared immediately Kirsten and Iain Anderson saw the county safely out of follow-on territory. Derbyshire had reached 252 for four – and Kirsten had scored 164 of those runs, unbeaten.

Surrey had a patchy second innings and declared on 144 for eight, leaving Derbyshire the stern task of scoring 294 in just over two hours plus 20 overs. They advanced to 240 for three before stumps were drawn, and Kirsten had again played the starring role. Seven minutes short of three hours after arriving at the crease, after Derbyshire had again lost an opener early, Kirsten registered his second century of the match, having helped himself to 123 not out.

Hampshire, who would retire with 43 first-class centuries to his name, fell 15 runs short this time, but had once again proved Kirsten's pillar of support. The 196 they added, equalling the best performance of a Derbyshire third-wicket pair against Surrey, ensured that the Londoners would not make much progress in the championship race in that match.

'I was stunned after that Surrey match when captain Barry Wood, dressed in gown and slippers, summoned John Hampshire and myself to his captain's cabin,' Kirsten remembers. 'He began chastising us – especially John – for slow play, believing us to have given up the run chase. Nothing was further from the truth especially with Clarke and Jackman in their attack. Barry had misread the situation.'

When the stalemate was declared, Kirsten stood on 123. Not out. In four days, he had taken 310 runs off Surrey at the small cost of one dismissal, and that in the Sunday League match.

It was the second time Kirsten had scored two centuries in a match, becoming the first Derbyshire player to do so in 17 years, and the second time he had matched Leslie Townsend's 1933 county record of six first-class hundreds in a season. And there were six first-class matches left in the 1982 campaign.

Twenty days later, on 23 August at Chesterfield, Kirsten got the better of influenza and a Sussex attack that included Garth le Roux to score his seventh century of the season and so claim sole ownership of the Derbyshire record.

Almost inevitably, he was not out, this time on 105. The record had fallen after just more than three hours' flawless batting, in which Kirsten hit 14 fours. Had two hours not been lost to bad light on the first day, which ended with Kirsten on 64, Wood might have been tempted to give Kirsten more time in the middle. But he was forced to declare when Derbyshire reached 300 for five in the ninety-ninth over to claim their last batting point.

While Le Roux gave some of Kirsten's middle order team-mates something hard to think about, the number three indulged in dashing strokeplay despite the dodgy light. Wright rediscovered his form to score 79, helping to add 49 for the second wicket, and Miller's 52 featured in the third-wicket stand of 85.

Sussex began their reply by racing to 50 off nine overs, but it took them a further 56 to reach 100. Bad light brought an early end to an aimless afternoon with Sussex having mustered 202 for four and rain prevented any play on the last day.

Having gleaned just five points against Sussex, Derbyshire sank to ninth place in the championship standings and they had already shot their bolt in the one-day competitions. Professional cricketer or not, for Kirsten the season was threatening to degenerate into a list of irrelevant games that had to be played.

So he and Wright, who felt much the same way, embarked on a run chase. Not cynically, nor with any disrespect intended towards the game. Just something to add spice to an otherwise bland end to the summer.

Wright struck the first blow, and it was a significant one. Kirsten, still stricken with flu, watched from the pavilion as Wright hit 107 against Hampshire at Derby on 1 September to chalk up his seventh century of the season.

What's this? Competition?

Derbyshire's next championship match, their penultimate first-class game of the season, was against Yorkshire at Scarborough. Kirsten hadn't scored a century in the nine matches he had played against Yorkshire since 1978.

He arrived in Scarborough to find doubtful weather and a pitch he liked the look of. But Derbyshire promptly collapsed to 137 all out, followed by Yorkshire for 217. The pitch was not the problem. Largely inept batting on both sides was exploited by the persistent seam bowling of, first, Arnold Sidebottom – who sent six Derbyshire batsmen back to the pavilion at a cost of 31 runs – and then Dallas Moir, who took six for 68 for Derbyshire.

The second innings would have been similarly disastrous for Derbyshire had it not been for Kirsten. Wickets tumbled about him as he played a solidly defensive innings in a bid to save the match.

Derbyshire had resumed on 126 for four – a lead of 46 – and with Wood and Kirsten intent on survival. But in the fourth over of the morning Wood, batting sixth, edged a simple catch to wicketkeeper David Bairstow, who was on his way to equalling the world record of 11 catches in a match. So ended an important partnership of 58 runs, and Derbyshire then battled to find a worthy partner for the solid Kirsten. Eventually Moir endured for one and a half hours in sharing a ninth-wicket stand of 65.

But its end was soon followed by the demise of the innings, totalling 237, and Yorkshire were left with the relatively uncomplicated job of scoring 158 in two and a half hours and 20 overs.

Kirsten, however, stood unbowed. Having more than just guarded his wicket for over four hours against bowlers of the calibre of Ray Illingworth and Chris Old, he deserved the respect he earned for his undefeated 140. The 18 fours and three sixes he hit were mere details. What mattered was his responsible, disciplined batting.

Out of the context of the match, it also mattered that he had snatched back the record from Wright. To have done so as part of a winning team would have made it more meaningful. But this was not to be, as Yorkshire cantered home by six wickets.

For Kirsten to score a century in his last county innings would have been bending the rules of most fairytales. But he nevertheless came within eight runs of doing so in the season's finale, the match against Glamorgan at Derby.

Glamorgan had been dismissed for 234 and Derbyshire made a fight of it with a reply of 281 for eight, thanks to 100 not out from Barnett. A somewhat negative approach from Glamorgan in their second innings saw them dawdle into the 153rd over before captain Barry Lloyd declared at 327 for nine.

Their lacklustre tactics lingered into Derbyshire's second innings when the field was dropped – five posted on the boundary – after just ten overs. But given good weather and a festive crowd knowing they were watching their last cricket for the year, Derbyshire made an enthusiastic effort to reach the distant target of 281 in one and a half hours and 20 overs.

Wright and Anderson shared an opening stand of 54 runs, 44 of which were Wright's, before Kirsten joined Anderson in the eleventh over to add exactly 100 for the second wicket. Anderson was then bowled for 38 by Rodney Ontong, and Colin Tunnicliffe was quickly caught at long-on.

But Hampshire halted any further decline, making liberal use of bottom-hand power to hit his 50 in 47 minutes and put on 63 for the fourth wicket with Kirsten.

The South African didn't spare the splendour of his batting in that last knock under Derbyshire's rose and crown. Out came the flashing cut, the cameo square drive and, once settled, the punchy cover drive. He went to his 50 in 51 minutes and looked sure to score what would have been a legendary ninth century when Eifion Jones stumped him off Charles Rowe for 92.

Jones had missed a stumping when Kirsten was on 69, and a half-chance had been put down at mid-on a run later. But Kirsten had lived through both to deliver 102 minutes of classy entertainment. His departure preceded a flurry of wickets as Derbyshire tried to score 42 off the last four overs. They fell just 13 short, totalling 268 for eight.

What turned out to be Kirsten's last season in England was also his most successful. An aggregate of 1941 first-class runs – the third highest in Derbyshire's history – at 64,70 tells its own story.

But it doesn't touch on the intense cricketer who had made Derby his winter home for five years, who had given as much of himself as of his cricketing talents to a grateful county. Kirsten has fond memories of his time with Derbyshire. He is grateful for the opportunity to have played there and to have known some wonderful people.

14

Sri Lankan Sop;
West Indian Whirlwind

There was but one arrow missing from the Kirsten quiver as he went into the 1982-83 season: the South African captaincy. Not that he sought it.

Both Mike Procter and Barry Richards, who had shared the South African leadership against the English rebels in 1982, were reaching the end of long and legendary first-class careers. With more unofficial tours in the offing, the South African Cricket Union had to give some thought to a more permanent choice as captain.

There were only two genuine candidates: Kirsten and Clive Rice. It wasn't an easy choice. Both had sound cricket brains and led by unquestionable example. Kirsten didn't exude quite as much presence as Rice did on the field, but Rice had shown an unfortunate penchant for speaking out in the press. It was also an important fact that Kirsten and Rice had taken over the captaincy of their respective provinces the season before – and there could be no wondering which of the two had made a better job of it.

So when the Arosa Sri Lankan side arrived out of nowhere in October, Kirsten was named the South African skipper. 'I had the full backing of Ali Bacher, which I really appreciated,' Kirsten says. '"Get out there and market yourself" were his exact words to me.'

Kirsten's appointment caused consternation in sections of the Transvaal press, which had unashamedly backed Rice for the job.

The tourists did not test Kirsten's skills and instincts as a captain, nor indeed those of any of the South Africans they came up against in the two four-day and four limited overs internationals. The visitors crashed to innings defeats in both the former and were similarly out-classed in the latter.

The Sri Lankans, captained by Test skipper Bandula Warnapura, played as if the gloom from the 25-year bans from all cricket which they had incurred for agreeing to play in South Africa had already been enforced. More than any of the teams that were to visit South Africa before readmission in 1991, the Sri Lankans were on a mission to make money.

The former British colony had been granted full Test status in 1981 and had by far the weakest team in the poorest country playing at the highest level. Consequently, they were not the most popular opponents at home or away, and a lucrative tour to South Africa was the best living any of their cricketers could make.

But, aside from several names unplayable to South African ears, they added nothing to the summer's cricket. As Lawrence Seeff notoriously remarked, 'It's not the real thing.' He was rapped over the knuckles for his honesty.

Any team that tries to win matches consistently in South Africa with just three recognised and none-too-threatening seam bowlers – in this case, Tony Opatha, Susanthe Karunaratne and Lanthra Fernando – is going to come second, especially if their much-vaunted spin attack doesn't fire. And though the Sri Lankans' batting was more competitive, they scored only two centuries as opposed to the deluge of 13 made against them.

Nor could the Sri Lankans win any of their plethora of provincial matches, their only non-failure being the drawn match against, ironically enough, Western Province. The only match they did win was a social affair organised by Nicky Oppenheimer.

Attendances at their matches dwindled, and by the time they left the country in December, hardly anyone not directly connected with cricket noticed. Those in the game hoped the next squad of rebels would be worth spending money to see.

They were not disappointed. With 1983 still fresh on the calendar, 16 West Indians did the unthinkable and arrived in South Africa on a cricket tour. The Sri Lankans might have been the first black international team to tour the apartheid state, but the West Indians took it a step further: they played invigorating, inspiring cricket, and were patently proud to be black.

They were also a very, very good side with 12 Test players – totalling 211 caps – among them.

Lawrence Rowe, the bright new West Indian batting hope, had given it up to captain the rebels, and the powerful Collis King emerged as the tourists' most successful batsman. Not surprisingly, the attack bristled with pace in the form of Sylvester Clarke and Colin Croft, who wasn't a factor because of a back injury, and Ezra Moseley. In addition, Franklyn Stephenson was an all-rounder to be treasured.

Desmond Haynes, Malcolm Marshall, David Murray and Hartley Alleyne were rumoured to be on their way from Australia, but in the end only Murray and Alleyne arrived.

Here, indeed, was a challenge for Kirsten and all those who took the West Indies on. And for the next five weeks South Africa was taken on by a travelling band of master entertainers who happened to include cricket in their repertoire.

Entertaining for the public, that is. For the South African teams who played against them, not quite. The hard, fast pitches and the West Indian pace bowlers were a perfect marriage for those who didn't have to face them.

Kirsten had an early taste of it when the tourists played Western Province in a 50-over match at Newlands on 15 January. Chasing 205 to win, Western Province were all out for 183 in the final over. Western Province had acquired Graham Gooch and John Emburey from the English rebel squad, and had it not been for Gooch's nine Tests' worth of experience against unbridled Caribbean wrath – which undoubtedly helped him in both opening the batting and scoring 64 in this match – the home side's total might have been something of an embarrassment.

Kenny McEwan, on the brink of a wonderful season of heroic batting, made the only other respectable score: 37.

Kirsten remembers the naked hostility of the bowling. Facing Joel Garner in one county match and Malcolm Marshall in another was difficult enough but it was manageable. Having to deal with the lethal likes of Croft, Clarke, Moseley and Stephenson all in the course of one torrid afternoon was a far tougher test.

The fact that the West Indians won their first match sent a sigh through the corridors of South African cricket power. After the incompetent display by the Sri Lankans, the focused competitiveness of the West Indians ensured good crowds. Six days of cricket on the tour were indeed sold out, half of them at the Wanderers. The tour still made a loss, and a significant one at

R26 795, but it didn't approach the R493 816 that went down the drain on the Sri Lankan venture.

But perhaps the real investment of that West Indian visit was the interest in the game which it evoked in black communities. The only area of South Africa where cricket had taken root and established a tradition among blacks was the Eastern Cape, due to the twin influences of British missionary schools in the area and the experiences migrant workers brought back from the Transvaal gold mines at the turn of the century.

But because of the larger malaise around them, black cricketers never had the opportunity to make the most of their talents. They had neither facilities comparable to those of their white counterparts, nor access to sponsorships that could improve their lot. Thus, to the majority of South Africans, cricket was a peculiarly genteel game played by those with a hankering after South Africa's colonial past.

In Natal, the substantial Asian population had ensured a cricketing culture of sorts among people other than whites, and there was a significant band of black players in the Eastern Province. These forgotten cricketers played in the Howa Bowl, named after the larger-than-life president of the non-racial South African Cricket Board of Control, Hassan Howa.

An uneasy, and ultimately unsuccessful, first attempt at unifying South African cricket had been made in 1977, leading to the formation of the South African Cricket Union. Commentators spoke proudly of the arrival of 'normal' cricket but, alas, not much had changed.

White and black cricket and cricketers were still poles apart. The Currie Cup, Datsun Shield and Benson and Hedges competitions glittered with talent and money and were played on either gracious or imposing grounds. The Howa Bowl made do with sub-standard pitches and bumpy outfields, not to mention a dearth of funds, guaranteed to douse the enthusiasm vital to the blossoming of any young player with an unopened gift for the game.

But whatever the politics involved, the success and vitality of the rebel West Indians added a promising glint to the stark reality of the times.

'Man, these West Indians can play' became one of the few notions of commonality between blacks and whites in the dark days of the early 1980s.

Curiously, while the game gathered a new following, its traditional audience was also undergoing an education. Even as apartheid was being measured for its coffin, white South Africans saw the world through the fog of institutionalised racism. But here were black cricketers who not only played the game wonderfully well, but went about it with an oh-so-cool swagger.

Indeed, the 1983 West Indian tour undoubtedly alienated further the racial factions in South African cricket, but it had the opposite effect on those in the stands or watching the matches on television. Finally, a grain of agreement between the races: 'Man, these West Indians can play.'

Not that it stopped black South Africans from steadfastly supporting the tourists, as was invariably the case before sports codes unified in the late 1980s and early 1990s.

To Kirsten, it seemed even white South Africans were more excited by seeing the opposition do well. Unwisely, he said so. In public.

After the four-day match at Newlands, Kirsten openly accused the crowd of supporting the West Indians. The charge sent a jar through more than just the quarters it was seemingly aimed at. Senior players in the side felt that top administrators had not shown sufficient appreciation of a convincing South African victory. As captain, Kirsten became their voice perhaps without due regard for the damage he was doing to his own image.

Then, after Clarke had taken 12 for 100 with a performance no less a heavyweight than Ali Bacher described as among the finest ever to grace the modern Wanderers, Kirsten made what some saw as an inexcusable gaffe.

'They didn't win the game. We lost it,' he announced to the silence of jaws dropping everywhere. Harmless naivety was one thing. This was something else.

Paradoxically, as guarded as Kirsten was on the field, he didn't always watch what he said off it; and to reporters, no less. They wrote up the story with gleeful smiles, unlike the committee men, who wore worried frowns.

But the West Indian supporters had much to smile about at the end of a hectic 30 days. Honours in the two-match four-day series were shared after South Africa won by five wickets at Newlands before the West Indies came back with a 29-run victory at the Wanderers, and South Africa had won four of the six limited overs matches.

But South Africa had come through a searching test with some of its myths clearly exploded. Richards and Pollock, at 37 and 38, were still the backbone of the batting. Each scored a century against the rebels: Pollock 100 in the first innings at Newlands and Richards 102 in the one-day match in Port Elizabeth.

They were, however, the only South Africans to get that far against the fearsome West Indian attack. Kirsten, still finding his Springbok captain's feet, managed 108 runs at 18,00 with a single half-century. McEwan's supreme temperament and technique helped him score 162 runs in the five limited overs internationals he played, but he was untried in the four-day

114

matches. Kourie showed outstanding fighting spirit lower down the order, but he was no frontline batsman.

Who, then, was the next South African master batsman? Kirsten was the obvious heir, though not on the evidence of his batting on that tour.

That the West Indians notched only one century in the four-day games, a crucial 101 by King in the first innings at the Wanderers, was compensated for by their match-winning attack.

The South African bowling was in better shape. Stephen Jefferies dispelled early doubts of his claims to a place in the side with important contributions in the second innings of both four-day matches, and Van der Bijl's performance could not be faulted. The wild and woolly Rupert Hanley, the Transvaal paceman who took the injured Garth le Roux's place, rocked the Wanderers with an explosive hat-trick in the fifth one-day match. And Kourie did a fine job in his primary role as a slow bowler, operating with remarkable accuracy against some of the most aggressive batsmen in the game.

The six one-day internationals whizzed by in the final nine days of the tour, followed by the rest of the interrupted domestic season. Going back to the comparatively drab provincial scene was akin to swapping a fine Bordeaux for a bottle of Tassies. So this is what we've been missing, the cricket establishment thought, as it bade farewell to the West Indians.

Despite the increased pressure to perform, Kirsten would gladly have kept the South African captaincy in exchange for the Western Province leadership that season. And not because of any deficiencies in his or his team's form.

Repeating the twin glories of 1981-82 was always going to be a miracle too far for Kirsten and his men. That they deserved their initial successes was unquestionable, but to do it again with a cluster of still-young players carrying so much of the workload was pushing things. This was common knowledge. But what frustrated Western Province no end was the fact that the presence of most of the players who had helped them win the double the season before didn't seem to count for much.

Lamb had gone, but Gooch was no less a batting force, scoring 597 runs at 39,80 and making two centuries towards the end of the campaign. With 36 wickets, Emburey was the most dangerous bowler in the Western Province attack. However, he was less successful at the Wanderers, where he found himself in six matches of one sort or another that season.

In terms of log points, Western Province's tally of 115 was just one worse than in 1981-82, but what mattered more was that they finished one outright victory short of the desired six. Three draws – against a mediocre Natal team, Transvaal and Northern Transvaal – cost them dearly, as did Transvaal's 122-run win in the New Year match, but they did enough to reach the four-day final against Transvaal at the Wanderers.

The idea of a Currie Cup final to decide the champion province in 1982-83 was not universally supported. The old argument about a final deciding a league competition – that a team which led the points table by a wide margin might see their season's work undone in just one match – was raised, but the marketing men pushed it aside.

In fact, Western Province went into the final at a distinct disadvantage to their opponents. By virtue of being runners-up, they had to take on the leaders at their home ground and beat them outright to win the trophy. A draw would make Transvaal the champions.

As it happened, Western Province did well to escape with a draw.

Rice won the toss, the prelude to the fifth time in seven home matches that season that Jimmy Cook and Henry Fotheringham put on a century partnership for the first wicket. Their separation only brought Kallicharran to the crease, and he left 151 runs later.

Kevin McKenzie's 92 pushed Transvaal into the unbeatable position offered by a first innings of 475. Le Roux's enforced absence was just what the Transvalers might have ordered, and Jefferies and Emburey were punished mercilessly. And it got better. For Transvaal, that is.

Western Province, despite a pair of worthy half-centuries from Pienaar and Henry, sank to 124 for seven before the latter and Jefferies coaxed 80 runs out of the dying innings. But a total of 228 didn't inspire confidence.

The visitors were duly asked to follow on. Even on the fourth day the pitch was a strip made for batting and the runs flowed. Kirsten, with seven half-centuries but no centuries behind his name that season, found rich form and stroked 137 runs for the second wicket with Seeff before sharing 181 with the equally ruthless McEwan. As the Transvaal attack tired, the runs came even more prolifically. McEwan was dropped twice, but went on to make a memorable 130. Kirsten went a few better. He saw it out, this last hurrah of a momentous season, and reached 168 before declaring and setting Transvaal a target of two hours and 20 overs.

But that was the end of the match as a contest. Knowing they had only to draw to win the Currie Cup, Transvaal were in no mood for a run chase and the rain which temporarily halted play before the home side totalled 97 for one seemed to concur.

Above: Wedding day: mother Lois on the left and father Noel on the right.

Below: Bestman to brother Andrew. A fine sportsman, Andrew played cricket for Western Province B and scrumhalf for Western Province senior team in many games.

Above: Kirsten with the late Stuart Leary ('Master'). They had a three-year partnership at Western Province from 1981 to 1984, Kirsten as captain and Leary as coach. (FRC Hammond, Western Province Cricket Union)

Below: Proud Derbyshire folk. Winners of the 1981 NatWest trophy – the club's first trophy since 1935.

Western Province Cricket Team, 1985/86. Winner of the Castle Currie Cup, Benson & Hedges Trophy, Protea Challenge and Firestone Challenge; runners-up in the Nissan Shield.

Above: The South African XI against Lawrence Rowe's 'rebel' West Indies XI. Kirsten captained the South African side. (Terry Haywood)

Below: 'Rub-a-dub-dub, three men in a tub …' Steve Jones, Kenny Watson and Peter Kirsten had a joint celebration for their 40th birthdays.

Above: Calcutta welcome for the South African team, just out of isolation, 1991.

Below: Man of the match in New Delhi, 1991. Kirsten (86 n.o.) and Ali Bacher.

Kirsten, eventually chosen for the World Cup squad in Australia and New Zealand in 1992, celebrates with wife Tuffy and daughter Leilah. (Gary Horlor, Daily Dispatch)

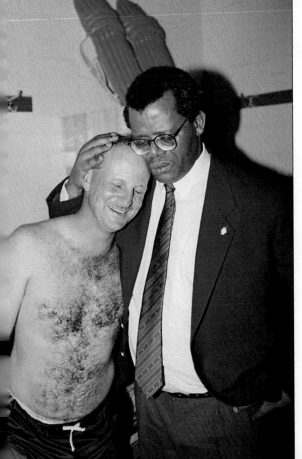

WORLD CUP 1992

Above: Away from the pressure: Kirsten finds a moment for a quiet cup of tea. (The Argus)

Left: 'Peter, you've saved the country.' An emotional Steve Tshwete embraces Kirsten after the South Africans' victory against Australia. (Allsport/Touchline)

WORLD CUP 1992. *Above left:* Great feeling, great country. (Allsport/Touchline)

Above right: 'Good throw, Hansie!' Kirsten and Cronjé are ecstatic at the run-out of David Boon in the match against Australia. (Allsport/Touchline)

Below: Kirsten tries to lift the run-rate in the match against Sri Lanka but, despite his 47 runs, Sri Lanka clinched their three-wicket victory in the final over. (The Argus)

WORLD CUP 1992. *Above:* Semi-final gloom – vs England in Sydney. Rain, rain, go away … (Allsport/Touchline)

Below. Victory in defeat. (The Argus)

MEMORABLE MEETINGS. *Above left:* Kirsten is introduced to Queen Elizabeth at Highclere in 1994.

Above right: Meeting Mother Teresa in Calcutta was a humbling experience. Kirsten comments: 'I've never known Ricey so speechless before!' (Allsport/Touchline)

Below: An inspiring moment, meeting President Nelson Mandela before a Test match. 'Ah, you're the older one,' he said to Kirsten.

Above: A relaxed moment on the England tour, 1994.

Below: Man of the match: the second Test at Headingley in 1994 when Kirsten scored his maiden Test century.

Border Cricket Team 1993/94 season. Back: A Lawson, B Fourie, G Thompson, A Badenhorst, K Bauermeister, G Victor, S Palframan, Q Still, F Cronjé, P Emslie. Front: B Osborne, P Botha, R Bauser (General Manager), S Jones (Coach), P Kirsten (Captain – A Team),

Western Province also found an easy route to the Datsun Shield final and Transvaal, with a total of 303 for five, were easy 109-run winners. The same teams met in the Benson and Hedges showpiece, and Transvaal won by six wickets in the face of fine batting by Gooch (85), Pienaar (61) and Jefferies (67).

No matter what they tried, Western Province almost invariably finished second to Transvaal. That they were undeniably the second-best team in the country was, of course, irrelevant. Frustration, utter frustration.

15

Trouble in Paradise

Whatever the events on the field during the 1982-83 season, there was much happening off it among South Africa's top cricketers. The rebels had ensured that money was an important consideration to every first-class cricketer.

The amounts the touring teams were being paid led, inevitably, to the South Africans questioning their lot in both the provincial and international arenas. The sudden arrival of a planeload of unexpected – or, rather, unannounced – rebel cricketers played havoc with the fixtures and invariably resulted in a congested season.

This led to problems with bosses, who had heard enough about their employees' precious cricket commitments. The South African cricketer clearly needed better management of his financial interests and security.

After the season, in April 1983, the five captains of the A section provinces and the executive of the South African Cricket Union met to discuss the following season. The subject was bound to come up: what about representation for the players? But the captains were not prepared and the president of the SACU, Joe Pamensky, issued a curt message to Kirsten as the national captain: 'Put your house in order, then come talk to us.'

Having finally severed his ties with Derbyshire, Kirsten had a free winter on his hands. And six months of activity between provincial captains and their players led to a mandate for the South African Professional Cricket

118

Players Association to be formed. Eddie Barlow might have retired from the playing field the season before, but he still had much to offer the game and was elected the new body's first president, with Mike Procter as his deputy.

The declaration of the constitution embodied the Association's guiding aim of ensuring every provincial cricketer was treated fairly. It spoke of better communication between players, administrators, umpires and sponsors, of reaching all the country's cricketers and of establishing a code of ethics to protect the game.

Kirsten, as national captain, Clive Rice, Procter, Peter Cooke and Barlow were central to the creation of the organisation and it was the first concrete evidence of long-held views on professionalism in cricket. More had to be done for the players, the heart of the game, the cogs in the machine that made it run.

The South African captain thus entrenched himself on the side of fairness as they squared up, without overt hostility, to those in control of the game and their careers. There were no lines drawn in the sand, but there it was: he had nailed his colours to his chosen mast.

Then, with the return of the West Indians for the second half of their contract imminent, press reports with Johannesburg datelines started wondering if he would retain the South African captaincy.

Retain it? What exactly had he done that would cause it to be taken away? Tactically he passed muster, though not without his detractors, and he had accomplished the none too shabby feat of sharing the spoils with a team infinitely more experienced than his own. He was no diplomat, but was not a captain's first priority – and the one which should govern the length and tone of his tenure – what he did in the field? Some, it seems, did not think so.

It seems the Transvaal cricket writers knew something that others didn't. Kirsten was duly reappointed to the captaincy – for the first three four-day matches. He was reappointed by Chris Burger, convener of selectors. Kirsten's own reply to Burger's tentative offer of the captaincy was, 'Yes, I would love to continue the captaincy, give me a chance to grow into the new level of responsibility during the next run of four-day Test matches. It would be an honour to captain South Africa during these sensitive times, see how I go.'

Even then, all was not well. Slowly, but unmistakably, the wheel of earned good fortune (if there is such a thing) was turning away from Kirsten. And it didn't help that the cracks in South African cricket were left gaping by that second West Indian visit.

Except for Kirsten and Pollock, the batting disintegrated as the results of isolation were rammed home for all to see. In the last season Garth le Roux had been injured; this time it was Stephen Jefferies, not in the best of form as it was, and so the attack suffered a similar amputation.

By contrast, the West Indians returned an even more coherent unit than the year before. Three-day matches against each of the five A section provinces before the first four-day international helped fine-tune their game for the series that lay ahead.

The rain-affected first four-day match, at Kingsmead, proved nothing beyond the fact that the tourists had improved their batting form. Their first innings total of 529 included 103 by Alvin Kallicharran and Lawrence Rowe's 157. South Africa winced.

Bolstered by Jimmy Cook's 69, 84 from Kirsten and Graeme Pollock's 62, the home side totalled 333 – not enough to avoid following on but enough to ensure the match would be drawn, with South Africa 59 without loss in their second innings.

The pressure on Kirsten mounted as the frowns on a few well-worn, well-meaning, but out of touch faces deepened. But they eased somewhat when South Africa won the second match, the New Year fixture at Newlands, by ten wickets. The tourists were bowled out for 252 and 268 and Kirsten featured strongly with 88, though in the shadow of Pollock's 102. Together, they withstood the physical and mental barrage that comes with taking on any West Indian attack to share 183 runs for the third wicket. Cook and Fotheringham, with unbeaten scores of 40 and 71 respectively, knocked off the 117 required in 21.2 overs as South Africa celebrated a consummate victory.

But the joy would not last. The West Indians had won the only one-day match played before the New Year match by two wickets, a competitive, typically pulsating affair at the Wanderers tainted, perhaps, by the tourists' refusal to wear the coloured clothing specially made for the day-night game in protest at a sponsorship row which, happily, blew over without much further ado.

However, the events of that balmy evening, which saw the West Indians appear at the crease in all manner of garish combinations of white and maroon, scarcely hinted at the acrimony which was to follow.

By the time the third four-day match was to be played, at the Wanderers, the limited overs scales had tilted strongly in the tourists' favour. They led 3-1 with two to play, and the exaggerated significance which one-day cricket still enjoys in South Africa became the slippery slope down which Kirsten's captaincy would slide.

The South African team for that third match showed three changes:

Kenny Watson and Rupert Hanley came in for Le Roux and Jefferies, while Adrian Kuiper was preferred to a second spinner, in this case Denys Hobson. They were all sensible moves calculated to bring out the best in the home side. Then the shock.

The appendage '(capt)' that had become a familiar shadow behind the name P N Kirsten was missing as the names of the selected team flashed around the country and beyond. Instead, one C E B Rice would lead the team at the Wanderers.

Losing the national captaincy jolted him, Kirsten admits, but he knew he was handing over to a fine leader. In Kirsten's words there were 'not many better' than the square-jawed, utterly committed Transvaal captain in the 1970s and '80s.

What was it like suddenly not to be the leader of a team which included some of his boyhood heroes, to be told abruptly that he would now be taking orders instead of issuing them? No problem, or at least a matter of much less significance than the difficulties of dealing with Clarke and Co.

It would be unfair to judge Rice's undoubted leadership qualities on the events of a series he walked in on halfway through, but the record books state starkly that the West Indians won the remaining two four-day matches, by one wicket and six wickets respectively, and duly wrapped up the limited overs contest in the fifth match before South Africa gained a consolation victory in the last.

The Wanderers four-day match featured the famous partnership between Kirsten and Graeme Pollock that began with South Africa in trouble at 10 for three and saw them to safety. The atmosphere created by the 25 000 spectators was electric.

Kirsten's personal contribution to the four-day series spoke volumes. He topped the averages with 304 runs at 50,67 and showed immense courage in the face of hostility – from both the opposing bowlers and his own administrators. His considerable reputation as a fielder – always attacking, invariably lethal – had been enhanced to the point where he was freely touted as the world's most dangerous man in the covers.

That Kirsten managed to perform to these levels despite the turmoil off the field was nothing short of miraculous. It was the fighter in him coming out the only way he knew – with cricket of the highest calibre.

But he could not deny that his sacking had crippled his confidence and proved singularly unhelpful in the crucial task of motivating his players. Before the West Indian tour, Western Province were unbeaten in a total of 13 limited overs and first-class matches, of which they had won ten.

Then came the tour and an interruption of two months in which Kirsten's perspective on the game was radically altered. Of the seven matches Western Province played following the resumption of domestic hostilities, they lost four. Among them were the Currie Cup final, lost to – who else – Transvaal by 141 runs at Newlands after Western Province had topped the final standings by nine points. That the competition had been reduced to a single round of four matches each made the margin for error far smaller, although it was always going to be a two-horse race.

And it seemed Western Province were destined invariably to finish second, as they did in the renamed Nissan Shield. There was a measure of variation in the Benson and Hedges series, in which they were fancied to beat Natal and qualify for the final but went down by six wickets in their first loss at Green Point stadium, the makeshift Cape Town venue for day-night cricket.

Natal went on to beat Eastern Province in a wet, lacklustre final at the Wanderers.

The same day the final was played, 30 March, the news broke nationwide: Kirsten had resigned the Western Province captaincy. In truth, he had been asked to leave. Fritz Bing, the selector who had argued for his elevation to the Western Province side in 1973, who had shown faith in the untried but gifted stripling, now sang a different tune.

'Are these statements you have made in the press true?' Bing asked. Kirsten had criticised some of his players and the administration in the Afrikaans press for not, as he saw it, giving their all. He confirmed he had not been misquoted.

'Then, regretfully, I have no option but to take the captaincy away.'

We think it would be better if you resigned, Peter. Adrian Kuiper will take over the captaincy.

How brutally quickly it had crumbled, the citadel Kirsten thought he had built out of stone but which turned out to be made of sand. Two summers previously he had been the saviour of Western Province cricket, blazing a triumphant trail for the new generation, those who would have to follow Barlow, Ackerman and Procter. The hero of Newlands, the scourge of the Wanderers, the prince of batsmen, awarded a benefit for the 1983-84 season …

As Kirsten discovered, it was a short fall from those heights to being 'the bugger who caused all the trouble', who dared to point out certain truths as he saw them.

Losing the national captaincy was undoubtedly a blow but this was worse, far worse. The province he had worked so hard with and for, shared sympathy with, celebrated with, and then been asked to lead, no longer considered him fit to captain them.

122

Not the players, mind, but the committee men.

Kirsten regrets the way his tenure at the helm came to an end. There was so much he still planned to do and he felt he had barely manoeuvred the myriad duties of a first-class captain into focus when they were whisked away.

Would it have been different had he been less volatile, less reckless, more inclined to see the game from the administrator's perspective, a better communicator? Would it have helped to have been groomed for the captaincy, instead of being handed it when the edges of the Kirsten gem still gleamed rough and dangerous with an awkward splendour? And that among players younger, or not much older, than himself.

Quite possibly not. But Kirsten nevertheless could not shake off the infuriating feeling that he had been made a scapegoat to turn the scalpel away from the major abscess.

He felt he had been sacked by people who weren't doing too wonderful a job themselves, the same people who had alienated Barlow and were to lose several priceless assets in years to come, among them Kirsten himself, Hylton Ackerman, Terence Lazard, John Commins, Stephen Jones, Stuart Leary, Omar Henry, Bob Woolmer, Daryll Cullinan and Kuiper.

At 26, Kirsten had been King Arthur, much loved and respected. At 28, he became the dreaded Mordred. And much as his batsman's instinct told him not to rub the red stain where this bouncer had struck him, he had to admit it: this one hurt.

Kirsten would contribute for another six seasons to Western Province's successes, all the while seeking a greater challenge. The culture of Newlands and the adulation of the Western Province cricketing public would always be part of him.

In November 1985 an Australian rebel team, who also returned for a second tour, became the latest rabbit the South African Cricket Union pulled from its hat. The initial plans for the tour had been hatched in 1982, but the Aussies had to take their place in a growing queue of cricketers eager to make what they could out of South African cricket.

Now they were in the country. Under Kim Hughes' leadership, the squad of 16 included Rod McCurdy, Steve Rixon and Terry Alderman, who were to have undertaken an Ashes tour that year. Legal action was taken against players contracted to the Australian Cricket Board, a list made up of Hughes, Graham Yallop, Rodney Hogg, Tom Hogan, Carl Rackemann, John Maguire, John Dyson and Steve Smith. The SACU managed to settle out of court.

Indeed, there was much consternation both at Lord's and the Melbourne Cricket Ground at the prospect of an Australian team touring outlawed South Africa.

Similar in outlook and the way they play their cricket, South Africa and Australia are natural enemies on the cricket field. Series between these two countries have invariably brought out the best of both teams.

But Kirsten, despite scoring 96 for Western Province against the rebels, was in patchy form in the three-match four-day series. He followed scores of two and five in the first match at Kingsmead with a solid but unspectacular 72 on a difficult Newlands pitch, sharing 132 runs with Cook for the second wicket, and he made 20 in the second innings. Both matches were drawn, with the tourists dominating the first and Hughes saving the second for his team by hitting a fighting, undefeated 97.

The decider, at the Wanderers, was played over five days, starting on 16 January, and it carried a purse of R30 000 for the winners. It unfolded into a spectacular advertisement for first-class cricket with South Africa eventually winning by 188 runs.

Hughes won the toss, asked South Africa to bat on the evidence of a well-grassed pitch, and no doubt patted himself on the back when Hogg broke through early to bowl Cook for five. But after he had bowled four overs, Hogg hobbled off with a hamstring injury.

Having left McCurdy out of his XI, Hughes was suddenly reduced to two fast bowlers, neither fully fit. Carl Rackemann was battling to shake off a chest virus and Terry Alderman had a painful back. Perhaps no one told the South African batsmen that the Australian attack had been effectively neutered. Kirsten's performance on the day – taking two consecutive deliveries from Rackemann on his knuckles, trying to hit back and being caught behind for 12 – was as good as most, as one South African after another contrived to get out in increasingly bizarre fashion.

Rackemann couldn't believe his luck. He certainly bowled outstandingly well, but not well enough to take eight for 84, six of them caught by Rixon, against a line-up like this. Only Kevin McKenzie batted with any authority, scoring a typically rumbustious 72 with a variety of strokes after coming to the crease with South Africa looking down the barrel at 86 for five.

He took the score to 166 before being eighth out and, after bad light ended play just less than two hours early, the innings ended on the second morning with South Africa having totalled 211.

Hugh Page had John Dyson caught at third slip by Rice 25 minutes before lunch with 45 runs on the board. An early breakthrough: perfect.

But it proved the portent of a South African disaster as Steve Smith cut loose with an aggressive brand of batsmanship to hammer 116 of the 159 runs that had been scored before he slashed at a ball from Corrie van Zyl and was well held by Pollock at second slip. Much of the Australian challenge departed with him and they were all out for 267. Much of the Australian challenge besides Greg Shipperd, that is.

Arriving at the crease on the second morning, he survived until the first session of the third day, having faced 199 balls for his 44 runs.

Success was spread around the South African attack. Van Zyl had bowled with rare zest in his first match for South Africa, taking four for 82; Rice sorted out the middle order and the tail in his three for 42; and Page had kept it admirably tight with two for 37 off 26.3 overs.

As always, Rice didn't ask his players to do what he was not comfortable doing himself. He hit Rackemann on his bowling arm with a distinctly malevolent ball and then dismissed the tall paceman and Hogg in consecutive deliveries. South Africa, outplayed earlier, had snuck back into the match. A good start in the second innings would go a long way to ensuring that R30 000 didn't leave the country …

Bang: Fotheringham caught behind for five. Twenty-five for one. Bang: Cook trapped in front for 21. Thirty-one for two. Bang: Kirsten castled for ten. Eighty for three. South Africa, 56 runs behind in the first innings, had seven wickets left with which to set a reasonable target.

One of those wickets belonged to the Master, Pollock, another to McKenzie, and a third to Rice. Between them, they scored 225 of the 306 runs South Africa mustered in their second innings, setting the Australians a target of 250 for victory.

Pollock, his ripping power disguising exquisite timing, was in the midst of one of his finest innings when a delivery from Rackemann pitched on a length, reared and hit the left-hander on his top hand, fracturing a bone above the knuckles. Having hit ten fours in reaching 51 off 41 balls, he was in no mood to call a truce, but he was soon forced to leave the field clutching his forearm.

Then Rackemann began to hyperventilate, caused by the chemistry of adrenalin and the medication he was on for his chest virus, and joined Pollock in sick bay. Hughes scratched his head. His pace attack had been reduced to Alderman and the medium pace of Peter Faulkner.

Rice struggled to find the groove, but with McKenzie he took South Africa to 192 for three at the close. The rest day that followed allowed Rackemann to recover to his devastating best and he began the fourth day by hitting Rice on the helmet and then having him caught behind.

Three more wickets fell before lunch arrived with South Africa staggering at 273 for eight. Mercifully, rain started falling during the interval and eventually denied the Australians the last two sessions.

Would Pollock return? McKenzie had hung on bravely for his unbeaten 95 and was South Africa's last hope. There was no choice. Pad up, Geeps. No second bidding was needed.

Van Zyl was caught behind on his overnight score of two early that fifth morning and a crowd of 3 000 roared like twice as many when they saw the well-set figure of Graeme Pollock make his way down the concrete stairs that lead from the Wanderers dressingroom to the boundary.

Genius was sometimes not enough to get the job done. Sometimes it needed a dash of courage as well. And Pollock showed plenty of courage as, his three pounds of finest English willow suspended from just his left hand, he helped McKenzie to a deserved century and then unashamedly farmed the strike. A priceless partnership of 31 later – which included consecutive one-handed boundaries off Alderman – McKenzie edged Rackemann to Alderman to wrap up his first century for South Africa at 116 off 144 balls with ten fours and a six.

The applause as the unlikely last-wicket pair walked off was warm and genuine. But everyone knew the Australians had more than two sessions at their disposal to chase 250 and the series honours. The pugnacious Smith was on the victory trail early, quickly reaching 14. Then Van Zyl heard the joyous sound of leather on the merest splinter of wood, and the Australians were 24 for one.

Shipperd and Dyson had scored just five runs together when they were parted. Shipperd's supporters would call him compact and watchful; the rest would say he was awkward and a stonewaller. Le Roux said nothing, but remembered that the diminutive, moustached Western Australian who batted in something akin to a modern suit of armour, wasn't that keen on the quicker ball.

The ball exploded through Shipperd's guard and Le Roux was in the throes of his follow-through when he saw the off-stump cartwheeling. Hughes arrived and promptly departed – caught behind when he got a bottom edge to another swift delivery. By the time Le Roux bounded in again, he had four slips, a gully and a man within spitting distance of the bat.

All was quiet. Then – THUMP. Le Roux never appealed for a wicket: he demanded it. It was the same this time. Arms high, blond mane wild, a bellow summoned from the very bottom of his huge frame. Umpire Ossie Schoof considered the evidence for what seemed an age before delivering his verdict: yup, that's plumb.

By then Le Roux was so far down the pitch that the first player to leap into his arms was Ray Jennings, the wicketkeeper. The rest of his team-mates soon followed as they realised that, with the Australians reduced to 36 for five, the big fast bowler had won the match and the series in the space of three deliveries.

Rice's own hat-trick shortly after lunch might have come after the back of the innings had been broken, but it was a deserved reward for the South African captain. With his first delivery in the second innings Rice, who had dismissed Rackemann and Hogg to end the first innings, nipped past Graham Yallop's bat and pads and into his stumps with a superb delivery. It was his first hat-trick in 17 summers of first-class cricket.

Between them, Rice and Page accounted for the other five wickets and South Africa, having bowled the Australians out for 61 in 28.4 overs, were victors by 188 runs.

Both teams knew they had been part of an epic match and, with a draining, competitive series at last behind them, they inevitably ended up in one or other dressingroom, sharing a beer and countless anecdotes, cricketing and otherwise.

The convener of the South African selectors, Peter van der Merwe, appeared at the door. Bespectacled and with the air of a musty academic about him, Van der Merwe had been respected in his playing days as a deep-thinking, analytical captain. He had proved it by leading South Africa to a series win over Bobby Simpson's Australians at home in 1966-67, and an away triumph over England in 1965, the first by a South African team for 30 years and the last to date.

Van der Merwe was undoubtedly an intelligent cricketer, whether on the field or in the committee room. A pity he was also among the most thoughtless.

He exchanged pleasantries with the players and then, within hearing of both teams, he brazenly told Kirsten he had been dropped for the first three matches of the one-day series.

By the way, Peter, you're out of the first three one-dayers.

Just like that. No quiet chat, no consideration of the fact that he was dealing with a senior player.

Kirsten, who has succeeded in hiding a sensitive personality under a shield of toughness, was quietly devastated. How could he be out? Sure, 121 runs at 20,16 isn't what you expect from your number three, but there were better ways of breaking the news that he would be on the bench next time round.

It wasn't the last time Kirsten would feel the sharp edge of Van der Merwe's tongue, nor his selection policy. But at least the next time he knew what he was dealing with.

Kirsten returned for the last three matches and got into the twenties each time as South Africa rallied to win 4-2.

Like other players who came to South Africa as part of unofficial teams and were banned from playing for or in their own countries, several Australians changed from being cricketing mercenaries to refugees as they served out their sentences in the Currie Cup.

Not only was South African cricket in the unhappy situation of having to recruit its international opposition surreptitiously, it inherited a significant percentage of the players who came initially in search of fortune.

It became too much for Kirsten, this farcical existence of provincial cricket propped up by the haphazard arrival of one bunch of rebels or another, some of whom then remained to take up places in teams which some thought should go to local players.

For the first time in 13 years of first-class cricket, Kirsten became bored with the game.

There seemed to be no future at Western Province. Indeed, no future in South Africa, what with P W Botha waving that dictatorial digit in the face of any argument against the iron fist of the apartheid state. Too much, too much ...

Winter, 1986. Kirsten looked out on a sunny, yellow-green oval. Marvellous place to play cricket, he thought. Wide spaces, endless azure sky, people who knew the game, and no politics getting in the way.

Yes, Australia is a grand place to play cricket. Australia ... AUSTRALIA? It had to happen. Despite the fact that Kuiper had led Western Province to the Currie Cup crown and their first Benson and Hedges title in 1985-86, Kirsten had had enough and decided to see just how much greener the grass was on the other side.

With the start of the South African season three months away, he was in Adelaide peering across a stretch of Aussie lawn, the picturesque ground the Cottesloe Cricket Club wanted him to come and play on.

Allan Lamb and Robin Smith had done it in England, and until the previous season Kepler Wessels had been based across the way in Queensland when he wasn't playing in green and gold of the Australian variety. Why shouldn't he see if he could play Test cricket? He was 31 and counting; the years were slipping away.

Kirsten had taken to the perhaps un-Australian atmosphere of Adelaide, and the Oval, headquarters of the South Australian Cricket Association, was all a batsman could hope for: a legendary batting pitch in one of the most attractive settings in world cricket. The people of this graciously colonial city were friendly and without the brashness that gives some the wrong idea about Australians.

Take a less focused look and it might be Cape Town. Yes, he could bring his family here.

Visas for Peter and Tuffy had been taken care of. All that was left to do was to sign the contract, the first step towards the ultimate for any cricketer, he told himself.

Or would it be treason? Kirsten had no trouble with other South Africans playing under a foreign flag. Like him, they were professionals entitled to earn their livelihood wherever they wished. The professional cricketer in him believed this fully, knew it was right.

But he wasn't just a cricketer – he was also a South African. And no matter how lucrative the offer and how confident he was of being selected to the Australian team, the prospect of disposing of his birthright was the greater consideration.

Kirsten couldn't sign that contract. He simply could not bring himself to abandon his roots, his family, his cricket as he had learned it, the special smell of boerewors on the braai, and the taste of a cold, cold Castle.

The telephone rang. Tuffy, her voice shaking. Peter, it's the old man. He's got stomach cancer. He's dying.

Noel Kirsten had spent much of his life urging his children to do their very best on the sportsfield. He was deservedly a proud father. When the frustration of being a top class cricketer in South Africa in the 1980s boiled over, it was Kirsten's father who cooled the temperature. 'Test cricket is coming. Hang on, Peter,' he would say.

Now, as he had done at Port Elizabeth airport all those years ago, and at various times in Kirsten's career, Noel Kirsten was helping his son see reason. Kirsten returned to South Africa.

An Australian? Never!

Western Province opened their Currie Cup campaign that 1986-87 season against Natal at Newlands on 25 October. After Natal had recovered from losing four wickets for 62 runs in the first session, mediocre bowling by both attacks on the flattest of pitches all but precluded a result. But that was by the by.

With Natal's eventual 338 their primary objective, Western Province made the right sort of start on the second morning by scoring 121 runs for the first wicket through Allan Elgar and Lawrence Seeff. Without the pitch on his side and with little venom from his team-mates coming into the mix, even Hartley Alleyne looked ordinary.

In the pavilion Kirsten sat padded up but thinking of his father, who had died, aged 59, on 30 September. We should have been closer, he lived just down the road, for goodness sake.

A cry of relief went up from the Natal side as Elgar's bails tumbled through the air. Rob Bentley's persistent medium pace bowling had paid off. Time to go to work. Gloves, bat ... and something else.

Kirsten is not a religious man, trusting in the concrete rather than the ethereal. But he felt he was not alone when he took guard that day. Whether it was his father's presence or the way his son, who found he was unable to get the tears out when Noel died, was finally expressing his grief will never be known. But it was inspiring to think that the father who, groundsman or not, could not bear to be in the ground when his son was at the crease, might be looking on as the runs flowed in lieu of tears.

The close saw Kirsten still busy on 114 – his first Currie Cup century in two seasons. All the magic was there as he commanded the ball to do his bidding with a consummate display of invincible batting.

That evening, the prospect of Kirsten's first double century in South Africa, following six for Derbyshire, hung in the air like mist over Table Mountain. If he did reach 200, he would share with Dave Nourse the record for double centuries by a South African.

The next day, with six and a half hours' immaculate batting behind him, Kirsten passed that milestone, having hit 27 fours and a six in getting there. The Newlands scoreboard read 'P N Kirsten not out 204'. Peter Kirsten's scoreboard read 'One for Noel'.

Predictably, Kuiper declared immediately and the match wound down to its fated draw, with Natal 193 for five in their second innings.

Despite reaching 50 four more times, Kirsten would not score another century for Western Province that season. And though Terence Lazard, Kenny McEwan and Seeff made up for that with eight tons between them, Western Province still emerged with just the night series trophy, as well as some of the minor offerings, in the cabinet.

Kirsten did, however, taste success against the returning Australians, despite being left out of the first two of four day-night internationals, which South

Africa won 2-1 with one rained out. After reaching 14 and 19 in the four-day match at the Wanderers, he grafted his way back in the drawn New Year match at Newlands, scoring 173 in the first innings and 103 not out in the second.

That made him one of only three South Africans – Alan Melville and Bruce Mitchell are the others – to score centuries for their country in both innings of a five-day match.

South Africa had won the first match by 49 runs and were happy to draw the remaining three for a 1-0 series win, and they then took the one-day series 3-1.

In 1987-88 Western Province became the first province to annex three Benson and Hedges titles, but their Currie Cup trail was littered with failure. Of their seven matches, Western Province won two and drew three.

The batting was substantially weakened by McEwan's move back to Eastern Province. Kirsten hit three half-centuries in a tally of 398 runs at 39,80 – good enough for second place in the Western Province averages, but not good enough for the man himself.

One of the brighter spots of the season was the first-class début of his half-brother, Gary, for Western Province B.

Kirsten scored marginally more runs (442) the next season, but slipped to an average of 31,57. Four half-centuries, still no tons. And in spite of signing a long-term contract the season before, there were rumours of flirtings with Northern Transvaal.

Western Province won the Nissan Shield and reached the final of the night series for the fourth consecutive time but in the arena that mattered, the Currie Cup, they were mournful. Four draws, two losses and a solitary win told of a team that had lost its way, whatever their limited overs success in the second half of the season. Midway through the winter Kuiper's reign as captain ended and Seeff took over.

Kuiper's feel for the one-day game simply did not translate into sound captaincy in first-class cricket. Infamously, he sent Eastern Province in at Newlands and they were still batting well into the second day after Mark Rushmere, Adrian Birrell and Wessels had all scored centuries. EP declared at 440 for eight and Western Province were promptly bowled out for 175 with Kuiper caught behind without scoring. And they were nine wickets down and still 52 runs behind when the match ended.

Both Stephen Jefferies and Garth le Roux were dropped from the Western Province team for the first time in their careers. Though Jefferies returned to the senior side, he was never again the bowler who had held South Africa's finest batsmen spellbound. Le Roux came back with some success but found himself merely going through the motions and announced his retirement from the game on the eve of the New Year match against Transvaal.

Kirsten hadn't reached the same dire straits but he could understand Le Roux's reasoning. Playing for Western Province, once an honour and a pleasure second only to representing his country, had lost its sparkle.

Crucially, there was no challenge. Much of Kirsten's spiritual bond with Western Province had been loosened the day he resigned the captaincy. He had been to the top and down again, and he had nowhere left to go – other than to another province.

The summer of 1989-90 was a tumultuous time for both Western Province and South African cricket. It was the summer of the infamous Gatting tour and all the unpleasantness that came with it. It marked the National Sports Congress's biggest victory over establishment sport – namely, the curtailment of the tour, and the opening of white eyes in the SACU.

There would be no more rebel tours. The only way forward was through complete, genuine unity and with a development programme that had grown too big and too successful for its once cosmetic boots.

Ali Bacher saw the light and made sure others saw it too. The darkest hour, of clandestine negotiations and thinly veiled hostility from black administrators towards whites, was yet to come but the breakthrough had been made. No more would the SACU tell itself what it wanted to hear, that cricket in South Africa had been normalised and that the International Cricket Council were a bunch of wimps who couldn't stand up to their governments.

Kirsten also found his political principles tested during the Gatting tour. Shortly after Kirsten taken part in a mass march for peace and an end to racism in South Africa, Ngconde Balfour, a senior man in the NSC, took him to lunch and asked him not to play for South Africa against the rebels.

Kirsten thought about it. He had never agreed with apartheid, could not understand the racism that permeated every sector of South African society. But he was a professional cricketer and he could not hope to maintain that status and his reputation if he refused to play on political grounds.

'I'm not that kind of hero,' he told the papers. No, he could not agree to boycott the Gatting tour.

Kirsten had a sub-par run in the one first-class and the four-match limited overs series played against the tourists. But he played himself into better form for Western Province. Two centuries – his first in three seasons – made the season bearable, as did sharing the Currie Cup with Eastern Province.

An outstanding memory from the Eastern Province match was setting the Province second-wicket partnership record with his brother Gary. Their 252, of which Gary scored 175 and Peter 128, is still in the books.

Although an honour of this nature would seem to be the preserve of a happy team, that wasn't the case with Western Province that season. They didn't come up to scratch in either limited overs competition and the extent of the dissatisfaction at Newlands was apparent at the end of the season when Robin Jackman was removed as coach.

Four days before he scored 185 in the first innings of the Boxing Day match against Free State, Kirsten had been in East London for a Benson and Hedges match against Border. And it wasn't any old match. It was Border's first at their new home, Buffalo Park. The unfinished ground, the work in progress of a dedicated band of administrators, was littered with scaffolding and rain threatened to spoil it all for a vocal home crowd ecstatic that the lights had finally been switched on in their backyard.

Kirsten was impressed by their enthusiasm. Even as the rain drenched them, the spectators kept up a steady racket. And when the players returned the cheers grew louder.

Chasing a reduced target of 134 off 31 overs, Border were just five runs shy as Meyrick Pringle took a B and H record six for 30 and Craig Matthews three for 34, bowling all his victims in one over. Kirsten had played a major role in his team's victory, hitting a fine 104 not out off 156 balls.

But defeat wasn't enough to take the wind out of the spectators' sails and they sang their way out of the ground. Kirsten was amazed, but not entirely surprised. This was the Border as he knew it, driven by plucky people who refused to accept they were anything but winners. The same positive vibe ran through their administration, where the white and black factions were well on the way to unity.

There were things happening here. Good things. One of them was that Robbie Muzzell, Stutterheim-born but like so many others lost to the bigger provinces during his playing years, had come home. The former Transvaal opening batsman would become the first president of the united Border Cricket Board in 1991, but at that stage he had another bee in his bonnet.

Let's bring Border's products back to the Border, was his idea.

And Kirsten was a prime target.

16

A New Challenge

'You are going to shorten your international career,' was Fritz Bing's parting shot to Kirsten as he prepared to put into action a decision that had stunned the Western Province Cricket Union executive a month previously.

Kirsten's contract with Western Province was due to expire in March 1991. But on 27 July 1990 he met with the executive, of which Bing was president, and requested that he be released from it. This was it: he was going. But where?

To East London.

East London? But that meant Border and the wilderness of the B section. Those to whom cricket was conveniently packaged into periods of six months at a time thought Kirsten had effectively put an end to his career. After all, South Africa's re-entry into Test cricket was imminent and surely he didn't expect to be selected for the national side on the strength of his performances against South African cricket's minnows and the second teams of the A section provinces.

And at 35 he couldn't gamble on making another move a few years down the line. But Kirsten was thinking bigger than that.

From his point of view, the major flaw in his contract with Western Province was that it took no cognisance of the winter months. Contrary to what some administrators seemed to think, cricketers did not go into hibernation after the season.

Kirsten had asked the WPCU for a 12-month contract for several years but there was no budging them. 'It's never been done,' seemed to be their sole response to the suggestion.

'It's very difficult to put a cricketer in a situation like that,' said Kevin Commins, the administrative director of the WPCU and father of Test opening batsman John Commins.

Companies in Cape Town were approached with a view to securing a permanent position for their star batsman. But the Union had let Kirsten drift too far. Despite the offer of a second benefit in 1991-92, he was going to East London and that was the end of it.

Border had succeeded where Western Province failed. In collaboration with the director of Rhodes University's East London campus, Ray Suttner, they had secured a position for Kirsten, and it was unmistakably up his alley. From 1 September 1990 he would be the 'administrative officer responsible for sport, public relations and school liaison', as the East London *Daily Dispatch* put it in gleeful reports on its front and back pages on 1 August.

In Johannesburg, Clive Rice admitted to being confused by Kirsten's move – and by the Western Province administrators who allowed him to make it.

'For Western Province to let him drift away to the B section when he's still got six years of A section and Test level cricket in him is hard to comprehend,' Rice told the *Cape Times*. 'Halfway through the season Western Province will be asking why they didn't keep him – you don't replace a brilliant player like that overnight.'

The sentimental tug of returning to his roots was never raised with the administrators but it certainly played a role in Kirsten's decision. At last he could go back to East London, where he first learned of the joy of cricket and rugby.

Kirsten expected leaving Cape Town to be a wrenching experience, and it was. Both he and Tuffy were transplanted to the Mother City – she, a granddaughter of legendary Test leg-spinner Ernie Vogler, from the Eastern Cape university town of Grahamstown – but that did not stop them from enjoying immensely the colourful palette Africa's southern tip presents its citizens. After 17 years, leaving it all behind for the less vibrant, somewhat apathetic lifestyle he would encounter in East London involved a personal paradigm shift.

But he made it gracefully enough and played some useful if low-key cricket in 1990-91. Border, anticipating a return to the A section, recruited players from other provinces and snatched back a few of their own who had left in search of brighter lights.

Opening batsman Brian Lones came back from Eastern Province and left-arm spinner Andrew Griffiths returned from Cape Town, where he had played for Western Province B. Mackie Hobson, a fast bowler who played for the South African Universities XI for three consecutive years, also donned Border colours, as did Kirsten's youngest brother Paul.

In addition, Kirsten was appointed vice-captain to Ian Howell, a clear indication that he would soon lead Border.

Border responded by sharing the Bowl, the B section championship, with Western Province B for the second consecutive summer to strengthen their claims for an A section berth.

The Western Province senior team was also successful, winning the Currie Cup and the Benson and Hedges crown. But that didn't stop the rumours from snaking through when Kirsten visited Cape Town directly after the season.

'Kirsten may return to WP,' warned the *Daily Dispatch*. He concurred: if Border were not granted A section status before the 1991-92 season he would consider going back to Cape Town.

'A section is important to a cricket career especially without international cricket looming,' he explained to the press. 'I want to stay in East London but my career has always been important to me and I would be silly if I didn't have a final shot at Test cricket.'

If Border's application failed, Kirsten added, it would not be a shock if he returned to Cape Town because he had repeatedly made his intentions clear – to help get Border into the A section.

The story might well have been the creation of bored reporters in East London as well as in Cape Town, where it originated. But it all came to nothing when, in the United Cricket Board executive meeting in Johannesburg on 4 May, it was decided that Border would rejoin the top flight in 1991-92.

Half of Kirsten's mission, to play A section cricket again, was thus on the brink of being accomplished. The other half, the dream of playing official international cricket for South Africa which he, like so many others, had carried with them for so long, emerged closer to reality on 23 October.

'I am delighted to announce that South Africa has been invited to play in the 1992 Benson and Hedges World Cup.' To South African ears, Colin Cowdrey, president of the International Cricket Council, had never sounded as positively chuffed as when he crackled across a telephone link-up in a Johannesburg hotel to deliver that wonderful message.

Cowdrey was in Sharjah in the United Arab Emirates, where the ICC had decided that South Africa had suffered enough and had done enough to return to world cricket. Kirsten was in East London, five days after scoring a fluent unbeaten 71 in a rain-contrived five-wicket loss to Northern Transvaal.

Silky timing had always been one of his most valuable attributes at the crease and now he had proved that he also had the knack for another kind of timing. Indeed, his move to Border, as risky as it had seemed, could not have been more timely. At Western Province he had been a respected senior player but still one of several batsmen expected to score big runs. At Border he was undoubtedly the star who glittered brightest. He could not be missed: not by the press nor by the national selectors.

The World Cup in Australia and New Zealand! Who would have thought …

17

Indian Adventure

Two days before Peter Kirsten heard the joyous news that he would be part of the first official South African team to represent their country in more than two decades, he was at the helm of a Border side which crashed to an ignominious defeat at the hands of his former team-mates, Western Province, in a Benson and Hedges match at Buffalo Park.

It had been an unhappy Friday evening. Border could not have been expected to take the Castle Cup (as the Currie Cup was now known) by storm in their first season back, but they had the benefit of two previous seasons' experience in the night series – some of their players had turned out for the Impalas before that – and should not have been bowled out for an embarrassing 47 runs.

The pitch had sweated under covers following rain and then warm, humid weather a few days before the match. But that could not detract from a superbly opportunistic seam bowling onslaught from Craig Matthews, Brian McMillan and Eric Simons, as well as inept batting by the home side.

With the ball caroming off the edge of every flaying Border bat, Simons took a sensational four for three off 2.1 overs (including a hat-trick), McMillan three for eight off seven, and Matthews two for 20 off nine. Even so, Gary Kirsten and Kenny Jackson took their bows early as Province wrapped up an eight-wicket win.

So it was a subdued Kirsten who packed his kit that night – just after

8 pm, almost three hours before the usual finishing time of a floodlit match – and contemplated his Saturday club match for Rhodes University. Like students everywhere, Rhodes were keen and adventurous on the field but seldom had the talent and skill available to turn grand plans into winning cricket. Kirsten enjoyed the spirit of that young Rhodes XI, but he was frustrated by their lack of seriousness.

Having sensed Kirsten's gloomy mood, a member of the Border Cricket Board executive, Rob Henderson, invited the skipper and his family to his home for a lazy Sunday afternoon of small talk around the barbecue fire.

Henderson had been one of the first Border administrators Kirsten had met when he moved to the area from the Western Cape and he had gained respect for him. An unpretentious man of action and of refreshingly informal mannerisms, the balding, square-shouldered Henderson can often be seen grooming the Buffalo Park pitch before the start of play. And it was fitting that a momentous chapter in Kirsten's career should have its beginnings in the presence of Henderson, a man he admires.

During that afternoon, Henderson mentioned that he had bought into a package deal for the trip to India. What trip to India, Kirsten wanted to know, completely unaware that his international career was about to be launched.

His hopes soared as Henderson, who would have had inside knowledge of South Africa's hastily arranged return to the international arena, explained the details of the tour. South Africa would play three limited overs matches against India at Calcutta, Gwalior and New Delhi. The touring party would be announced that evening.

At last, an opportunity to perform on the world stage, and without the stigma that had dogged some of the rebel series.

But first, the squad. At 36, was he too old? No, the selectors would have to go with experience. And he had been playing well, as well as anyone with similarly legitimate claims to a place in the side.

Minutes after the Kirstens arrived at their Vincent home that evening, the telephone rang. It was me.

'Tell your husband to pack his bags,' I told Tuffy Kirsten, unable to wait for Kirsten himself to be handed the phone. 'He's going to India.'

An electric pause, and then a frantic, 'Kirsy, Kirsy, you're in!'

Kirsten came on the line, bubbling in defiance of his usual caution. He said the necessary and we finished our conversation.

Seconds after he had put the phone down, it rang again, and again, and again … The press, friends and the public wanted to be part of that moment, when Kirsten's ship finally came in.

The Kirsten household was wall to wall with well-wishers that night and the party begun at the Hendersons' house continued there. The mood was of celebration, of talent and discipline rewarded. Like Clive Rice and Jimmy Cook, he had hung on, sometimes solely on the threads of the conviction that he could play and prosper at the very highest levels even though there was no way to prove it.

Now there was indeed a way.

In the midst of all the festivity, Kirsten recalled a more sombre occasion, though he kept the memory to himself. He remembered that meeting with the Western Province executive at which he had told them of his intended move to Border.

Fritz Bing's words, that he would 'shorten' his 'international career' by taking up the immense challenge of playing for a B section province like Border while trying to remain in the national selectors' plans, suddenly held no more sting.

Kirsten found that attitude typical of the short-sightedness which had driven a wedge between himself and the Newlands hierarchy. And he resolved to prove them wrong.

For him, his selection to the tour squad was vindication of his decision. Indeed, as the only bona fide star in the Border team he stuck out more than he would have done at Province. The load was squarely on his shoulders and he put the pressure to good, positive use. The risk he had taken proved worth it.

He would become the first Border player to represent South Africa since Buster Farrer played six Test matches against New Zealand, three each in 1962 and 1964.

But there was no time for such delicious whimsy. Kirsten had a tour to prepare for. Who would have thought it would be a tour to India, he marvelled.

A breathtaking transformation from the wretched days of isolation was upon South African sport and the country itself: no more rebel rabble, this was indeed the real thing. And to be part of it filled the emotional Kirsten with patriotic and personal pride.

That the tour had come about was an accident, a fortuitous one. Pakistan had been scheduled to visit India but had pulled out due to concern for the safety of their players. India, who were to embark on a Test tour of Australia, suddenly found themselves short of opponents to help them prepare for the venture.

South Africa seemed the obvious choice. India, the first country to take an official stand against apartheid, had also entered the proposal which ushered South Africa back into the ICC. The idea was a good one. The problem was the timing. The South Africans were given mere days to accept the invitation and select a team.

A routine national selectors' strategy meeting on Sunday, 3 November 1991 became the historic gathering which would pick the 14 men who would break the drought of their country's isolation from world sport.

Their names – some still playing, others not – ring with history: Clive Rice (captain), Jimmy Cook, Andrew Hudson, Mandy Yachad, Kepler Wessels, Peter Kirsten, Adrian Kuiper, Brian McMillan, Dave Richardson, Tim Shaw, Clive Eksteen, Richard Snell, Allan Donald and Craig Matthews. The manager: Ali Bacher.

Four days later, decked out in unfamiliar navy blue blazers, they boarded a plane and embarked on, as Kirsten puts it, 'One week of emotional chaos.'

It began when Calcutta poured out its heart to the tourists. A trip from Dumdum airport to the South Africans' hotel, the Oberoi, which would normally take 20 minutes, ground on for three hours. Perhaps not all Calcutta's 11 million inhabitants managed to squeeze on to the squalid streets to welcome their visitors, but the fair percentage who did make it were not about to melt away into the sweet, steamy air without making their presence felt.

This surging city, where the awkward proximity of poverty and opulence were to astound Kirsten, was at once deliriously ecstatic and proud to host such a memorable event.

The next morning the team met Mother Teresa, followed by a net at Eden Gardens.

The empty stadium, an almost avant-garde collaboration of concrete and metal, echoed to the sterile sound of bat on ball that afternoon. The next day, however, somewhere between 98 000 and 102 000 screaming, crazy, firework-tossing people crammed into the ground to witness the return of the cricketing prodigals. Crowd estimates swayed between these two vast figures with perhaps the only certainty being that there were far more in the stadium than its official capacity of 92 000.

Rice would have given much to field first that day, mainly to give his star-struck players a chance to settle down in front of the awesome crowd. But Mohammad Azharuddin, no doubt aware of the anxiety in the South African camp, called correctly: 'We'll bowl.'

Their fate thus sealed, the South Africans hoped a walk into the middle before the start of play, ostensibly to show their appreciation of the incredible support given them, would banish the butterflies.

141

However, when Hudson, his face almost as pale as his whites, and Cook, a calmer if also awed débutant, ventured out to open the batting, the confidence that is part of newly discovered talent or proven experience drowned in a flood of nerves.

Hudson, his polished batsmanship evaporated, endured a truly frightening début and was caught behind off Kapil Dev in the first over: South Africa three for one, and enter Wessels. Then Cook, trapped in front by Javagal Srinath, became the first victim of an outlandishly low and slow pitch: South Africa 38 for two, enter Kirsten.

The size and volume of the crowd didn't help. A Newlands full-house of 15 000 or 25 000 at the Wanderers was one thing. This was decidedly another. Intent on surviving for at least half an hour, Kirsten made just seven runs before being bowled to give Venkapathy Raju his only wicket of the match as South Africa stumbled to a barely mediocre total of 177 for eight off 47 overs, the Indians falling behind in the over rate.

Batting third, Wessels, who had gained experience of the demanding Indian conditions when he toured the subcontinent with Australia in 1984, wrought a 50 and Kuiper made 43.

For the rest, it was a sub-par performance for a team which might just as well have been playing on the moon. And the disappointment was only heightened by the wristy relish with which the innovative Indian batsmen set about becoming the first team to beat the New South Africa, by three wickets with more than six overs in hand, despite Donald's superb effort of five for 29.

But to dwell on such matters is to prolong the sense of failure and early the next morning the tourists were whisked away to Agra where, somewhat tousled and tired, they lined up for the cameras in front of the Taj Mahal before moving on to Gwalior, scene of the second match.

South Africa lost again, this time by 38 runs after being bowled out for 185, of which Wessels scored 71 and Kirsten just two, in search of 224.

In the midst of the gloom came an ugly backlash. After 30 overs of the South African innings in Calcutta the ball began to swing diabolically. Upon inspection, one side of the ball was found to be normal, while the other seemed to have been scraped with a sharp object.

Bacher had spoken to the Indian cricket authorities privately about the matter. But when a similar situation arose in Gwalior, it reached the public and a hasty – some would say grovelling – apology was issued by then UCB president Geoff Dakin.

Off the field, the South Africans were in great demand. Hardly an evening went by without some or other official engagement. And while Rice understood and was eager to fulfil his role as captain beyond the boundary, the diplomatic workload began to tell on South Africa's 42-year-old leader.

For Kirsten, a personal storm had started to brew. In the press and among certain selectors his failure in the first two matches had made him an apparent certainty for the chop when the squad was selected for the World Cup in Australasia the next year. This unsettled Kirsten, and he felt the fact that he was relatively out of sight on the Border during the domestic season would aid his detractors in their efforts to put an end to his international career after just two games.

The chips were truly down. He needed to answer the critics who would seek to take away what he had worked towards for two decades.

His spotlight waited in New Delhi, although his stage wasn't quite a cricketer's.

The Jawaharlal Nehru stadium is a well-equipped venue for athletics and soccer, but its architects didn't envisage too many important cricket matches being played there. So the pitch is artificial and much of the outfield consists of synthetic running track.

Kirsten had gained experience of a similar surface when Western Province played their provincial Benson and Hedges matches at Greenpoint Stadium in Cape Town before the lights went up at Newlands. Moreover, this pitch was more in tune with the South African batting line-up's timing than the dusty, barren strips they had floundered on in Calcutta and Gwalior.

But it also proved attractive to the Indian batsmen, Ravi Shastri and Sanjay Manjrekar carving 109 and 105 respectively as India treated the South African attack with disturbing disrespect to total 287 for four off 50 overs.

It was India's highest total in a limited overs international and it certainly looked insurmountable to the South African public watching the match on television. Oh no, the groans went, not another loss. If they couldn't reach 200, how were they going to get closer to 300?

But what was not apparent from the substandard television pictures was the beginning of the metamorphosis in the South African team from accidental tourists into the professionally run, focused unit that was soon to come agonisingly close to reaching the World Cup final.

The lessons of India were learned as much off the field as on it. As has so often happened in this era of South African cricket, the first lesson was delivered by Ali Bacher.

It will just not do to go home having been thumped three times, he told the team before the New Delhi match. Get your act together. There is plenty to celebrate but we are primarily here to play, and win, cricket matches.

Stop dreaming and play some cricket.

Kirsten's description of Bacher's plea is more blunt: 'He crapped on us.'

Bacher's concern was, however, well-founded. The South Africans were caught up in the romance of what was happening and the mystery, the otherness of India, at the expense of their playing priorities. Though it never came second, cricket battled to keep up with the other demands being placed on the tourists.

But under the glow of the Nehru stadium's floodlights that night, there was much cricket to be seen, and the best of it was played by South Africans.

Besides the official dubbing of the Indian adventure as the 'Goodwill Tour', there was an element of the same quality, a paying of dues, in the selection of the South African teams for the first two matches. However, the XI who took the field on 14 November were indeed the best the country had to offer. Cook and Wessels, elevated a place in the order, opened and made immediate progress in climbing the mountain of runs blocking their team's path to victory.

When Cook got out for 35, having helped in a stand of 72, South Africa were, incredibly, one run behind the required run rate. Wessels, in unusually fluent form, seemed to be moving inexorably to a century when, just ten runs short, he was given out to a full toss delivered by Raju.

But Wessels would be the last South African to be dismissed on the night.

Moved up to number three, a suddenly smooth-stroking Kirsten had hungrily added 111 runs for the second wicket with Wessels. Though their partnership was brisk, it was the sterling work of two players for whom mere slogging has never been the answer. Solid, grooved strokes are hallmarks of their play.

But when Kuiper joined Kirsten, finesse stepped aside for the fiery batsmanship of two players lusting after a long dreamed of triumph.

Kirsten looked for runs with more intensity but largely stuck to his compact approach, sometimes summoning his more expansive shots. Kuiper, however, blazed as only Kuiper can. In the 12 overs they were at the crease, Kirsten and Kuiper lashed 105 runs as South Africa strode to a comprehensive win with 3.2 overs to spare.

Kirsten was not out on 86; Kuiper unbeaten with 63. But the South African dressingroom after the match was no place for crowing about the feats of individuals.

For Kirsten, the moment is captured as a group of cricketers who had been trapped in the confines of lukewarm domestic competitions for so long they had neglected to communicate with one another, finally celebrating the triumph of a shared victory.

The cosy paddock that was the Castle Cup had turned the natural fences of provincial boundaries into divisive walls between teams, captains and players. It had, after all, been the only honour to play for.

But India, and especially the power of the win in New Delhi, had smashed those divisions and used the bricks to build another, more significant wall. And it was green and gold.

The World Cup loomed not quite as daunting as before the Indian tour, but it would be a stern test of cricket's prodigals none the less. Although Wessels was then quite unaware that he would lead his country on that epic mission, his success in India was to be reaccepted as a South African cricketer. Eighteen months earlier he had opted out of the rebel scene after it became apparent that his defection to Australia in search of a Test cap had not been forgotten by cricketers who had stayed loyal to South Africa through the dark years.

But the guts and commitment Wessels had shown in India, apart from his contributions of 50, 71 and 90, as well as in pushing Eastern Province to the top of the domestic heap, cemented his place in the South African team as far as both the selectors and his team-mates were concerned.

18

Selection Rollercoaster

The Kirstens' retreat at Yellowsands, a resort 20 km to the east of East London, has served them well as a refuge from the public eye. Even on the Border, a province caught between rural obscurity and the metropolitan glare, fame has its price.

But at Yellowsands, with a fishing rod in one hand and a beer in the other, Kirsten didn't have to be the master batsman, or the Border captain – as he had become at the start of the 1991-92 season – or one of South Africa's returning heroes from India. Here he was plain Peter, or Kirsy if you like.

So it was not surprising that Kirsten headed for Yellowsands as soon as he could after the announcement on 29 December of South Africa's initial squad of 20 for the World Cup.

Despite the events in India six weeks before, Kirsten was not in the squad. Nor were Clive Rice, Jimmy Cook, Mandy Yachad and Clive Eksteen, who had also made the trip to India.

Kepler Wessels was the new South African captain and, apart from Adrian Kuiper, Dave Richardson and Tim Shaw, he was also the only member of the squad with any lengthy experience.

The 20 named were not to be considered the final touring party, the United Cricket Board was quick to point out. The organisers need 20 names by the end of December to go ahead with preparations for the tournament.

The squad could change before the final group of 16 was announced on 19 January.

The omission of Yachad and Eksteen was expected, but certainly not the axing of the three veterans. Besides his batting and bowling talents, Rice's level-headed captaincy would be of obvious value to a team going into the unknown territory of the World Cup. Kirsten was having a solid enough season with the bat – he scored 107 and 54 against Northern Transvaal the very weekend the squad of 20 was announced – and while Cook was struggling to adjust to South African conditions in general and a seaming Wanderers pitch in particular after his third sparkling season with Somerset, he was still among the best opening batsmen in the country.

Rice had defied the selectors during the second rebel West Indian tour in 1983-84 by refusing to accept the team for the final four-day international in Port Elizabeth because Kenny McEwan had been left out. McEwan was eventually included and underlined his captain's wisdom by scoring a century. But seven years later, when Mike Gatting's rebels arrived, Rice was inexplicably dropped and the captaincy awarded to Cook. Rice returned for four limited overs internationals, but played them under Cook.

Peter van der Merwe was a member of the selection panel in 1983-84 and by 1990 he was the convener. The coincidence is difficult to ignore, although it should be remembered that Van der Merwe would have approved Rice leading South Africa in India.

The reaction from the Transvaal was swift and, in some cases, unseemly. A photograph of Rice pushing Cook in a wheelchair, both of them sporting false beards, appeared in the *Sunday Times*, and Cook was quoted as saying the selectors had come up with a list of athletes, not cricketers. He later denied saying this.

Worse than any allegations of bungling was the inference that provincialism was at work. Van der Merwe was an Eastern Province man, as was the president of the UCB Geoff Dakin, and, of course, Wessels.

But there was never any evidence to substantiate this. Wessels was a thoughtful choice as captain. He had led EP with distinction since his return in 1986-87, proving he deserved to reclaim his South African citizenship with Currie Cup titles in 1988-89 (shared with Western Province) as well as the Nissan Shield in 1987-88 and 1989-90, the season EP also won the Benson and Hedges series for the first time.

Kirsten fumed as much as Rice and Cook at his non-selection. But he kept his head and contacted one of his longest-standing allies in the game, Ali Bacher. The Test captain turned world class administrator's advice was simple and sound: say nothing to the press and hang in there. This thing isn't over.

So Kirsten's comment to the media consisted of the fact that he was 'disappointed'. Privately, he wasn't as demure and attacked what he saw as 'the age thing'. It was a plausible theory. Rice was 42, Cook 38 and Kirsten 36. It was natural to wonder if South Africa could afford to have three of only 16 places in the squad taken up by players in the autumn of their careers, and that in a squad which was going to work harder than any South African team before it.

But the scenario changes when all three happen to be key players with no obvious replacements. And what was so unbearable about the over-35s anyway? Kirsten and Cook were still sharp in the field and Rice bowled himself as hard as any of his players, although he had replaced much of his pace with dastardly cunning.

Whatever his own claims for a place in the side, Kirsten felt particular sympathy for Rice. Picked for the cancelled 1970 tour of Australia, Rice stayed loyal to South Africa throughout the gloomy years of isolation, living with the uncertainty of it all, wondering when the tunnel was going to light up.

'Then he gets a week in India and he's dumped.'

As the plane landed at Jan Smuts airport after the Indian adventure, all aboard were naturally euphoric. Bacher said over the address system, 'Thank you, everybody, for making this trip so worth while and thank you, Clive, you have just played your greatest innings for South Africa.'

Kirsten regrets not having been able to play more international cricket with Rice, and feels that South Africa's return to international cricket might have been even more explosive had he been at the helm. But Van der Merwe and his selectors didn't see it that way.

Much of Kirsten's soul searching was done during three depressing days at Yellowsands. He pondered his future in the game, wondered if it had all been worth it. His spirit ebbed with the tide as he watched it go out.

To his eternal credit, however, Kirsten said nothing in public. Five years previously that would probably not have been the case, but he had learned a few things over the years.

Behind the scenes, forces were moving in Kirsten's favour. Wessels, vice-captain Kuiper and the South African coach, Mike Procter, quietly but firmly campaigned for his inclusion. Wessels and Procter also felt strongly that Cook should be in the party.

Wessels also telephoned Kirsten and hinted that he should be 'enthusiastic in the field'.

But there wasn't much support for Rice. As Dakin, not a man to mince his words or concern himself with diplomacy, had said, the forthright all-rounder had dug his own grave immediately after the announcement of the squad of 20 with his angry outbursts in the newspapers and in a strained television interview.

Wessels undoubtedly wanted Kirsten at the World Cup for his batting and his experience. He might also have remembered a day in 1990 when he discovered first-hand that Kirsten had the character to match his prodigious cricketing talents.

It was during the Gatting tour and there was growing unhappiness in the team that Wessels had been selected despite having represented the Australian rebels just three years earlier. Cook, Kirsten, Rice, Roy Pienaar and Kuiper had met with Bacher, then managing director of the South African Cricket Union, to discuss the matter.

They were simply protecting their turf, territory they had guarded religiously through the difficult years, and were not about to take kindly to sharing it with someone whom they saw as having taken the easier option.

We were loyal, Wessels took the Australian option, was the gist of their argument. He's a fine player and we need him, was the upshot of Bacher's reply.

Kirsten felt uneasy with the way Wessels was being treated. There may have been valid grounds for dissension in the ranks, but that didn't justify giving a team-mate the cold shoulder. So he did something about it.

The South Africans were in Johannesburg for the only four-day international played on that tour. Ominously, it was over after three days.

After a training session at the Wanderers on the eve of the match, Kirsten went up to Wessels. Feel like a run back to the hotel? he proposed.

Wessels agreed and the two set off into leafy Corlett Drive. As they ran, Kirsten laid out the whole story. Wessels listened, said nothing. Kirsten tried to explain the feelings of the South African team, without insulting Wessels, without making him feel like an unwelcome prodigal son. Just the facts from his side of the fence.

It is unlikely Wessels heard anything new as he and Kirsten chugged through the streets of Johannesburg. After all, the players' grievances were easy enough to figure out, but at last someone had the guts to face him instead of whispering behind his back.

Having spent the summer of 1976-77 as strong-willed, serious young stars in the Western Province team, Wessels and Kirsten now found they had matured into men of similar character. They respected each other.

Wessels' integrity wouldn't allow him to forget that run and the rather one-way conversation which took place. Here was someone he could trust.

Kirsten was beginning to feel he had hatched a hundred ulcers when 19 January arrived. Surely no Sunday afternoon had ever been quite so tense, certainly not in the Kirsten household.

He watched and heard Dakin alternately booming and beaming live on television from the pavilion at St George's Park.

'And the squad is: Kepler Wessels, Eastern Province, captain; Adrian Kuiper, Western Province, vice-captain; Tertius Bosch, Northern Transvaal; Hansie Cronje, Free State; Allan Donald, Free State; Omar Henry, Free State; Andrew Hudson, Natal; Peter Kirs...'

The rest was drowned in whoops of unbridled celebration as Peter and Tuffy were released from the tension of the previous two weeks. He had done it. It was all worth it.

The remaining names – Brian McMillan, Meyrick Pringle, Jonty Rhodes, Dave Richardson, Mark Rushmere and Richard Snell – were still echoing around the country when Kirsten's telephone rang. But this time he expected it and resigned himself to fielding more than a few calls that afternoon, between gulps of bubbly and answering the door, of course.

19

Warming Up

The colonial setting of the Harare Sports Club is a long way from the spacious, modern Australian and New Zealand grounds on which South Africa captured the cricketing world's imagination at the 1992 World Cup.

But Kirsten, around whose flashing blade South Africa's challenge revolved, traces the source of his immense success in that tournament to the Zimbabwean capital on a hot Wednesday afternoon. It was here amid marquees and a quaint gabled clubhouse that he felt the tensions of the previous few weeks slip away completely.

The likes of Peter van der Merwe were out of his life and the people that really mattered – Kepler Wessels, Adrian Kuiper, Mike Procter – had made his role clear to him. Kirsy, you're the number three batsman – go out and do the job.

He knew where he stood; he liked where he stood. And he communicated the fact to the record crowd of 9 000 with an at first cautious but then more fluent 64 as South Africa coasted to victory over Zimbabwe by six wickets.

Wessels had won the toss and decided to put the home side in because of the morning cloud cover. The new ball duly seamed and swung and, fortunately for the crowd, the Zimbabweans recovered from a jittery start to make a game of it and total 170 off 49.3 overs with Donald taking three for 29 but sending down 10 wides in the process.

South Africa lost Wessels and Andrew Hudson early but Kirsten and Hansie Cronje kept them on track with a third-wicket stand of 99. Kuiper hit the winning runs, with four balls to spare. It was a good enough beginning, although not as effortless a victory as some had hoped for.

Kirsten embarked on the nine-hour flight the next evening glowing in anticipation of a dream on the verge of being fulfilled. Andre Abrahams, his coach at SACS, had been a vocal admirer of the Australian approach to cricket and consequently Kirsten was well versed in the exploits of the antipodean greats. Names and places that had been only names and places for so long were about to become part of his first-hand experience.

He remembered his trip Down Under in 1986 and noted how different it was this time. Then he had been trying to escape to a better future. Now he was part of an infinitely better future.

The first South African team to venture overseas in 27 years touched down in Perth on 7 February. Ironically, the Western Australian capital had become a haven for the country's well-heeled expatriates. But this planeload of South Africans was different: they were proud to be there, proud to be from the land of the springbok – even though they were playing under the United Cricket Board's purposefully generic logo – and eager to go back with a far more prestigious trophy than a bottle of Mrs Ball's chutney.

The South Africans went into the day-night match against Western Australia at the WACA on 9 February, a Sunday, rain having interfered with their pre-match training. Kim Hughes was on hand to advise the tourists not to make winning the top priority. Instead, they should stick to playing sound cricket on what was acknowledged as one of the quickest pitches in the world. They didn't listen well.

Five South Africans, including Kirsten, were caught behind for minor scores as South Africa slumped to 66 for five before totalling 157 for eight thanks to a sixth-wicket stand of 66 between Jonty Rhodes and Brian McMillan. The home side won by three wickets with five balls to spare.

A defeat, but not a disaster. The bowlers, relishing the conditions, had tightened up considerably – reducing the extras from 30 to 16 – although the batsmen had still not provided conclusive proof that they were ready for what lay ahead.

Two days later a match against the Australian Academy in Adelaide was rained out but the next day South Africa won an additional match, arranged because the management was concerned about the amount of preparation time being lost to the weather, by 45 runs with Kirsten scoring a handsome 63.

Minor but significant tension arose between Wessels and Omar Henry during this match. The Adelaide Oval is aptly named because the square boundaries are shortish, while a batsman going for a straight six finds himself having to heave the ball close to 100 metres.

A bowler of Henry's pace and type invites the odd swipe across the line and the Academy batsmen, bred on the aggression of their mentor, Rod Marsh, took great delight in repeatedly smashing the left-arm spinner over the short fence for six. As far as Henry was concerned, he didn't get the support he deserved from his captain, and he said so.

Wessels, on the other hand, was adamant he had done what he could to protect Henry's figures. It was nothing like a major altercation and Kirsten realised that Wessels' introspective character was showing itself. He knew first-hand just what Wessels was having to come to terms with – the responsibility, the weight of expectation.

Wessels had not been in the best of form in any of the four matches played until then, and it was getting to him. But Kirsten knew it would only take a good knock to get him right. Not only was Wessels new to the national captaincy, but the team was unaccustomed to his style of leadership. It took some getting used to his all-or-nothing approach, but once they did the way became smoother.

Fortunately, there were no truly disruptive characters in the squad, and perhaps it was a blessing that for most of the three weeks building up to the opening match the captain seemed more unhappy with himself than anyone else.

Kirsten, on the other hand, struck the perfect psychological chord. Less than three months away from his 37th birthday, he told himself, he was about to step on to the world stage. Unlike the selectors, he turned his age into a positive factor.

There would certainly be pressure on him as the number three batsman, but he had shed the burdens of leadership he carried with Border. All he had to do was bat. He was in form, he had confidence in the abilities of the players around him, and there was no doubting he faced a challenge. Just the way he liked it.

Motivation? Not a problem.

Kirsten didn't have sole rights to the positive vibe. An impressive 17-run win over Pakistan in Canberra – where Wessels broke through with an innings of 72 off 114 balls – was followed by victory over Tasmania by seven wickets in Hobart on 17 February.

Two matches to go before South Africa's début World Cup game against the holders, Australia, at the Sydney Cricket Ground on 26 February. But a cyclone at sea and the continuous rain it brought prevented the game against

Queensland at the Gabba in Brisbane from taking place, and the Bowral encounter with the Sir Donald Bradman XI was also rained out.

Losing the last two opportunities for fine-tuning was a setback, but the team had worked hard and felt ready. It had all come together nicely. All the major batsmen had tasted a biggish innings and the bowlers were performing with impressive discipline.

Then came the first big shock. Unfancied New Zealand beat Australia by 37 runs in the opening match in Auckland. Kirsten didn't take too much notice. This is one-day cricket, he told himself, and anything can happen.

20

The Wizard of Aussie

It wasn't easy to be the number three batsman for the first 19 overs of South Africa's innings on that balmy Wednesday night at the SCG, the night 22 years of frustration was swept away by a gloriously irresistible green wave.

Kirsten, the batsman in question, sat padded up on the players' balcony with itchy hands, feet and anything else that might have come into play if he could only get to the crease. Trouble was, a couple of blokes called Wessels and Hudson were in no mood to leave the field.

The former had almost made an early exit, scoring 23 before edging a delivery from Mick Whitney to stand-in wicketkeeper David Boon, who took over the gloves when Ian Healy pulled a hamstring while batting. The unlikely looking stumper made contact but couldn't hold it.

Ah well, better luck next time. Only there wasn't a next time as the South African captain accumulated runs within the confines of his familiar bluecollar batsmanship. A dab here, a stab there, and plenty of sensible run gathering in between.

Hudson was unrecognisable from the frightened rabbit who had frozen in the electric atmosphere of Eden Gardens six weeks before. Sweet drive followed sweet drive as he found the confidence to let his imagination rule his batting.

The crowd of 39 789 who had filled every nook of the picturesque SCG would no doubt have been happy if all the evening's entertainment consisted of was Wessels and Hudson thrashing the Australian bowling. But so much had happened before.

There was that thrilling first ball from Allan Donald, which everyone in the ground except umpire Brian Aldridge knew had hit Geoff Marsh's bat; there was a South African fielding performance of such all-round intensity that it drew the odd favourable comment from the notoriously Australian members of the Channel 9 commentary team; there was Allan Border's first-baller, a viciously swinging delivery from Adrian Kuiper; there was Jonty Rhodes' swoop-dive-throw run-out of Craig McDermott.

Most important of all, there were only 170 runs forthcoming from the much-vaunted Australian batsmen. And after 19 overs, Wessels and Hudson had knocked off 74 of them as South Africa cruised inexorably to a famous victory.

Peter Taylor stepped up to bowl his off-spinners in over number 20. Hudson stuck his courage to its sticking place once more and advanced down the pitch – only to miss the full delivery completely. It bit hard into the Sydney turf and crashed into his stumps.

On the players' balcony, 19 years of waiting – of wondering whether the moment would ever arrive when he would take on the Australian giants – came to an end as Kirsten rose. Gloves, bat: time to go to work. Ninety-seven runs to get, almost 30 overs to get them in. No problem.

He had a quick word with Wessels but it was really just a courtesy between two old stags who had come a long way, if not always together. Besides, the captain and the senior pro didn't need tactical discussions at this stage. They knew what had to be done.

'Two leg, please.' He looked around, studied the field as he had done countless times before. But it was never quite like this. Kirsten, the best player of spin bowling in the squad, was none the less respectful of Taylor and scored just two runs off the first 10 balls he faced.

Quietly, efficiently, they got on with the job, easing into top gear as they approached the modest summit. Kirsten was happy with the secondary role, rotating the strike, leaving the bigger hitting to the senior partner.

With three overs to go, 11 runs were required, and Wessels clipped all of them off five deliveries. The final shot of the match was his cameo open-faced dab down to third man. The SCG, which had been buzzing with disbelief and anticipation all evening, erupted into celebration as the South Africans in the crowd bayed their approval.

For Australia, who wore the look of a comprehensively beaten team, it was an unmitigated disaster. Played two, lost two: this was not the way to get to the semi-finals. Their faces looked all the more sullen for their daffodil-yellow pyjamas as they solemnly congratulated their conquerors – Wessels, 81 not out, and Kirsten, 49 not out. When Kirsten telephoned home that night, Tuffy enquired, 'Why didn't you get 50?'

If there were 11 unhappy cricketers on the field, there were none in the South African dressingroom. Champagne and smiles were much in evidence as the VIPs streamed in to be part of the moment. Ali Bacher was there, as was the African National Congress's Steve Tshwete, not yet Minister of Sport. Tshwete's passion for sport streamed down his cheeks that night as he hugged both Wessels and Kirsten. 'Peter, you've saved the country,' he blubbed, oblivious of the fact that his dignity had gone out of the window.

But he hadn't exaggerated. South Africa stood on the verge of a referendum that would decide its very future. Should reform continue, was the simple question F W de Klerk was asking the white electorate.

The feel-good value of an event like a nine-wicket victory over the world champions was infinite, and there can be no doubt that South Africa's overall performance in the tournament gave the politicians the kind of publicity they couldn't buy with the entire budget.

Another familiar figure appeared, ostensibly to offer his congratulations. But when he got to Kirsten, who was by now undressing and starting to unwind emotionally from the drama, he mouthed something about the selectors having got it right after all. Another Van der Merwe joke, thought Kirsten. Kirsten later learned that Van der Merwe had not wanted him in the squad, and that he preferred Dave Richardson for the number three batting spot. If he had known then …

A day that ended so merrily had started in utter silence for the South Africans. But Kirsten remembers as a positive tension the deathly quiet that reigned as the team bus made its way to the stadium. They knew the country was watching them: they simply had to win.

The faxes and telegrams from people who mattered, from De Klerk and Mandela, told them the same thing.

Kirsten also remembers the contribution that manager Alan Jordaan made to the victory. A relaxed, likeable Afrikaner from the Northern Transvaal, Jordaan has a remarkable talent for making himself understood simply and humorously. After Wessels had said his piece before the match, it was over to the manager.

Typically, Jordaan was brief and clear: '*Manne, al wat ek kan sê is vat hulle laag en fok hulle op!*'

The South Africans had done just that, and opened a wide path to the semi-finals. They were to face New Zealand in Auckland three days later and Sri Lanka in Wellington two days after that. Easy games, surely.

Not quite. Going from Sydney to Auckland was like exchanging a day on a Durban beach for a week on the back of the moon. Though there had been rain about in Australia, the weather in New Zealand had an antarctic edge to it when the South Africans arrived an hour late following a flight delay.

Representatives of the Halt All Racist Tours (HART) organisation, which had put a spoke in the wheel of the 1981 Springbok rugby tour of New Zealand, were on hand to demand that the players sign a political declaration, part of which slammed the fact that only whites would take part in the impending referendum. Tshwete intervened deftly, essentially telling HART to wake up and smell the democracy that was around the corner in South Africa.

And while the World Cup hype was unavoidable further north, the Kiwis seemed nonplussed about the fact that one of the world's great sporting events had crossed their borders. Unlike their more extrovert neighbours, New Zealanders are no-frills people. 'Get on with it' could be their national motto.

The South Africans' first impressions of the country were not improved when they arrived at Eden Park for a scheduled net practice only to find the New Zealanders already at it. Several players became agitated, perhaps showing their inexperience of touring. A more seasoned team would not have allowed a hamstrung net session to cast a cloud of negativity over their sunny mood.

Kirsten refused to let it get him down and instead sought out his former Derbyshire team-mate and friend, John Wright, an integral member of the New Zealand squad although an injury would keep him out of the match. A pleasant barbecue ensued and the pair reminisced almost as much as they laughed in wonder at the way it had all turned out.

The South African camp had done their homework on Eden Park and the New Zealand tactics. They knew the sluggish pitch was singularly unhelpful to front-foot players and fast bowlers. The home side, therefore, would be happy merely to bowl straight with as little pace on the ball as possible, thus forcing the batsmen to take risks by hitting out.

South Africa knew this, and yet they still came badly short, losing by seven wickets. Wessels won the toss but he and Hudson lasted just six overs together before the Natalian went in a similar fashion to his Sydney dismissal. This time Dipak Patel, to whom New Zealand skipper Martin Crowe had cleverly tossed the new ball, was the lucky bowler.

The lack of life in the pitch had clearly hampered the momentum Wessels and Hudson hoped to generate. But when Kirsten arrived, he decided he wasn't that far away from home after all.

Hello, Buffalo Park, fancy meeting you here. The pitch was uncannily similar to what he had become used to in the past one and a half seasons in East London and he showed it by late cutting Patel for a couple. But Watson immediately had Wessels, who was trying to cut too close to his body, caught behind, and Hansie Cronje lasted just 22 deliveries before he fell to Chris Harris from a similar shot.

Suddenly it was 29 for three in the sixteenth over and the supposed favourites knew they had a game on their hands. The New Zealand plan was working perfectly: slow it all down and frustration will get the better of them.

The dependable Richardson was sent up the order to calm things down. It worked well enough and although the scoring rate slowed down at first, they had put on 79 off 115 balls when Richardson failed to master a delivery from Chris Cairns and was caught at mid-on in the thirty-fifth over.

Kirsten was remarkably unaffected by what was happening around him. He didn't panic and try to get what he could before the roof fell in, nor did he retreat into a defensive shell. He simply played his game, with due adjustment to the pace of the pitch, and was scoring runs with as much ease as frequency.

Kuiper replaced Richardson and faced two balls before departing under bizarre circumstances. Cairns' second delivery to him was dug in short and Kuiper got a top edge which was safely held by wicketkeeper Ian Smith. By the time the catch was taken Kuiper was halfway down the pitch. He looked back to make sure he had indeed been dismissed, and continued towards the dressingroom.

No one noticed umpire Khizar Hayat standing at square leg with his arm parallel to the ground. And no one had heard him call no-ball when the delivery climbed above Kuiper's shoulder. Cairns was the first to realise what had happened. He ran to the stumps and demanded the ball but eventually Harris, backing up, removed the bails. Kuiper had also caught on and tried to get back, but too late.

Rhodes wasn't there long before Crowe brought off a diving catch at midwicket. At 121 for six South Africa desperately needed a man to stick with Kirsten for the remainder of the innings. McMillan stepped into the vacancy and helped Kirsten add 41 for the seventh wicket before the latter, having employed the lofted drive to great effect, was caught at long-on.

Kirsten's superb 90 had come off 129 balls with 10 fours. He patently deserved those 10 missing runs, but he had none the less announced his presence to every bowler and captain in the tournament.

South Africa totalled 190 for seven and thought it could be a competitive score on that pitch. But opener Mark Greatbatch, who replaced Wright, blew that notion out of the water with 80 minutes of barely controlled aggression. The hulking left-hander crashed the bowling all round the ground to score 68 off 60 balls with nine fours and three sixes. He might have been the first to go, but the 114 runs he and Rod Latham hammered off 107 balls left South Africa with hardly any options.

Kirsten, who eventually bowled the frenzied Greatbatch, was Wessels' seventh bowler – and that in the eighteenth over. The faster Donald, Richard Snell, McMillan and Tertius Bosch bowled on that pitch, the faster the ball disappeared towards the boundaries of what is essentially a rugby stadium. Medium pace, as the South Africans bowled it, didn't do much good either. Cronje went for 14 off two overs and Kuiper capped an unhappy outing by watching Greatbatch slam three fours and a six off his only over.

The most effective bowler was Kirsten, who returned a respectable one for 22 off seven and, with McMillan, was the only South African to bowl a maiden over. Mercifully, it was all over in 34.2 overs. At the inevitable post-mortem, Kirsten said he felt South Africa should have played Henry. He made the comment constructively and without trying to criticise Wessels' tactics.

So he was understandably surprised when, on the morning of the match against Sri Lanka, his captain called him aside and said he wanted total support, especially from his senior players. Back me, or else, was Wessels' clear, all-or-nothing message. Kirsten certainly had grounds for a retort – he was the senior player – and a younger Kirsten might have delivered one unthinkingly and stuff the consequences.

But he was wiser now, and a team man. And at least Wessels had come out with his gripe, not brooded on it.

'That's fine. I'm grateful to you for helping to get me into this squad in the first place,' Kirsten replied. 'I'm here to bat, but if you need any help I'm here for that too.'

Kirsten knew the pressure was on Wessels to succeed, and that losses to teams like New Zealand didn't help. The younger players in the squad also needed an experienced team-mate to look up to, and though Wessels set an admirable example, it was virtually impossible to follow.

So Kirsten became something of a sergeant-major to the troops, once memorably telling Rhodes, who had idolised him throughout his boyhood, that he talked too much. 'Do you eat budgie seed for breakfast?' he joked.

But before things got better, they became worse. No sooner had South Africa accepted that they had lost to the Kiwis than they went down to lowly Sri Lanka at the Basin Reserve in Wellington. Another plasticine pitch, a cold and windy day, and an unsettled South African line-up led to an unlikely three-wicket loss.

Henry duly came into the team for Bosch, and Kuiper was promoted to the top of the order in an attempt to profit from the 15-over fielding regulations.

Aravinda de Silva, who captained a team of useful batsmen but mediocre bowlers, won the toss and put South Africa in. Fourteen overs later Kuiper was out, bowled by left-armer Don Anurasiri after managing to hit just three boundaries off the 44 balls he faced for his 18 runs.

Kirsten heralded his arrival with a zinging straight six off Anurasiri but, with Wessels doing nothing more than propping up an end, runs were scarce. Kirsten was eventually caught in the deep for 47 off 81 balls, and Wessels followed in the next over having struggled to 40 off 94.

Rhodes hit a bright 28 and McMillan a useful 18 not out, but South Africa fell five runs short of their hoped-for total of 200 when Allan Donald was run out off the last ball of the innings.

Donald took three quick wickets to raise South Africa's hopes but opener Roshan Mahanama stood firm and found a worthy ally in Arjuna Ranatunga. They shared 67 runs for the fifth wicket before Mahanama was caught behind in the forty-third over. Sri Lanka went into the last over needing seven runs and, despite losing their seventh wicket, were home with a ball to spare.

Ranatunga and Champaka Ramanayake, the not out batsmen, couldn't wait until they were off the field to celebrate, throwing their arms around each other in the middle of the pitch. Wessels and Kirsten knew exactly how they felt, but that was five days ago – five days which seemed so far away.

Another loss would make it extremely difficult to fulfil the South African dream of reaching the semi-finals at the first attempt, and during the three days between the match against Sri Lanka and what had become the crunch encounter against the mighty West Indies at Lancaster Park in Christchurch, it seemed that the country had already given up on the team hailed as 'World Champs 1970-1992 (unbeaten)' on a banner in the crowd at Sydney.

Over the years, Kirsten has developed a simple test of public opinion of his performances while on the road. If he finds a wad of telegrams and faxes jammed under the door when he returns to his hotel room in the evening, he knows his efforts have been appreciated and the messages are invariably congratulatory. Nothing under the door is indicative of a mediocre run of form.

After the Sri Lanka disaster, Wessels wasn't lucky enough to be simply ignored. No, he had to confront faxes which were distinctly less than complimentary. To make matters worse, Wessels fired a broadside at what he considered unfair comment in some South African newspapers. The press in South Africa is indeed capable of alarming fickleness, but most of it is perpetrated by news reporters more interested in a front page by-line than cricket. However, Wessels wasn't to distinguish between cricket writers and non-cricket writers, and tarred the lot with the same broad brush.

The wheels were in danger of coming off South Africa's World Cup campaign as that fateful Thursday loomed. This was it: they had to win it.

Lancaster Park is unmistakably a New Zealand venue, complete with all the attendant impediments for foreign players. But it does boast a tad more grass and the ground itself is firmer, more like what South Africans would call a cricket pitch.

West Indian skipper Richie Richardson was well aware of that and when the day dawned grey he knew his bowlers would be eager to have a go at a batting line-up hungry for runs – perhaps too hungry. So he was happy to let South Africa take guard after he won the toss.

Hudson was back in the team, but he didn't have the company of Wessels for long. In the fourth over, the left-hander tried to work a delivery from Malcolm Marshall to the leg side, only to have it pop up on the off. Desmond Haynes did the necessary at point.

From the pavilion, Kirsten had seen how the openers had battled to middle Marshall's deliveries. The crafty veteran had the ball skidding off an already slow surface at an awkward angle. And the cloud cover was helping him to swerve it this way and that with disconcerting regularity. Bowling from the other end was the human skyscraper, Curtly Ambrose, who was also bothering the batsmen with the angle of his deliveries from the pitch. But while Marshall's scooted through at or below knee height, Ambrose was likely to bury the ball in someone's armpit.

Kirsten knew it was not going to be easy. Got to be careful here: this buck might bloody well stop with me. But he and Hudson couldn't afford to protect the partnership too well and both found the boundary before Ambrose and Marshall had finished their first spell.

Winston Benjamin and Anderson Cummins didn't look quite as lethal as their predecessors but it was Cummins who made the breakthrough, with the help of Brian Lara at deep gully who dived to pluck from the air a ball

Hudson had cut with particular venom.

Hudson's 22 was followed by Mark Rushmere's 10 off 24 balls, but Kuiper then joined Kirsten for a handy fourth-wicket stand of 46. Up against world class seam bowling, Kirsten didn't have the freedom to chase the runs and he managed just two fours before he was fifth out for 56, which came off 91 balls. But there was no denying he had played one of the crucial innings of South Africa's World Cup campaign.

'Under the circumstances, this was my best innings of the World Cup,' Kirsten said later.

Rhodes scored 22, McMillan 20 and Richardson 20 not out as the men in green totalled a competitive though not unreachable 200 for eight. However, their efforts would have meant little without the foundation Kirsten provided. That he had batted on despite feeling the familiar pull of an old calf muscle injury only earned him more respect.

But it was to be with the ball rather than the bat that South Africa heaved their challenge back on track. Meyrick Pringle's ability to move the ball through the air became the match-winning factor as he removed no less a quartet than Lara, Richardson, Hooper and Arthurton. Pringle, left out for the two preceding matches, booked his place in the team for the rest of the tournament with an astonishing 11-ball spell in which he took all four of his wickets without conceding a run. He would finish with four for 11 off eight spectacular overs, half of which went scoreless.

The first of his victims, Lara, fell to a magical catch by Rhodes at point. Lara unleashed his second flying square cut – the first had sped to the boundary – only to have Rhodes somehow get hands to the ball just above the turf. The anger of the shot knocked him clean off his feet, but he clung to the ball to effect perhaps the most important dismissal of the match.

At 19 for four, only the immense presence of Desmond Haynes could resuscitate the West Indies' hopes of winning. The veteran opener was hit on the right index finger by Donald but, until Snell forced him from the field by worsening the injury, he batted with all the poise that had made him the world's leading batsman in limited overs cricket.

Haynes, 13 not out when he retired in search of medical attention, returned to the fray when he heard Marshall had gone and the West Indies were reduced to 70 for five. Content to let the brave Gus Logie hunt the boundaries while he kept an end quiet, Haynes was eventually seventh out for 30 after sharing a partnership of 46 and fanning the embers of the contest. Logie went a run later – 117 for eight – followed shortly by Ambrose and Cummins.

And that was that: victory to South Africa by 64 runs.

Played four, won two. Good enough to keep the dream alive. So New Zealand isn't that bad a place when you are winning. But the South Africans were nevertheless glad to be on their way back to Australia, where the playing conditions were much closer to those they were familiar with.

The win also had a marked effect on Wessels' mood. Gone was the tense gloom he had projected after the trials of Auckland and Wellington. In its place was a serious but more relaxed determination to finish the job.

Kirsten, with scores of 49 not out, 90, 47 and 56, was on a roll, and he sensed the rest of the team were also picking up the invigorating momentum that only comes with success. Crucially, South Africa began believing they could reach the semi-finals, as opposed to merely saying, thinking or hearing they could.

They had turned the corner at Christchurch, but there were a few more twists in the plot. One of these involved Kirsten's calf muscle. Team physiotherapist Craig Smith would eventually call Kirsten his 'best customer' and not for nothing. The time Kirsten spent with Smith began to rival the hours he was putting in at the crease and it was a constant battle to keep up the running repairs.

The first sign that the injury was going to upset South Africa's plans was when Kirsten was forced to withdraw from the next match, against second favourites Pakistan at the Gabba in Brisbane.

South Africa were a point up on Imran Khan's team going into the match, and both teams knew a third loss would be the limit if they wanted to stay in the running. Pakistan had not had the best of tournaments, beating Zimbabwe but losing to the West Indies by all of 10 wickets and to India by 43 runs. And they had been shot out for 74 by England when rain washed out play.

World champions in the making? Not on 8 March, when they lost to South Africa by 20 runs after rain had led to the revision of the original target of 211 to 194 off 36 overs.

Solid batting through the order by Hudson (54), Rushmere (35), Cronje (47 not out) – all three players' highest scores for South Africa at that stage – and McMillan (33) did half the job. The rest was thanks to the budding colossus that was Rhodes.

The Pakistan batting had been hampered by the withdrawal of Kirsten's one-time Sussex team-mate, Javed Miandad, with a stomach injury. In fact, their selectors had nothing to do before this match – of the 13 remaining members of their squad, batsman Rameez Raja had shoulder problems and all-rounder Wasim Haider was battling a thigh strain.

And the cruel equation that reshaped the match when the torrential rain relented all but put them out of the match. But the game will be remembered for the run-out that launched a thousand television highlights packages: Rhodes' headlong dive to remove a subsequently flabbergasted Inzamam-ul-Haq.

That the same dynamo later ran 30 metres before finding his bearings to topple over backwards and pull off an unbelievable catch to send Ijaz Ahmed packing was lost in the hype. But they were both vital dismissals at important stages of the game.

Kirsten ruled himself fit for South Africa's next match, against lowly Zimbabwe at the Manuka Oval in Canberra two days later. It might have been a virtually irrelevant game, he explained to the press, but he didn't want to endanger the glorious form he had been blessed with. Besides, Craig Smith was getting bored.

If it had been a more important fixture, it might have been dubbed 'Kirsten's Match', as was the wont of Victorian cricketers. Although he received unintended assistance from the Zimbabwean batsmen, Kirsten emerged as something of a demon off-spinner. The midwicket boundary at Manuka seemed to stretch into the next time zone, but that didn't deter Andy Waller and captain Dave Houghton from trying to hit the makeshift offie into the following week.

Cronje was on hand to dismiss both an over apart. And Houghton was still taking off his pads when Ali Shah, a left-hander, popped an easy catch to Wessels in the covers. In the space of nine balls, Kirsten had sent three batsmen on their way.

The honeymoon didn't last, however, and he finished with three for 31 off five overs as Zimbabwe were dismissed for 163 in 48.3 overs. Then Kirsten and Wessels combined for the major partnership of the South African innings, scoring 112 for the second wicket before Wessels was bowled for 70 (127 balls) with nine overs remaining.

Kirsten ended up unbeaten on 62 off 105 deliveries, deservedly winning man of the match honours.

In one sense, the victory over Zimbabwe took pressure off South Africa as it meant they had to win just one of their remaining league matches against England and India to qualify for the semis – if it came down to a simple race for points. But what was seen as slowish batting in Canberra would have influenced their overall run-rate, the quotient of the total number of runs they scored in the tournament divided by the overs faced. If teams finished on level points, overall run-rate would be employed to separate them.

And when South Africa lost to England by three wickets in another rain-affected match at the Melbourne Cricket Ground two days later, the pressure was on again like never before. In order to escape the vagaries of the calculator, they would have to beat India in their last league match.

England were disrupted by injuries for the match against South Africa. Most significantly, captain Graham Gooch was out with hamstring problems, as was Allan Lamb. All-rounder Chris Lewis had a side strain and was unable to bowl.

Lamb's unavailability was a let-down for Kirsten, who had been looking forward to clashing swords with his old mate. As it was, they got together for a pint and a chat about the old days. As with Wright, the conversation invariably turned to the wonder of it all, the fairytale finish to South Africa's long years of isolation.

Despite a perfect MCG batting pitch and the prospect of rain, Alec Stewart, England's stand-in captain, asked Wessels to bat after winning the toss. Hudson and Wessels got off to a quiet start but the 50 was up in the fifteenth over and the 100 followed in the twenty-eighth.

At last, South Africa seemed to be on their way to a total which would give their bowlers some breathing space. The first-wicket pair took it to 151 before Hudson, who had made an attractive 79 off 115 balls with seven boundaries, pushed up a simple return catch to Graeme Hick in the thirty-sixth over.

Kirsten leapt at the chance to get going on what had now been shown to be a pitch full of runs. He began with a booming straight six off left-arm spinner Richard Illingworth, but had only reached 11 when he was caught near the square leg fence by Robin Smith off Phil DeFreitas. Had the match been played in South Africa, the ball would no doubt have crashed into the fifth row of the stands. But this was Australia, the cricketing equivalent of Texas.

But even Kirsten's first failure of the tournament had a touch of poetry about it. There was the paradox of not making a major contribution to what would be South Africa's biggest total of the tournament, and the irony of being caught by a former compatriot. The Kirsten story, a saga which could so easily have been one of eternal frustration and unfulfilled ambition, was finally unfolding the way it deserved to – as a story of triumph.

But the England episode didn't go according to plan. Kuiper's potential was wasted as he only got to the crease in the forty-sixth over and didn't have the opportunity to take charge of an innings that should have weighed in at more than its eventual 236 for four.

For once, Wessels had left his critics no ammunition to fire back at him. His 85 was his highest score of the competition, but it was the efficiency with which he rattled up his runs off 126 balls that impressed most. Never hurried, but never bogged down, the South African captain had played the model limited overs innings.

The rain drove the players from the field 12 overs into the England innings with the total an ominous 62 without loss. Forty minutes later they were back, but now England needed 164 more runs off the remaining 29 overs.

And when McMillan and Snell got rid of Ian Botham, Smith and Hick in the space of seven deliveries to reduce England to 64 for three, the poms were more than a little worried.

Enter Neil Fairbrother and, with him, more than two hours of enterprising batting. He and Stewart shared 68 runs for the fourth wicket before the captain was run out by razor-sharp Rhodes. Stewart had placed the ball immaculately in his 77 off 88 balls, including seven boundaries.

His dismissal seemed to hand the initiative back to South Africa but Fairbrother, who hit an unbeaten 75 off 83 deliveries with six fours, and Lewis (33) refused to give in and embarked on a rollicking sixth-wicket stand of 50 to all but steer England to victory with a ball to spare. And this despite sensible, tight bowling by the South Africans.

The loss to England dented South Africa's resolve somewhat because it was the first game in which they had played well but were still beaten. India, the team who had run them ragged in two out of three games just four months before, looked to be just as tough a proposition, especially on the run-filled Adelaide Oval.

But if a week is a long time in politics, four months can span an education in one-day cricket. And both sides knew panic was not an option when rain reduced the match to a 30-overs-a-side bash.

It didn't matter to the Indians, as they had no hope of making the semi-finals. But asking South Africa to pin their hopes on 60 hectic overs was like asking a skydiver to click his heels on a ten-cent piece – there would be no margin for error and the insignificant developments of a 50-over game would take on overpowering importance.

Wessels won the toss and put India in. Round one to the novices. But loose bowling, along with the Indians' legendary talent for inventive strokeplay, quickly wiped out that advantage.

With their captain Mohammad Azharuddin in sublime form, all India needed to do was find him a steady partner. Sanjay Manjrekar stayed for a second-wicket stand of 78 but battled with his timing. Then Sachin Tendulkar hit 14 runs off as many balls before being caught at mid-on.

But Kapil Dev and his supreme confidence was what India required, and they got it in a highly concentrated form. With his captain, he thrashed the bowling in a menacing partnership of 71 off 48 deliveries. India lost three wickets during the final, insane nine deliveries – one of them Azharuddin for a superb 79 off 77 balls with six fours – but were happy with their total of 180 for six. Kapil had struck 42 of those runs – off 29 balls with three fours and a six.

Wessels looked at the asking rate of six runs an over and then at the batsman most likely to put his team within range of it from the start. Fancy opening the batting, Kirsy?

From not being amongst the first 20 in the country to heading up the batting with a World Cup semi-final berth on the line: funny game, cricket. Wessels read the situation well. He knew he was not the man to score at the required rate, and he was big enough to hand the responsibility to someone he thought could.

Bat, gloves: time to make history. Kirsten had had a good feeling about the Adelaide Oval since visiting it in 1986 as it reminded him of Newlands. Hudson faced Kapil's opening over and notched a single, then he played out a maiden to Manoj Prabhakar.

The third over, and Kirsten to face. Kapil stormed in, arms crossing with that curious rhythm as he delivered. As if born to it, Kirsten leaned on his back foot and sent the ball searing through the covers for four.

Let the games begin.

South Africa matched India with uncanny precision in those early overs, especially once Hudson began hitting over the top of the ring of fielders shackled to the circle for the first 15 overs. It was a belter of a pitch, the ball coming on cleanly from the seamers and the left-arm spinner, Venkapathy Raju, having to look to variations of pace rather than turn. Kirsten twinkled up and down the strip to plunder Raju, and with no scant success. Only Tendulkar, whose mundane medium pace could have qualified him for New Zealand citizenship, managed to stop the haemorrhage.

Kirsten had sensed the depth of Hudson's ability and was thrilled to see it realised that night. When in form, there are few better drivers of the ball than the elegant Natalian and Kirsten felt privileged to watch him in action

168

from 22 yards. Bowled for a stylish 53 struck off 66 balls, Hudson departed with just 53 runs left to be scored, though off only 40 balls.

Not surprisingly, Kuiper was promoted up the order, but he had faced just six balls when Kirsten's adrenalin got the better of him. The Indians went up for a leg-before appeal with Kirsten facing. It was turned down, by which time he was well into hustling a leg-bye. Kuiper just couldn't get there and was run out.

Kirsten was anything but silenced by the loss and found himself down the pitch to Kapil in the next over. Willow met leather with an awesome crack and the ball flew over extra cover and into the boundary for four. He tried the same thing with the next delivery, but it swung in and bowled him.

He had given it his best shot, though he would have liked to be there at the end. At the age of 36, he knew moments like this would not be his to savour for much longer. The man who, if some had had their way, would have been watching the drama at home on television, had become the star of the show. Kirsten had wanted it so badly, and here it was – in his grasp and just as wonderful as he had hoped it would be.

Eighty-four runs off 86 balls, including seven fours, should translate into a match-winning innings. But there was work to do yet. South Africa needed 24 off 19 balls. There were, however, hands eager to finish the job.

In came Wessels to steer the ship home. Rhodes hit Prabhakar for a glorious six over square leg and then played a square cut with similar aggression only to be caught at point. No matter: he had hit seven runs off three balls.

Cronje joined Wessels and together they whittled away at the target. With seven balls left, South African needed eight. Kapil delivered, too full, and Wessels sent it crashing into the cover boundary. At last, with an over left, South Africa required fewer runs than they had deliveries in hand. Cronje didn't need to add it all up – he needed four runs and he took them off Prabhakar's first ball, pulling it to midwicket.

India, not long before so superior to South Africa in almost every aspect of the one-day game, had been soundly beaten by six wickets. Kirsten picked up his second man of the match award, a decision which might not have pleased Azharuddin but one with which he couldn't disagree.

'I can't believe he wasn't in your original squad, but that's selection for you,' the Indian captain said afterwards. 'He's a great player.'

Wessels concurred: 'I like him because he's a fighter, and he's a real great one-day player.'

The statisticians agreed. At that stage, Kirsten was the tournament's most prolific batsman, having scored 399 runs at 79,80 with four half-centuries, and he was in line to win a luxury car along with the grand title of 'World Cup Player of the Tournament'. But Martin Crowe would eventually take the honours.

Such mundanities weren't a factor then as South Africa waited for their semi-final fate to be decided. New Zealand finished top of the table on 14 points, followed by England (11), South Africa (10) and Pakistan (9).

New Zealand thus earned a semi-final against Pakistan at Auckland – a prospect South Africa were happy to escape from – and South Africa would take on England at the SCG a day later. Nice place; a shame about the opposition.

If any of their eight opponents had unsettled South Africa, it had been England. They were limited overs experts and Kirsten remembers a sense of wariness in the South African camp before the match, despite the embarrassing loss England had suffered to Zimbabwe in their last, admittedly irrelevant, league match.

But the South Africans were confident enough. We've come this far, how much tougher can it get?

Now, if the weather would only play ball …

21

Victory in Defeat

The South African dressingroom had known better moments than directly after they had been declared the losers, by 19 runs, of the World Cup semi-final against England on 22 March.

England had scored 252 for six off the 45 overs South Africa had managed to send down in the allotted three and a half hours. Had they been given a fair chance to better that and lost, it wouldn't have been as difficult to swallow.

But what unfolded that unjust afternoon and evening was as far removed from the spirit of cricket, the glue that holds the game together, as Kerry Packer and his gaudy creation could make it.

There was plenty of entertaining limited overs cricket played, but the dreaded rain lurked like a mugger in an alley. The match had started 30 minutes late because of the weather, and the rain returned as Chris Lewis ran in to bowl the first ball of the forty-third over.

South Africa had chased hard to stay within range of England's useful total and they needed 32 off the last 18 balls. A big ask, as an Australian would say. But it was far from a lost cause as the seventh-wicket pair, Brian McMillan and Dave Richardson, proved by scrambling 10 runs off the first five balls of that fateful over.

Twenty-two off 13? Tough but not impossible. Then the rain began to fall in ominous grey sheets and the umpires, Brian Aldridge and Steve

Randell, looked at each other and then to the batsmen. We'll stay, came their inevitable reply. Graham Gooch passed the buck back to the umpires, asking if the conditions were fit for play. No, was their opinion and off they went with McMillan protesting and Richardson visibly crestfallen.

It was over. South Africa's World Cup challenge had drowned in a bucket. The infamous message 'South Africa to win need 22 runs off 1 ball' that flashed on to the giant scoreboard just before the resumption and brought angry jeers from the fervently anti-pom Australians, was inaccurate as well as irrelevant.

In fact, they needed 21 off the only delivery that hadn't been obliterated by the rain rules, which were formulated entirely around the broadcasting requirements of the omnipotent Packer's Channel 9 television station.

But the match as a contest ended when Aldridge and Randell made the decision to leave the field. Would playing the game to a fair conclusion in spite of the conditions have been so wrong?

The principle involved is not new to cricketers and umpires who, when they are pulled into this argument, invariably and understandably ask, 'What if someone breaks his leg out there? Who's to blame?' It's a valid defence for calling off a club match, perhaps less so for ruining the World Cup semi-final.

England had qualified to meet Pakistan in the final. Imran Khan's team had come back from a shaky league section to beat New Zealand by four wickets in their Auckland semi-final the previous day and they would go on to a 22-run win over England in the final. But that was three days hence ...

'Oh God, I don't believe it,' was Kirsten's involuntary reaction from the players' balcony as the tragedy played out below him. He had had his off-stump removed by Phil DeFreitas for 11 almost two hours earlier and was perhaps able to think more clearly than those nearer the fire of indignation ignited by the farcical end to the match.

The mood in the South African dressingroom was of almost tangible bitterness, utter despair. We had come so far, we were so close ... how could they! Meyrick Pringle was openly distraught. Wessels sank into a deep, dark sulk.

Then, as the walls seemed to close in, there came one brave voice: 'Come on, guys. We've had a great tournament and done really well. Let's get out there and say thanks to the crowd.'

It wasn't Wessels talking, nor Kuiper, Procter or Jordaan, the official leadership of the squad. It was Kirsten, who knew the difference between triumph and defeat as well as anyone else in the team.

And this was not defeat. England might have won the match, but South

Africa hadn't lost it.

'I could see the boys were upset and it was important to lift them,' Kirsten explained. 'But to me there was no gloom; we had played so well.'

And so, with Wessels a reluctant participant, Kirsten led the vanquished troops back on to the field to say farewell to the crowd. That the applause which greeted every step of their lap of honour was far warmer than that begrudged the England team showed where the majority of the 28 410 spectators' sympathies lay.

Kirsten loped in front, waving and smiling; Rhodes emerged with a towel around his waist, and Pringle battled to see where he was going through his tears. The crowd, whether they were brandishing South African or British flags, was on its feet as one, shouting and applauding as they acknowledged the significance of the gesture.

That's better. Let's end this thing in celebration, not mourning.

The romance continued when the team returned home. Jan Smuts airport was crammed with ordinary South Africans, come to honour the heroes they needed but had been deprived of for so long – shining heroes without shadows.

'The country needed to get rid of the disgrace of the past,' was how Kirsten saw it.

Three years later, at a Rugby World Cup match between Western Samoa and Argentina in East London, Kirsten saw the effect a similar gesture by the Samoans had on the crowd. He recognised the emotion of the occasion.

The public had a less direct but more entertaining way of saying their piece, via the banners seen at the airport. 'Omar Henry en Oupa Kirsten' said one, and 'Kirsten for President' said another. Rhodes had his own fans: 'Marry me, Jonty'.

A few days later came the official recognition in the form of a ticker tape parade through the streets of Johannesburg, streets that were crowded with people of all colours who, before the World Cup, had never known what it was like to stand together and shout for one brave team.

On a personal level, Kirsten was understandably pleased with his performance, which translated into 410 runs at 68,25. It was quite the best of the South Africans, and the third highest aggregate in the tournament after Martin Crowe and Javed Miandad.

He doesn't have a technical theory for his success, saying simply, 'When things are going well, age doesn't come into it. The psychological well-being takes over, the adrenalin pumps and you're on your way.'

Five days after coming home, Kirsten and the rest of the South African team were indeed on their way – to the West Indies.

22

Caribbean Clash

'Tell your boys that the last day at Kensington Oval always belongs to us,' the veteran Bajan cricket watcher cackled as the dust settled on South Africa's remarkable re-entry to Test cricket. Moments before, Curtly Ambrose had bowled Allan Donald first ball, prompting the home side's wild celebrations of an improbable victory.

The West Indies had beaten South Africa by 52 runs after the visitors went into the fifth day needing 79 runs with eight wickets standing and their most experienced batsmen, Wessels and Kirsten, seemingly set for a match-winning partnership. But the match was over 21.4 overs into the day's play as South Africa, bowled out for 148 after resuming on 122 for two, somehow failed to become the first foreign team to win a Test in Barbados since 1935.

Among the South Africans, only Kirsten emerged from the fifth day with credit. His 52 in almost four hours was exactly the kind of fighting innings South Africa needed to win, or at least salvage, the match. But Wessels' early dismissal for his overnight score of 74 in three and a half hours was the beginning of the end, as one young batsman after another succumbed to the best pace bowling they had ever been subjected to.

Bowling on a pitch that harboured a demon or two on the final two days, Curtly Ambrose from one end and Courtney Walsh from the other would have made any target difficult to reach for even the most experienced batsmen. And when Kirsten chopped Walsh on to his stumps to make it 142 for six, a West Indies victory was a matter of time.

Ambrose and Walsh had no runs to play with going into the fifth day and bowled accordingly. Virtually every delivery forced a defensive response from the batsmen, either in resignation to another scoreless ball or in a desperate attempt to stay at the crease. They weren't particularly hostile, letting the variable bounce provide the nightmares, and concentrated instead on maintaining a watertight line and length.

Kirsten, 36 not out overnight, knew an overly defensive approach would be suicide. 'Let's be positive,' he told Cronje and Kuiper. 'The ball is there to be hit.'

Inside the Sir Garfield Sobers Pavilion, the man himself warned Jackie McGlew that South Africa were going about things too defensively. But neither Kuiper's charisma nor Richardson's experience was of any use and the younger players around them choked badly as Ambrose took six for 34, while Walsh picked up the other four wickets for 31.

The normally unflappable Richardson's reaction to a particular delivery from Ambrose summed up the way South Africa had gone off the rails. The ball pitched on a length but climbed alarmingly until it was at least 30 cm above the batsman's head. Instead of letting it pass harmlessly, Richardson invented what could only be described as a head-high forward defensive.

However, it would be unfair to single out South Africa's hard-working stumper for one of his few lapses in three gruelling months of virtually non-stop cricket. The West Indian tour, though it included South Africa's return to the Test arena, was more important politically than from a cricketing perspective and the welfare of the players took a back seat to the diplomacy at work.

When the International Cricket Council voted South Africa back into international competition in 1991, the West Indies Cricket Board of Control was the only full member to abstain. They had also opposed South Africa playing in the World Cup. Both decisions were made on the basis of the WICBC not having a mandate from its six affiliates.

So when Clyde Walcott and Steve Camacho, president and executive secretary respectively of the WICBC, invited South Africa and an Under 19 team to tour the West Indies directly after the World Cup, the United Cricket Board couldn't refuse. Preparations for the visit were only finalised after the UCB found a sponsor midway through the World Cup.

Then, three days before the South African teams embarked on the tour, Brian McMillan withdrew due to a nagging Achilles tendon problem. Apart from his contributions with bat and ball, as well as in the slips, the giant all-rounder was a reliable barometer of the team's well-being. His aggressive, positive presence seemed to reassure the rest of the side.

His absence had the opposite effect and although his replacement for the tour, Corrie van Zyl, is a talented cricketer, he did not fill the gap. In fact, one of the first comments Wessels made in the post-Test press conference was that the team had badly missed McMillan.

South Africa, weary or not, had given their all in the Test match – and controlled much of the first four days – but they were not at their sharpest in the three one-day internationals.

Kirsten puts it down to being unable to sustain the high they reached at the World Cup. One miracle at a time, please, was the cry from a team still feeling their way around the international circuit. Even a single warm-up match would have benefited the tourists, as only Wessels had played in the West Indies before – for Australia in 1983. But it was straight into the international series.

Wessels said as much and more to Bacher in Port of Spain, Trinidad, where South Africa were outplayed by ten and seven wickets on consecutive days in front of a packed Queen's Park Oval, and this after they had been thumped by 107 runs at Kingston's famous Sabina Park.

The South African captain was concerned that his team would lose the aura of their performance at the World Cup if they performed poorly in the Caribbean. Don't worry about the results; this tour is bigger than that, said Bacher while understandingly trying to keep one foot in the player's world and the other in the administrator's.

Coming from the first-world luxury of Australia, where the entire infrastructure seemed geared towards cricket, to the distinctly third-world reality of Jamaica also helped burst South Africa's bubble. Whatever its history, Sabina Park features more concrete than character, and the outfield during that tour would not have passed muster at most South African club grounds.

Air travel, which had been so effortless in Australia, was rather less so in the West Indies. On the day the teams left Jamaica for Trinidad, the vintage Boeing 707 carrying both South African teams and the West Indies squad, as well as the media and the administrators on tour, veered alarmingly to starboard shortly after take-off as its passengers watched the Caribbean Sea come rather closer than they wanted it to be just then.

'Ladies and gentlemen, we have a problem and will return to Norman Manley airport,' droned the British West Indian Airways pilot in that irresistible Caribbean lilt, sounding far too confident of getting there. But he did, and the problem was efficiently identified and dealt with. But not before the locals had informed their foreign travelling companions what BWIA really stands for – 'But Will It Arrive?'

Perhaps the most difficult aspect of the West Indian tour had been explaining to wives, girlfriends and especially children that two months away from home was about to become three. But South Africa's cricketers had to face the fact that they were now in the real world, where contracted players are employees doing a job which often entails overtime. The game in South Africa had burst its banks, and for those first few months it was sink or swim.

Paradoxically, when the tour reached Barbados, the South Africans saw it as a chance to unwind from the stresses of the one-day carnival. Not that practice and hard work disappeared off the agenda in the three days before the start of the match. On the contrary, the tourists headed straight from Grantley Adams airport, where they were met by Sir Garfield Sobers, among others, to the nets at Kensington Oval. But there was a feeling of relief that they could at last take a break from the mindless grind of carbon copy limited overs matches.

By contrast, the Bajan public were up in arms about the omission of fast bowler Anderson Cummins from the Test squad of 13. The highly effective boycott they mounted in protest resulted in only 6 000 people witnessing the most intense and dramatic cricket match in my experience to date.

'No Cummins. No Going. No Kensington. It's principles,' according to a placard displayed by a disgruntled Bajan on the front page of the *Barbados Advocate*.

On the back page was evidence that the South Africans were just as unfamiliar to international cricket as it was to them. Below a photograph taken at the airport the day before and clearly depicting Mike Procter, Bacher, Sir Garfield and Bacher's wife Shira, the caption read: 'History in the making: The first ever South African cricket team to visit the region touched down on Barbadian soil yesterday. The significance of the moment did not appear to overawe (left to right) manager of the team Allan [sic] Jordaan, managing director of the United Cricket Board of South Africa Ali Bacher, Barbadian cricketing legend Sir Garfield Sobers and a female South African supporter, shortly after the team's BWIA flight landed at the Grantley Adams International Airport.'

The essence of the debate about Cummins, a useful enough one-day player but not an obvious Test star, was the perhaps unavoidable insularity of the West Indies. There is no sovereign state called the West Indies: it is a region made up of island countries stretching from Jamaica, just south of Cuba, to Guyana on the mainland of South America. It is a vast area straddling two time zones.

So it is not surprising that the West Indian selectors' decisions are not always universally accepted. In African terms, they would have to choose one Test team from all the players produced by South Africa, Zimbabwe, Namibia, Botswana, Kenya and Uganda, each country's team being of roughly equal strength.

And each West Indian nation seems to have its own axe to grind. In Jamaica, Richie Richardson, an Antiguan, was shamefully booed when he walked out to bat, and that in his first 'home' match as captain, as a reaction to the West Indies' poor form at the World Cup. In Trinidad, the proud producers of Brian Lara and Phil Simmons, the atmosphere at the cricket was more settled but every cab driver, upon hearing that his fare had previously been in Jamaica, quipped, 'You'll like Trinidad better.'

Cummins' axing wasn't the only bone Bajans had to pick with the selectors. It seems many people in the country which has supplied the West Indies team with the bulk of its members over the years believe Barbados consistently gets a raw deal. And why did Desmond Haynes have only four Test captaincies to his credit …?

Even the cricket writers were pulled into the Cummins controversy. On the first day of the Test, the recognised world authority on West Indies cricket, Tony Cozier, found himself the target of a fan's anger.

'Cozier supports the boycott but he's here,' an irate man yelled from the Three Ws stand to the adjacent pressbox. Cozier, who heard the charge as plainly as the rest of us, didn't allow his attention to be diverted from the cricket.

South Africa had their own problems going into their first Test in 22 years. Meyrick Pringle, whose destructive burst against the West Indies in Christchurch had earned him wide respect in the islands themselves, was a doubtful starter with a rib cartilage injury which had prevented him from bowling his last five overs in the second match in Port of Spain. But he was declared fit to play two days before the match.

Being the Caribbean, the urge to go with four seamers won through and Omar Henry, who took one for 94 off 14.5 overs in the first two limited overs matches, sat it out. If there was any spin bowling to be done, the ball would go to Kirsten. Jonty Rhodes would have given anything to play, but became the game's most enthusiastic twelfth man.

A serene Good Friday only put the following day's tension in stark relief as the Test got going. Wessels won the toss and, on the strength of Kensington Oval's reputation for offering help to the seamers on the first day, asked the West Indies to bat.

However, the opposing theory held that batting on the last day in

Barbados was to be avoided if at all possible. The second and third days were fine, said the experts, but towards the end of the fourth day the bounce will start to vary. How right they were.

Half-centuries from Haynes and Keith Arthurton, Simmons' 35 and Richardson's 44 took the West Indies to a mediocre 262. Donald, at last freed from the box limited overs cricket squeezed his immense talent into, found his rhythm and bowled well enough to earn approving nods from some of the 1 000 spectators who had turned up to see the first session of Test cricket between these two teams.

Pringle looked to be holding something back, and Richard Snell alternated genuine wicket-taking deliveries with overpitched offerings. Happily, none of the South African bowlers went wicketless in their first Test innings.

Hudson and Rushmere ambled to 13 without loss in the 30 minutes they faced before the close, but an over into the second day's play the latter nicked a lifting ball from Ambrose to Lara at first slip and South Africa were 14 for one. Instead of inhibiting himself after the early loss of his opening partner, Hudson began to play more aggressively as he found his groove against the pace bowling he is so adept at converting into attractively scored runs.

However, on 22 he hooked Ambrose straight to Walsh at deep fine leg, in front of the pressbox. Most of the reporters behind Walsh, including former England captain Mike Brearley, would have fancied their chances of taking what looked a straightforward catch. But the Jamaican somehow made a hash of it and then suffered the embarrassment of watching the ball trickle over the boundary.

It would prove a most expensive slip, as would the second life Hudson had when, on 66, he edged Patrick Patterson against wicketkeeper David Williams' right glove. The ball rebounded to Lara, but he couldn't hold it.

Before offering his second chance, Hudson had bidden farewell to Wessels. The South African captain played with rare attacking fire to hit 59 in just less than two and a half hours, driving and pulling with aplomb against an attack that begrudged precious few loose deliveries.

The 125 runs they put on for the second wicket proved to the West Indians that what they had seen in Jamaica and Trinidad was not the whole truth of South African cricket. Kirsten and Cronje, both caught in the slips, shared a total of 48 runs with Hudson before he embarked on the next major partnership, an eventual 92 for the fifth wicket with Kuiper.

Hudson, playing with ever increasing authority, had advanced to 93 at tea. The last session included 13 overs with the second new ball, but he and

Kuiper were in complete control despite having to endure an additional 20 minutes as the growing frustration of the West Indian bowlers made it difficult for them to stick to the required over rate.

At the close, Hudson had become the first South African to score a century on début in Test cricket and the first foreigner to do so in Bridgetown. He stood unbeaten on 135 and Kuiper was 19 not out.

Twenty-five runs into the third day Kuiper, who had grafted for three and a quarter hours for his 34, was caught behind. Hudson helped take the score to 311, as South Africa built their lead, before he was yorked by Kenneth Benjamin.

More than eight and a half hours of superb batsmanship had ended with Hudson having scored 163, including 20 boundaries. The tail followed and South Africa totalled 345 – a lead of 83, good enough to build a victory around, but first they would need quick wickets.

That was just what they achieved, reducing the West Indies to 174 for seven before Test débutant Jimmy Adams, who had taken four for 43 with harmless-looking left-arm spin, and Benjamin halted the damage. With 184 on the board, putting them 101 ahead, and just three wickets standing the home side were indeed staring down both barrels.

The next day was a rest day and while the South Africans knew they still had work to do to win the match, they were confident they could do it. That evening, the WICBC invited the entire tour party, apart from the U19s, to a sea cruise on the Bajan Queen, a pleasure boat. Offered a rare opportunity to relax, the South Africans took it up with gusto. The West Indians were noticeably less festive. Kirsten remembers a tall West Indian introducing himself: 'Hello, I'm Michael Holding, Whispering Death'.

Nothing that would give a tabloid hack an excuse to grab a headline took place on the boat – a few drinks, dinner and some good-natured chorus line stuff, sans shirts – and it was all over in a few hours.

Besides, they had all of the next day to recover. What harm could it do?

But Kirsten feels that it did do harm. When the match resumed, South Africa's cricket lacked the hard edge that had taken them so near to a decisive advantage.

The seventh and eighth wickets fell quickly enough but then Adams, who was earning respect by the minute, and Patterson mounted a frustrating last-wicket stand of 62 in just short of one and a half hours. Wayward bowling didn't help, and when Tertius Bosch yorked Patterson South Africa needed 201 in nine hours, a somewhat less simple task than they had thought they would face.

Adams had battled his way to a memorable 79 not out in more than three

Just married: firmly caught in the slips by wife Tuffy, 1983. (The Argus)

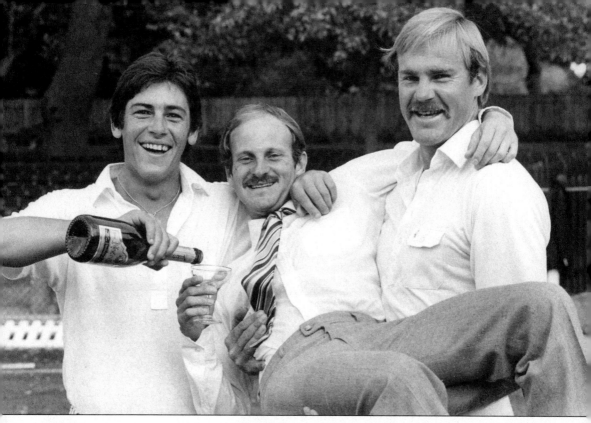

Above: With Stephen Jefferies and Garth le Roux: all three selected for South Africa against Graham Gooch's English 'rebels', 1982. (Pierre Schoeman, Die Burger)

Below: The formation of the South African Professional Cricket Players' Association in 1983 was an attempt, with the aid of Eddie Barlow and Peter Cooke, to streamline communication between players and administration. In time to come the Association would no longer be needed.

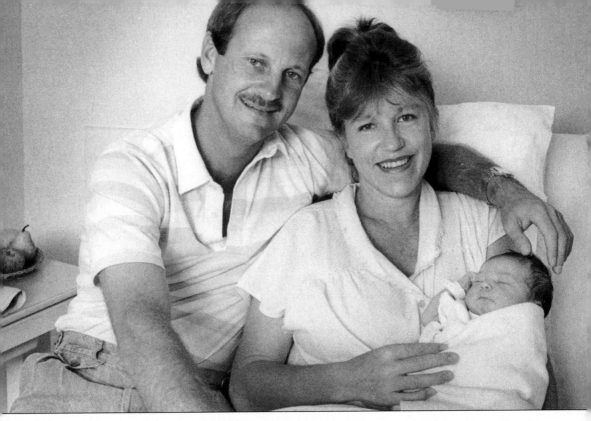

Above: Welcome delivery: with wife Tuffy and daughter Leilah, born in March 1986. (Cape Times)

Below: Winelands Sportsman of the Year, 1977: Kirsten receiving the trophy from Morné du Plessis. (The Argus)

Above: Khaya Majola, development cricket kingpin (right), with two 'greats' of yesteryear, Conrad Hunte (left) and Jackie McGlew, in Kingston, 1992.

Below: Sixes, Hong Kong: relaxed moments with Adrian Kuiper and Richie Richardson.

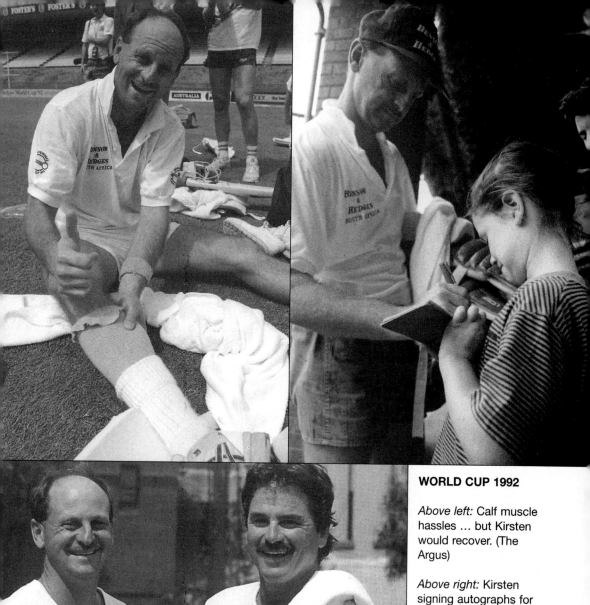

WORLD CUP 1992

Above left: Calf muscle hassles ... but Kirsten would recover. (The Argus)

Above right: Kirsten signing autographs for young admirers. (The Argus)

Left: Old friends and former Western Province team-mates, Kirsten and Allan Lamb meet before the semi-final against England. (The Argus)

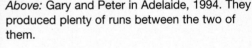

Above: Gary and Peter in Adelaide, 1994. They produced plenty of runs between the two of them.

Left: Robbie Muzzell, president of Border Cricket Board and manager of the South African squad to Australia, 1993/94.

Gary and Peter. Spot the difference?

The English press records
Kirsten's maiden Test century at
Headingley, 1994.

and a half hours, although few suspected then that his was the match-winning effort.

But there were many shocks in store. The first came when Hudson unwisely tried to cut the second ball he faced, from Ambrose, and steered a catch to Lara. Rushmere seemed to abandon completely the prospect of trying to score the odd run and, eventually rendered strokeless, he was bowled by Ambrose having laboured for 40 minutes over three runs.

This was trouble: 27 on the board, both openers back in the hut, a pitch that was starting to behave erratically and four sessions left for one of the world's best pace attacks to shoot the other eight wickets down. But Wessels and Kirsten came together with the sure-footedness of an old firm and the South African situation gradually brightened.

It was far from flowing cricket, but the currency of choice had ceased to be simply runs as the last session became a game of chess. A shot placed perfectly ... a fielder moved to close the gap ... a shot exactly where he was in the first place ... a bouncer fired in indignation. So it went on, and the South Africans could feel the initiative coming their way.

Kirsten proclaimed Wessels' batting in both innings as the best he had seen him play in a Test match. Altogether uncharacteristically, Wessels batted with something approaching abandon, as for once his attacking strokes outnumbered his defensive prods.

Kirsten also played no small role in getting South Africa to the close of the fourth day without further loss. But the next morning the third-wicket stand was broken at 96, followed by the disaster of the fifth day, black Wednesday. The lesson of that match, according to Kirsten, was that to relax for one second in a Test is folly.

Subdued but happy that their marathon season was finally over, the South Africans boarded the flight home later that night. Most of them were planning to go back to five months of anything but cricket.

23

From Knysna to Brisbane, and Beyond

Five months off! Since he stopped playing county cricket Kirsten had enjoyed his winters of relative inactivity. After a busy summer, his time was at last his own and he could look to his life as husband and father and potter about blissfully if he felt like it.

The summer of 1991-92 had started with a bang and featured one cricketing explosion after the next until, at the end of April, a ceasefire was called. Kirsten was as emotionally and physically drained as the rest of the South African team and expected to enjoy a few months of getting his life back.

Instead, he found it a strenuous period mentally. The euphoria of the World Cup was almost addictive, and the process of trying to settle down to a normal South African life brought with it something akin to withdrawal.

Consequently, his preparation for the 1992-93 season suffered. Despite being named vice-captain for South Africa's home series against India, he had a thoroughly forgettable season, averaging 12,66 in the four Test matches – sneaking in above Brett Schultz – and while his form in the seven-match limited overs series was better he was far from the batsman he could still be.

The cricket wasn't of an inspirational variety either. Although South

Africa's first home series against a country other than England, Australia or New Zealand was of historical significance, it produced what Wisden aptly called 'a great deal of humdrum cricket'.

South Africa won the third Test, in Port Elizabeth, by nine wickets on the back of Allan Donald's 12 wickets and Hansie Cronje's 135 in the first innings. But the other matches dwindled to the most boring kind of draws, particularly the Newlands Test in which runs came at the mournful pace of 1,83 an over.

Though South Africa were proud to win their first series of the new era, they played better, brighter cricket in the limited overs matches and were 5-2 victors.

However, Kirsten will remember the one-day series against India for the drama of the second match at Port Elizabeth. Kapil Dev had warned him about not backing up on three occasions in other matches during the tour. Kirsten drove the last ball of an over from Manoj Prabhakar for four. Then, without a previous warning in the match Kapil, instead of delivering the first ball of the next over to Wessels, changed hands and removed the bails with Kirsten out of his ground.

The crowd, their adrenalin stirred by South Africa having bowled out the opposition for just 147, couldn't believe what they were seeing. Kapil Dev, one of the game's greats, was sending another player with significant claims to that title on his way in the most underhand way.

Kapil appealed matter of factly and umpire Cyril Mitchley – who sensibly twice asked the bowler if he was sure he wanted him to proceed – had no option but to give Kirsten out.

'I know Paddy Clift was happy when he saw that happen,' Kirsten would say afterwards.

As the inevitable booing reached a crescendo, Kirsten turned on Kapil and spewed verbal abuse for several seconds. The helmet and grille Kirsten wore looked as if it was protecting Kapil from being bitten rather than keeping the batsman's head safe.

Once in the dressingroom, he threw his bat about in rage as the frustrations of the season boiled over. Did Kapil really think he was trying to steal ground? Crap! He had been so locked into the match he wasn't concentrating on how far down the pitch he had come.

Kirsten then ran into Amit Mathur, the Indian manager, and gave him a similar earful.

Out in the middle, Wessels was incensed at Kapil's action. While turning for a second run in the same over, his bat hit Kapil on the shins. It was the Indians' turn to get indignant and they duly lodged a complaint with the match referee, Clive Lloyd, citing both Wessels and Kirsten. As he had not seen the incident and television replays were inconclusive, Lloyd decided there was reasonable doubt whether Wessels had struck Kapil intentionally. Kirsten was fined 50 per cent of his match fee.

Wessels maintained that he had hit Kapil by accident, but Kirsten was pleased his captain had stood up for him. Kapil later apologised to Kirsten, saying they were both getting on in years.

Kirsten kept his place in the squad for the Triangular Series of limited overs matches which followed, involving the West Indies and Pakistan. But he knew for sure that he was on thin ice when Ali Bacher invited him to his hotel room in Port Elizabeth before the second match, against the West Indies.

You've got to do well in this one, Kirsy, otherwise you're out. Kirsten appreciated Bacher's effort, as he had done throughout his career. He had made only 18 in that first match against Pakistan, in which South Africa collapsed to lose by 10 runs, but fared better in the second, scoring an unbeaten 45 on a difficult Port Elizabeth pitch in a six-wicket win over the West Indies.

He totalled 139 runs in six matches for an average of 27,80 and wondered if he had done enough to be selected for the winter tour to Sri Lanka. The question was answered for him when he fractured his right index finger in a club match and missed Border's last six day-night series matches.

He was fit by the time the team was announced on 8 April, but his name wasn't there.

So, it had come to this. National hero the previous year, discard the next. Kirsten was a month away from his thirty-eighth birthday and not many would have been surprised if he had decided to pack it in as far as international cricket was concerned. He had enjoyed a remarkable renaissance at the World Cup and proved his mettle in the West Indies Test. What more could a cricketer who should have missed the international boat want?

Much more. Striving to push further the limits of his talent has been one of the dominant themes of Kirsten's career. Without it, he would have found it difficult to score many of his 100 first-class half-centuries, not to mention turning 51 of those into centuries, and eight centuries into double centuries, so far.

Kirsten's character does not allow him to give up. His central talent as a batsman is not his timing or his range of off-side strokes. It is the ability to steer the middle course whether the seas are rough or calm, to clear his mind of intrusions as he goes about doing what is best for his team. It is at once what he brings to his batsmanship and what cricket has done for him. He never gorges himself on runs, taking instead the maximum available to a player who refuses to bash.

Similarly, on a bad pitch or against attacking bowling, his ability to survive until the ball becomes older or the bowlers tire has led to many of those 50s becoming centuries and has been the guiding factor in all the double centuries.

Kirsten didn't lose these qualities in the 1992-93 season. He simply mislaid them.

Even in the midst of the gloom following the tour by India, he had ambitions: 'If I can hang in for the 1994 tour of England I would have done very well.'

The goal was thus set. Gloves, bat: time to go to work.

Kirsten revisited the basics of the game in the winter of 1993. With Border coaches Stephen Jones and Kenny Watson drilling him to peak fitness and hammering out the dents that had crept into his technique, he was free to think himself back into Test form.

And he was free to dream – as he and Gary did during a week of fishing and brotherly quality time in Knysna, a pristine haven of natural beauty on the south coast of South Africa. Imagine playing international cricket together, they mused while floating in a dinghy on the Knysna lagoon, lines dangling limp in the water, a couple of beers in the boat.

P N Kirsten and G Kirsten together on one scorecard, or even opening the batting. The old man would have enjoyed seeing that …

One of Kirsten's major priorities that season was to help turn Border into a winning side. Since their acceptance into the A section, they had become better acquainted with mediocrity than victory. One of the previous season's problems was the lack of an opening batsman comfortable with both defending and attacking.

No problem. I'll open the batting. Kirsten also knew his best chance of getting back into the South African team, at least in the one-day games, was as an opener. As he saw it, Hansie Cronje had battened down the number three spot and Daryll Cullinan was the obvious number four.

His intentions were made emphatically clear when he hit an undefeated 134 to lead Border to a handsome five-wicket win over Northern Transvaal in Verwoerdburg (now Centurion) in their night series opener, an early success on the way to their first semi-final berth in this competition and a respectable middle-of-the-table finish in the Castle Cup. Although he was dropped early on, Kirsten went on to play an innings against Northerns that was crammed with the best of his batting.

Nine days earlier he had also been the crucial Border batsman, but this time in a defensive role, as his team fought out a draw with Eastern Province in Port Elizabeth. While the middle order crumbled around him, Kirsten batted for more than eight hours in the second innings to see Border to safety. He faced 461 balls and hit a six and 24 fours before being caught behind for 181 – tantalisingly close to what would have been his eighth double ton.

While he was at the crease, the South African team to tour India and Australia was announced on the public address system.

There was no Peter Kirsten.

Nine days later, South Africa played their first match in the Hero Cup, a limited overs tournament in India also featuring the West Indies, Sri Lanka and Zimbabwe. It was the first part of a three-month trip that would see them take on Australia in three Tests and a three-way World Series Cup involving New Zealand.

When Border started their New Year match against Northerns at Buffalo Park, the first Test in Melbourne had been reduced to a one-innings dud by rain and the start of the second, in Sydney, was a day away. South Africa had also lost three of the four one-day matches they had played.

Half a world away in East London, Kirsten lost the toss and was asked to field. Less than 70 overs later Northerns were all out for 146 following bristling top and tail bowling by Brenden Fourie and Alan Badenhorst, who took seven for 59 between them, and Ian Howell, who relied on perseverance and frustration to pick off the other three wickets.

At 3.35 pm on that first day, Kirsten walked to the wicket to open the Border innings with Andrew Lawson. He was 44 not out that evening, but offered a chance three runs after reaching his half-century the next morning. It was to be the last blemish on Kirsten's innings until a catch was put down on the third morning. By then he had reached 190.

Earlier that day at the SCG, South Africa had been bowled out for 169.

Eleven minutes into the afternoon of the third day, Kirsten's epic innings came to an end when he wearily lifted a drive to mid-off. He had a right to be tired – he had scored 271, the innings that put Border on track for the innings victory they secured the next day.

The records tumbled. It was his highest first-class score and the best by a Border player; no other South African had scored eight double centuries; it was the thirteenth highest first-class score made in South Africa and the eighth highest by a South African in South Africa; and the 188 runs Kirsten shared with Pieter Strydom for the fourth wicket was a Border record.

Statistics make sterile reading, but the thought of batting for 10 hours and 40 minutes, facing 534 deliveries and hitting 22 fours should be enough to make most cynics look interested. The more cricket-minded, and there were only 250 of them at Buffalo Park that third day, knew they had seen somewhat more than the completion of a remarkable innings. They had witnessed one brave man's victory over age, youth and the widely held view that he was not good enough for the international arena.

The traits Kirsten had etched into his finest batting over the years were there for all to see. He exploited almost every opportunity to score, but didn't seem perturbed to have to go through long dry spells against a new ball or when the bowlers had been refreshed by an interval. He rode the waves as well as the troughs with the maturity of a batsman who had been there before.

When Kirsten's wicket fell it was just after 8 pm in Sydney and the South African team had endured a tough day in the field as the Australians took their time building a solid first innings.

Kirsten went home tired but satisfied. He was back – and how. Everything had gone so well, from his first winter training run to this latest feat. You know, if someone gets injured in Aussie …

As the sun peeped over the horizon the next day the urgent ring of the telephone shook Kirsten from his armchair slumber. He had turned on the television to watch the third day's play in Sydney, which continued through the South African night, and had fallen asleep during the second session.

'Hello,' he mouthed, still half asleep. It was Stephen Jones, making some joke about kangaroos.

'What?'

Kirsten shook himself awake while Jones explained. Robbie Muzzell, the South African manager on that trip, had appeared on television during the tea interval. Wessels had sustained his second injury – a fractured finger to go with his twisted knee – and could take no further part in the tour. Cronje would take over the captaincy for the rest of the Australian tour.

'And we have asked for Peter Kirsten to be sent out to join the tour,' Muzzell had announced while Kirsten snored. He was concerned at the loss of Wessels but was nevertheless bursting to break the news of a fellow Border man's success. As she had been three years before – when he had scored 291 in a club match – Kirsten's mother Lois, visiting from Cape Town, was there at a great moment in her son's career.

Predictably, the telephone then rang off the hook with congratulatory calls and Kirsten arrived late at Buffalo Park for the final day of the Castle

Cup match. At the entrance to the pavilion he found a poster saying 'Go show 'em how, Kirsy. Best of luck'. Inside, the walls were plastered with posters saying similar things.

Half an hour after the start of play, Kirsten emerged on to the field to relieve the twelfth man of fielding duties. Northerns were defeated just before the scheduled lunch break and it was back to the hurly-burly of making arrangements and talking to the media.

At 8.20 pm Kirsten boarded a plane in East London en route to Johannesburg and then Sydney. Peace at last. Or so he thought. After taking off from Johannesburg, he asked a stewardess to keep him up to date with the Test score, which could be obtained on the aircraft's radio system.

South Africa went into the last day needing to bowl Australia out for less than 116 to win. An inspired Fanie de Villiers had reduced them to 63 for four by the close of the fourth day, but it would still take a near-miracle for South Africa to win it.

But each time the stewardess visited Kirsten the news was better. Eventually, with Australia 75 for eight, he was invited into the cockpit to listen to the commentary. Kirsten could hardly believe his ears when the last two wickets went down for a South African victory by the scant margin of five runs.

He had thought he would be joining a glum team, but instead he walked in on a celebration. And his presence seemed to enhance the party as the World Cup glory shone again. One of the more enthusiastic revellers was Gary Kirsten, who had replaced the injured Brian McMillan after the first Test to make his Test début at the SCG.

Kirsten's first match on tour was the World Series game against New Zealand in Brisbane. He proved his value as an opener wasn't limited to the provincial arena with a pulsating innings of 97 struck off 108 balls, although lack of support down the order saw South Africa lose a rain-affected match by nine runs.

Gary Kirsten opened with Cronje against Australia at the same ground the next day, and South Africa went down by 48 runs. .

14 January 1994: a proud day for the Kirsten family. The first two names on the South African scorecard in the match against New Zealand in Perth represented a dream come true: P N Kirsten, G Kirsten.

The first scored 50, the second 31, and together they gave South Africa a fine start by sharing 80 runs off 112 balls. Hot stuff from the South African attack on the helpful WACA pitch had earlier removed New Zealand for 150 and, with Cronje banging a quick 40, it took just 30.3 overs for South Africa to register their first limited overs win against the Kiwis.

Two days later, disaster against Australia at the same ground. Kirsten had scored five runs when the pitch and gangly Australian fast bowler Glenn McGrath combined to put him in hospital. The delivery in question hit a crack in the pitch and reared, following him as he tried to sway out of its path. It crashed into his cheekbone and Kirsten crumpled, motionless. Dramatic scenes followed as he was stretchered into an ambulance.

'This can't happen,' he remembers telling himself. 'I've just arrived.'

De Villiers took one look at his dented cheekbone and said, '*Pietertjie, jy gaan nou huistoe.*'

He was diagnosed as having sustained a depressed fracture of the cheekbone. That was the bad news. The good news was that immediate keyhole surgery would ensure he could stay on the tour.

However, the Australians learned from the episode and bowled a straighter line to Kirsten after that.

Despite their poor start, South Africa sneaked into the best-of-three finals against Australia, and were comfortable winners by 28 runs in the first match at the MCG. But the Australians came back with a vengeance to win the last two, both at the SCG, by 69 and 35 runs. The Kirstens opened in all three matches, Gary starring with a commanding 112 not out off 137 balls in the first.

But the real business of Peter Kirsten's late call-up lay ahead in the third test in Adelaide. For many South Africans, a Test series victory over Australia in Australia is as close to heaven as cricket gets. That South Africa's results from five tours are three drawn series and two lost is half the allure – it has never been done.

The 1993-94 South Africans, 1-0 up going into the decider, gave it their best shot against powerful opponents but were to return home with just a share of the spoils.

Much has been said and written about Kirsten's supposed role in nullifying Shane Warne in the third Test. The revolutionary leg-spinner had taken 12 for 128 at the SCG and several of South Africa's frontline batsmen looked clumsy against him. Kirsten, considered one of South Africa's best players against spin bowling, was being sent on a mission to negate 'the Warne factor', some newspapers had it. Not quite, but he knew Warne had to be overcome if he was going to make a success of the chance he had to cement his place in the Test side.

Though he had not faced him before, Kirsten was confident of his ability to bat profitably against Warne. His technique against spin is to look for ones and twos rather than to pull or cut, so he wasn't tempted to hit against the turn when facing a leg-spinner.

The flipper, Warne's devastating quicker, bottom-of-the-hand delivery, had to be mastered and Kirsten felt his approach of trying to scavenge off spin bowling rather than attempt to dominate it would be the key. Reacting quickly to the flipper seemed the way to go, not driving through it.

An hour after tea on the second day, Allan Border, in his last Test on Australian soil, declared on 469 for seven. Steve Waugh had reclaimed his place in the Australian Test side in no uncertain terms, scoring an impressive 164 and putting on 208 runs for the fifth wicket with his captain.

Hudson and Gary Kirsten shared 100 runs for the first wicket before the latter was caught by Tim May off Craig McDermott. Then Cronje, whose form was affected by his sudden elevation to the captaincy, was caught behind without scoring.

In came Peter Kirsten, and he proved to be the wedge between South Africa and the follow-on. Waugh emerged as the innings wrecker, gaining a decidedly dodgy leg-before decision to remove Hudson for 90 after he and Kirsten had added 73 runs between lunch and tea, before snuffing out the innings of Rhodes, Daryll Cullinan and McMillan as South Africa slumped to 203 for six – still 67 runs short of avoiding following on.

The delivery which dismissed Hudson looked to be veering down leg and Kirsten was shocked when umpire Darryl Hair upheld the appeal. 'How can you give that out?' he asked Hair. It was a question that would earn him the first of his two fines from match referee Jackie Hendriks and it would not be the last time in the match that the Australian umpire would get under the South Africans' skin.

Kirsten's introduction to Warne's flipper had come, as he expected, early in his innings. In fact, he recognised the second delivery he received from the Victorian as the dreaded ball, but it was wide of his off-stump and he could let it pass harmlessly. With his partners concentrating on not getting out, it was left to Kirsten to get South Africa to 270. He was ninth out for 79, then his highest Test score, on that very total, and the last wicket fell three runs later.

Australia's lead of 196 became 320 before Border declared and at the close of the fourth day South Africa were reeling at 18 for three. Warne had bowled Gary Kirsten with a viciously turning delivery and general opinion was that he would finish South Africa off without much fuss on the final day.

But, again, it was Kirsten who added respectability to South Africa's performance. The stout-hearted De Villiers had come in as nightwatchman and although he and Kirsten made an unlikely pair, they batted past lunch and halfway through the second session in an effort to save the match. De Villiers had broken a bone in his right thumb while batting in the first innings, but he soldiered on until fatigue and the effects of the pain took over.

'*Jislaaik, Pietertjie, dis seer jong,*' was the fast bowler's lament during a mid-pitch conference.

'*Kak, daar is geen pyn. Jy moet net kolf,*' came Kirsten's swift reply.

They stayed together for just longer than three and a quarter hours and put on 82 runs for the fourth wicket before Craig McDermott broke the partnership and snapped up two more wickets, including Kirsten's, as South Africa tumbled to 129 all out and defeat by 191 runs.

Umpire Hair's leg-before decision to remove Kirsten prompted what Hendriks saw as dissent by the batsman, and he subsequently received his second fine of the match.

While he was at the crease scoring 42 and frustrating the Australians, Kirsten came into contact with the Australian art of 'sledging', a term applied when the fielding side employs sharp minds and even sharper tongues in their strategy to bowl the opposition out.

A delivery from Tim May drew Kirsten forward and while the ball missed everything that mattered, there was a noise and the Australians went up – only to be turned down. From behind his back, where David Boon was stationed under the helmet, Kirsten heard: 'Ya little weasel, don't ya dare do that again.' Later, after he had blocked Warne out of the attack, the blond bombshell was heard to implore from mid-on, 'Hey, desert head, how much longer are you going to stay here?'

Weasel, desert head, whatever. It didn't affect his game then nor when the Australians arrived in South Africa for a return series of three Tests and eight limited overs internationals. Despite Wessels' return to the side at number four, Kirsten fitted in well as number five in the Tests, scoring two half-centuries and a 49 in his five innings.

In six one-dayers, he scored 174 runs at 29,00 as an opener, but was disappointed to be dropped for the last two matches.

After demolishing Australia in the first Test at the Wanderers to win by 197 runs, South Africa faded as the tour went on, losing by nine wickets with a lacklustre performance at Newlands and being unable to break through the Australian second innings in Durban.

In six Tests, South Africa and Australia had thus played to a 2-2 deadlock, while the limited overs series in South Africa was also drawn, 4-4.

South Africa's tendency to fall away in the second half of the series worried Kirsten, though he was happy with his personal form and reasonably sure of reaching his stated goal – the 1994 tour of England.

He felt this in spite of what Tony Greig, back in South Africa as part of the Channel 9 commentary team, had said to him. 'Of course, you know that you're not going to England,' said Greig, with his trademark lack of diplomacy.

Kirsten didn't bat an eyelid. 'Don't worry, Greigy, I've heard it all before.'

24

England Revisited – Triumph and Disappointment

K irsten had no doubts that he would be selected to tour England with the first South African team to make the trip since 1965. That belief would have been laughed out of print in the aftermath of the India tour in 1992.

- Then there had been the gloom of a job not done well enough, of opportunity wasted. Two years later, however, there was only confidence and eagerness to return to England, this time wearing green and gold.

The year 1994 was to be 'my year', Kirsten had decided, and with good reason.

The character he had shown against the Australians made him the perfect senior pro. He was exactly the player most captains would have wanted holding their middle order together with know-how and still sound technique. What he had lost in reflexes and aggression to his 39 years, he had made up for with experience.

So it was a happy Kirsten who arrived in England in June with the rest of the South African squad – a Kirsten who had worked extremely hard to get there.

There was pressure on him, but it was the kind which motivated him. The mercurial Daryll Cullinan, who did not play against Australia in South Africa, had been included in the squad for England and to Kirsten's thinking they would be competing for one middle-order berth in the Test team.

It would be Cullinan's surge to form after a fitful start to the tour that would sketch all too clearly for Kirsten one of the biggest dilemmas he had faced in his career.

Border had signed Cullinan, originally from Queenstown, from Transvaal after the 1993-94 season and he and Kirsten had spent much of the two and a half months between the departure of the Australians and the beginning of the England tour training in East London.

Like Kirsten, Cullinan had risen to prominence as a schoolboy, perhaps too young, and his path to the top had not been as smooth as many thought it would be. Having begun his A section career with Western Province in 1985 before moving north, Cullinan was happy to be back near his roots.

Both he and Kirsten were serious and sometimes introspective about their cricket and found each other's company beneficial as the long winter's sweat now glistened in the pale sunshine of spring.

Kirsten was fit and he was happy – and he couldn't wait to play in England again. When he last took guard for Derbyshire in 1982, he had been part of an isolated group of players in search of the variety and challenge of international cricket denied them by apartheid and the world's reaction to it. He remembers being called 'scum' from the boundary because of his nationality.

But South Africa had changed. It had jettisoned its old ways and embraced democracy under the warm touch and gaze of Nelson Mandela. The events of 27 April 1994 didn't liberate only oppressed black South Africans: the country's élite sportsmen were also given back their freedom.

And the rest of the world wanted to share in the glow, as evidenced by Peter Hain, the former anti-apartheid activist who became a British Labour Party MP, meeting the team at Heathrow with his hand outstretched, bearing friendship instead of a protest sign.

For Kirsten, it was magnificent to be welcomed as a South African in England. The dinners and functions in London which preceded the start of the real business of the tour could easily have been an endless round of boring meals taken in boring company. But he found the people he met interesting and interested in his country.

Then, a problem. The day after the South Africans arrived in the country, they had trained at the Oval. Perhaps Kirsten should have regarded as a bad omen the one and a half hour traffic jam the team bus was caught in en route to the ground as a result of a gay rights march.

But keen as a player 20 years his junior, he pushed himself a touch too hard and felt a twinge in his right calf muscle. The management were taking no chances and left him out of the first match of the tour, a social affair at John Paul Getty's magnificent private ground, Wormsley. No problem, just a twinge.

He was also unable to play in the traditional fixture against the Earl of Carnarvon's XI at Highclere but, frustrating though the inactivity was, he knew he had to let the injury, an old bugbear, settle down. But when he was forced to sit out the first county match, against Kent in Canterbury, Kirsten began to fret. Was his England tour over before it had begun?

He would have to play against Sussex at Hove in the match which started two days after the Kent game, he told himself. OK, Kirsy, strap on those pads.

It didn't take long for Kirsten to rediscover his England touch and it felt good to score a century, which grew to 130, in his first innings back. His calf was fine and he knew he had struck an important blow in keeping his Test berth.

Four matches later – some of them victims of the English weather – South Africa played Northamptonshire in their last game before the first Test, at Lord's. As history would have it, Allan Lamb celebrated his fortieth birthday the same weekend. It probably wasn't the best preparation for a Test match, but Kirsten spent much of his spare time in Northampton at Lamb's home, meeting a range of people his friend had invited to what began as a standard birthday party and evolved into an extended weekend of celebration.

Wisely, Lamb had made himself unavailable for the tour match against the South Africans. Kirsten didn't clock much time at the crease, scoring nine and 19 not out, but already the adrenalin was pumping and he knew he was ready for his first Test match in England.

Lord's was polished by sunshine as Andrew Hudson and Gary Kirsten emerged from that famous pavilion flanked by a forest of custard-and-cranberry MCC ties and panama hats adorned with I Zingari hatbands. The applause of a ground sold out months before swelled warmly as they made their way to the middle of the game's most recognisable arena to end South Africa's 34-year absence there.

In the team's hotel the previous evening, Wessels had stopped to have a chat with Kirsten and Craig Matthews, who were sharing a room. Wessels, whom Kirsten recalls as being remarkably relaxed in public on that tour, was in a confident mood. 'We're going to win the toss and we're going to bat,' he had announced.

And that was just the first of the many victories that went to make up South Africa's unblemished triumph in the Lord's Test. Four days later it was all over – South Africa had produced a stunning performance to win by all of 356 runs.

With the Sydney victory, this ranked as South Africa's finest hour in the new era. Michael Atherton's sand-in-the-pocket problems somewhat disappointingly grabbed the headlines in a country where an England defeat had long since ceased to stand on its own as a story, but there was unreserved praise for South Africa as well.

The only note of discord from a South African point of view was when Anglican Archbishop Desmond Tutu found that his clerical collar wasn't enough to gain him entry to the pavilion. No, sir, I'm afraid you require a jacket.

Kirsten's personal contribution was scores of eight and 42, as well as the catch which dismissed Phil DeFreitas in the second innings. But he would hold the spotlight later.

This one was reserved for Wessels. If the South African captain had been asked to script his idea of the perfect Test match, it would be no surprise if he plagiarised the saga of the Lord's Test of 1994. His century, off 217 balls and including 15 fours, was the centrepiece of a consummate batting performance which saw South Africa total 357.

England, with totals of 180 and 99, were barely in the match and the crowds which annexed the field immediately after the last English wicket fell were joyously, proudly South African.

The momentum flowed into the next match, against Nottinghamshire at Trent Bridge, where South Africa sailed home by 134 runs. Kirsten couldn't recall a time in his career when he felt fitter. It showed in his batting, and he scored 57 and 21 not out in his last outing before the second Test at Headingley.

Lord's might be the hallowed home of the game, but it's in Yorkshire and Lancashire that cricket courses strongest through the blood. Kirsten enjoyed the Headingley crowd. They were knowledgeable, unpretentious, and they appreciated his kind of cultured batsmanship.

But it is doubtful whether they could have foreseen the trouble ahead for South Africa, trouble which began the very minute Atherton won the toss and elected to bat.

How to bowl effectively at Headingley is a mystery of cricket that was only partly uncovered when, paradoxically, the TCCB declared that England's pitches should be covered. And the South African bowlers, hampered by Allan Donald being on light duty with a foot injury, were still in the dark when England declared at 477 for nine. Three half-centuries and a clutch of 20s and 30s gave the home side a total they could work with.

With the pitch's help, they were working with it far too well for South Africa's liking on the third day when the fall of the fourth wicket, with 91 runs on the board, summoned Kirsten to the crease.

Incredibly, in the light of their inept performance at Lord's, England had opened a chink in South Africa's armour which could conceivably lead them to squaring the series.

Really? Not if Peter Noel Kirsten had anything to do with it. South Africa needed guts, a steady hand and a master at the crease that day. In Kirsten, they got all three, and much more.

He remembered Geoff Boycott's advice to him for batting at Yorkshire headquarters: 'Get those feet dancin'.' And he did so, ultimately putting on 94 runs for the sixth wicket with Rhodes and 115 for the seventh with McMillan.

Kirsten's strokes might not have been as sound as 12 years previously and his timing seemed to come and go at will, but somehow he stayed in control.

The pitch was unusual, even for Headingley. It seemed to gain pace as the match progressed and increasingly variable bounce made shot selection a lottery. But Kirsten knew that if he got out early South Africa would find it extremely difficult to stay in the match and he hung on, sometimes by a coat of varnish that wasn't on his bat, sometimes through the instinct of what stroke to play. Lunch brought temporary relief from one of the toughest matches he had played.

Then, shortly after tea, with his 50 in the book, Kirsten took his eye off a bouncer from Darren Gough and it caromed off his helmet, sending him earthwards. Was that the end of it, this wonderfully defiant innings?

For the minutes that he lay on the turf receiving medical attention it certainly seemed so. But he wondered how many more chances he was going to have to complete a Test century and pull his country out of trouble. So …

He rose. Gloves, bat: time to go back to work.

Soon he was playing with confidence again and as the runs mounted the edge of the woods came back into view.

Into the 90s, and nervousness froze the blood in his veins. So close, so far. Come on!

The light was fading by the time DeFreitas started the third last over of the day, but there was enough left for Kirsten to stroke the ball into the covers and claim his maiden Test century. At 39, he was the second oldest man to do so. Headingley was on its feet; back home, South Africa was on its feet.

Then, having advanced to 104, DeFreitas found the shoulder of Kirsten's bat and the ball flew to point where Alec Stewart took a fine diving catch.

Kirsten, upset that he would not be able to bat on the next day, walked off to deafening cheers. He had spent almost five hours at the crease, facing 226 balls and hitting 13 fours.

That DeFreitas should have taken his wicket held sweet irony. He and Kirsten had talked of playing against each other in a Test match when they met while DeFreitas was playing for Boland in 1993-94. In the Castle Cup match against Border in East London, DeFreitas had bashed his way to a rare first-class century.

But this was Kirsten's moment. The reception in the dressingroom was chaotic. What a pity he hadn't scored his century at Lord's, he joked, so that he could have his name on the boards that record every player who makes a century or takes five wickets at the home of cricket. No problem, said Hansie Cronje, and promptly wrote up Kirsten's feat on the dressingroom wall.

The English press were waiting when he reached his hotel room, and he only escaped at 9.15 pm. Then the South African press invited him to the pub for three cheers and a drink. Somewhere in between Kirsten telephoned Tuffy and received a call from Allan Lamb.

It was heady stuff, all this sudden fame. The faxes poured in, one of them from Dr Jan van der Merwe who had operated on his knee in 1974 and told him to give up rugby, saying: 'Congratulations! I'm pleased you followed my advice.'

Kirsten had saved the match for South Africa, even if it did only end two days later when he collected his man of the match champagne. But the Headingley Test was also the turning point of the tour for South Africa. When they left Leeds, their fortunes plummeted.

And Kirsten was not to know then that it would be the last time he would have anything to celebrate on that tour.

Kirsten's last match before the Oval Test was against Minor Counties in Torquay. Though it wasn't quite the way to prepare for a series-deciding Test match, he was sure he was ready for it. After all, what could go wrong?

An edgy Wessels asked to have a word with him. Would he open the batting at the Oval, his captain wanted to know. Andrew Hudson, in pitiful form with 30 runs from his four Test innings, had lost confidence completely and didn't want to play in the match. Wessels, the obvious choice, said he wasn't keen to open as he wanted to keep the left-right contrast at the top of the order. Nobody else wanted the job.

'All right, I'll open.'

Looking back on that decision, Kirsten says, 'What I should have said was no way, I'm staying at number five. But you're approached to do a job and you do it for your team and your country.'

He also knew that Peter Pollock was keen to bring Cullinan, who had by now caught fire with the bat, into the side and he wondered if, in the process, his place would be on the line.

As it happened, the batting order was irrelevant as England won the match via two explosive events – Steve Rhodes and Phil DeFreitas thrashing an ailing Donald all round the ground to knock up 70 runs in 50 minutes for the eighth wicket on the third evening, which helped England reach 304 in reply to South Africa's 332, and Devon Malcolm's crushing 16.3-over burst that brought him nine for 57 on the fourth and last day.

The fourth best bowling analysis in England's history took them to victory by eight wickets.

Four days later South Africa went down by six wickets at Edgbaston in the first of two one-day internationals. The triumph at Lord's seemed a million miles away. The spirit the South Africans had created in that match felt just as far away. Wessels had retreated into his shell and there was a lack of control and guidance in the ranks.

The night before the first one-day match Dave Richardson, who was on the tour selection committee, had said to Kirsten, 'Make this the best innings you've ever played in a one-day game.'

Not quite. He was caught behind for eight. And when the team for the match at Old Trafford was announced, there was only one Kirsten in it – and it wasn't P N.

Kirsten marched on to Old Trafford on the morning of the match and confronted Mike Procter about his axing. Procter responded by telling him he was no longer in South Africa's one-day plans, according to Peter Pollock and the national selectors. It turned into an ugly slanging match.

Wessels approached Kirsten: 'If at this stage of your career you're going to be upset by being left out, you may as well retire now.' His words stung Kirsten, who watched from the boundary as South Africa went down by four wickets.

Surely it couldn't end like this? Oh no, there was worse to come.

The last match of what had by now become a morbid tour was against Holland in The Hague. It was a meaningless fixture – until South Africa lost by nine wickets, and to some it became the only match that mattered. South Africa were rudderless by then, not least because Wessels and Procter did not make the trip across the Channel for the game. The next time Kirsten saw Wessels was at Heathrow as the team prepared at last to return home. 'Kirsy,' Wessels asked worriedly, 'were there any dramas?'

It was a long flight home. Some slept; others talked quietly.

Kirsten spent the hours alone with his thoughts.

It would have been easy to let the negatives cloud the genuine victories of the England tour. He remembered the success and excitement of the first two Tests. He thought of the people he had met as well as the interrupted friendships that had been reconnected.

There had been good times, many of them.

But what ultimately banished any lingering bitterness was the realisation that in his country's colours he had accomplished much more than he could have dreamed possible. Isolation had denied many of his countrymen of similar age the opportunity to prove their worth on the international stage.

While Kirsten might have returned in the nick of time, he had found the reserves of talent and determination to make the most of his short time at the top. A lesser player – one of weaker will, of inferior skill – would not have made it that far. Many didn't, and others had sought honour and fame under foreign flags.

Kirsten had remained loyal to his country and to himself. He played his cricket to the limits of his gift for the game: the absence of Test cricket did not breed in him a lack of respect for the provincial game. All along the way, he had given his all – for his school, his provinces, and then for his country.

There were no regrets.

Peter Kirsten's Personal Team Selections

Peter Kirsten's selections include only players with and against whom he has played during his first-class career (1973-1996). He has chosen them on absolute merit and their general approach to the game. Slip fielding and agility in the field won the day for some!

South African Squad for Five-Day Tests

1	Barry Richards	– Technically, the master. A genius.
2	Jimmy Cook	– Determined and solid, and a fine fielder.
3	Kepler Wessels	– A gutsy fighter and a great slip fielder.
4	Graeme Pollock	– A simply brilliant, unorthodox genius.
5	Eddie Barlow	– Enthusiastic, with terrific presence on the field. A supreme slip fielder and a great all-rounder.
6	Kenny McEwan	– Wonderful flair; superb player of spin.
7	Clive Rice (captain)	– A great all-rounder: positive, disciplined and competitive.
8	Dave Richardson	– A highly efficient keeper and batsman.
9	Mike Procter	– Highly talented all-rounder.
10	Vince van der Bijl	– A fantastic bowler.
11	Allan Donald	– Exciting super-quick super-striker.
12	Garth le Roux	– Exciting, aggressive bowler with a killer instinct – and a fair batsman too.
13	Stephen Jefferies	– Brilliant left-arm swinger and quick.
14	Denys Hobson	– A match-winning leg-spinner for all occasions.
15	Pat Symcox	– An underrated off-spinner and effective batsman.

South African Squad for One-Day Internationals
1   Barry Richards
2   Jimmy Cook
3   Kenny McEwan
4   Graeme Pollock
5   Adrian Kuiper
6   Eddie Barlow
7   Clive Rice (captain)
8   Dave Richardson
9   Mike Procter
10   Vince van der Bijl
11   Garth le Roux
12   Denys Hobson
13   Jonty Rhodes
14   Hansie Cronje
15   Pat Symcox

World Squad for Five-Day Tests
1   Barry Richards
2   Gordon Greenidge
3   Brian Lara
4   Graeme Pollock
5   Viv Richards
6   Clive Lloyd (captain)
7   Ian Botham
8   Richard Hadlee
9   Malcolm Marshall
10   Ian Healy
11   Andy Roberts
12   Shane Warne
13   Allan Border
14   Allan Donald
15   Derek Underwood

Peter Kirsten's
Career Statistics

Compiled by Andrew Samson

Test Record: Match by Match

No.	Season	Against	Venue	How out	Score	Cts
1	1991/92	West Indies	Bridgetown	c Lara b Benjamin b Walsh	11 52	2
2	1992/93	India	Durban	c More b Srinath not out	13 11	
3	1992/93	India	Johannesburg	lbw b Prabhakar b Kumble	0 26	
4	1992/93	India	Port Elizabeth	c More b Venkatapathy Raju	0	1
5	1992/93	India	Cape Town	c More b Kapil Dev c Manjrekar b Kapil Dev	13 13	1
6	1993/94	Australia	Adelaide	c ME Waugh b Warne lbw b McDermott	79 42	
7	1993/94	Australia	Johannesburg	b May c Boon b May	12 53	
8	1993/94	Australia	Cape Town	lbw b Warne c Taylor b Warne	70 3	3
9	1993/94	Australia	Durban	lbw b SR Waugh	49	1
10	1994	England	Lord's	c Rhodes b Gough b Gough	8 42	
11	1994	England	Leeds	c Stewart b DeFreitas not out	104 8	
12	1994	England	The Oval	b Malcolm c DeFreitas b Malcolm	16 1	

Test Record: Series by Series

Season	Series	M	Inns	NO	Runs	HS	Ave	100	50	Ct	Balls	Runs	Wkts	Ave	BB	5I
1991/92	West Indies in West Indies	1	2	0	63	52	31.50	0	1	2	0	0	0	-	-	0
1992/93	India in South Africa	4	7	1	76	26	12.67	0	0	2	30	13	0	-	-	0
1993/94	Australia in Australia	1	2	0	121	79	60.50	0	1	0	24	17	0	-	-	0
1993/94	Australia in South Africa	3	5	0	187	70	37.40	0	2	4	0	0	0	-	-	0
1994	England in England	3	6	1	179	104	35.80	1	0	0	0	0	0	-	-	0
Totals		**12**	**22**	**2**	**626**	**104**	**31.30**	**1**	**4**	**8**	**54**	**30**	**0**	**-**	**-**	**0**

First-class Career Record – Season by Season

Season	Teams	M	Inns	NO	Runs	HS	Ave	100	50	Ct	Balls	Runs	Wkts	Ave	BB	5I
1973/74	WP	5	10	0	259	74	25.90	0	2	4	0	0	0	-	-	0
1974/75	WP	8	15	1	345	48*	24.64	0	0	8	114	35	2	17.50	2-15	0
1975	Sus	1	1	0	31	31	31.00	0	0	0	0	0	0	-	-	0
1975/76	WP/Inv XI	10	19	2	656	128*	38.59	2	2	5	0	0	0	-	-	0
1976/77	WP/SAU	9	15	1	1074	173*	76.71	6	1	8	108	38	2	19.00	2-20	0
1977/78	WP/SAU	9	15	1	579	106	41.36	3	1	7	265	99	1	99.00	1-70	0
1978	Derbs	20	35	4	1133	206*	36.55	2	7	11	1246	581	18	32.28	4-51	0
1978/79	WP	9	17	1	732	197	45.75	2	3	1	168	65	0	-	-	0
1979	Derbs	23	38	2	1148	135*	31.89	2	5	21	1617	752	19	39.58	4-44	0
1979/80	WP	8	14	2	551	93	45.92	0	4	3	342	166	6	27.67	2-7	0
1980	Derbs	21	36	6	1895	213*	63.17	6	8	12	173	90	1	90.00	1-44	0
1980/81	WP	7	13	6	337	73	25.92	0	3	3	18	9	0	-	-	0
1981	Derbs	21	35	6	1605	228	55.34	3	7	11	192	98	2	49.00	1-7	0
1981/82	WP/SA	12	19	3	948	151	59.25	4	3	11	150	60	2	30.00	1-0	0
1982	Derbs	21	37	7	1941	164*	64.70	8	6	12	726	348	9	38.67	3-25	0
1982/83	WP/SA	14	22	3	837	168	44.05	1	7	6	333	143	4	35.75	1-5	0
1983/84	WP/SA	11	19	1	805	100	44.72	1	9	6	168	87	2	43.50	1-14	0
1984/85	WP	8	14	2	511	133	42.58	2	2	5	660	330	5	66.00	2-29	0
1985/86	WP/SA	10	17	1	516	83	32.25	0	5	4	843	380	12	31.67	6-48	1
1986/87	WP/SA	12	21	2	921	204*	48.47	3	4	8	1437	659	7	94.14	2-24	0
1987/88	WP	7	12	2	398	82	39.80	0	3	4	318	135	2	67.50	2-46	0
1988/89	WP	7	14	0	442	66	31.57	0	4	4	60	39	0	-	-	0
1989/90	WP/SA	9	17	1	590	185	36.88	2	1	5	156	54	2	27.00	1-0	0
1990/91	Bdr	5	8	1	278	105	39.71	1	1	4	509	145	14	10.36	5-40	1
1991/92	Bdr	3	6	1	267	107	53.40	1	2	1	120	54	1	54.00	1-24	0
1991/92	SA in WI	1	2	0	63	52	31.50	0	1	2	0	0	0	-	-	0
1992/93	Bdr/SA	9	17	1	516	158	32.25	1	2	4	330	156	4	39.00	2-21	0
1993/94	Bdr/SA	9	14	0	872	271	62.29	2	4	6	36	33	0	-	-	0
1993/94	SA in Aus	1	2	0	121	79	60.50	0	1	6	24	17	0	-	-	0
1994	SA in Eng	10	16	5	549	130	49.91	2	1	5	108	76	2	38.00	1-23	0
1994/95	Bdr	9	15	2	350	60	26.92	0	2	4	66	33	0	-	-	0
Totals		309	535	58	21270	271	44.59	53	101	185	10287	4682	117	40.02	6-48	2

First-class Career Record – Each Competition

Competition	M	Inns	NO	Runs	HS	Ave	100	50	Ct	Balls	Runs	Wkts	Ave	BB	5I
Tests	12	22	2	626	104	31.30	1	4	8	54	30	0	-	-	0
Castle Cup	149	263	17	10260	271	41.71	24	51	82	4158	1926	35	55.03	6-48	1
UCB Bowl	5	8	1	278	105	39.71	1	1	4	509	145	14	10.36	5-40	1
County Championship	101	172	25	7535	228	51.26	20	32	63	3816	1811	45	40.24	4-44	0
Unofficial Tests	19	32	3	1192	173	41.10	3	7	10	985	422	13	32.46	3-61	0
Other First-class	23	38	10	1379	197	49.25	4	6	18	765	348	10	34.80	3-7	0

First-class Career Record – For each Team

Team	M	Inns	NO	Runs	HS	Ave	100	50	Ct	Balls	Runs	Wkts	Ave	BB	5I
Western Province	133	236	19	9087	204*	41.88	21	47	78	4128	1875	34	55.15	6-48	1
Derbyshire	106	181	25	7722	228	49.50	20	33	67	3954	1869	49	38.14	4-44	0
South Africa	38	64	9	2188	173	39.78	5	12	23	1147	528	15	35.20	3-61	0
Border	28	48	4	2020	271	45.91	5	9	13	1031	408	19	21.47	5-40	1
SA Universities	2	3	1	209	107	104.50	2	0	3	27	2	0	-	-	0
Sussex	1	1	0	31	31	31.00	0	0	0	0	0	0	-	-	0
Invitation XI	1	2	0	13	11	6.50	0	0	1	0	0	0	-	-	0

First-class Career Record – Against Each Team

Team	M	Inns	NO	Runs	HS	Ave	100	50	Ct	Balls	Runs	Wkts	Ave	BB	5I
Boland	5	6	0	163	105	27.17	1	0	4	438	136	10	13.60	4-7	0
Border	2	3	0	155	83	51.67	0	2	0	149	90	1	90.00	1-10	0
Eastern Province	36	62	4	2568	181	44.28	8	10	23	879	373	2	186.50	1-11	0
Griqualand West	2	3	1	107	74	53.50	0	1	0	293	100	8	12.50	5-40	1
Natal	33	61	5	1946	204*	34.75	4	11	20	915	377	8	47.13	2-7	0
Northern Transvaal	20	35	4	1556	271	50.19	4	7	14	627	347	10	34.70	2-29	1
Orange Free State	10	16	0	691	185	43.19	2	2	7	243	117	6	19.50	6-48	0
Rhodesia	12	21	3	838	128*	46.56	2	2	9	342	140	3	46.67	2-15	0
Transvaal	34	63	2	2602	168	42.66	6	16	10	1030	484	5	96.80	2-20	0
Western Province	2	4	0	98	51	24.50	0	1	1	0	0	0	-	-	0
Western Province B	1	2	0	56	41	28.00	0	0	2	0	0	0	-	-	0
SA Universities	1	2	1	200	197	200.00	1	0	0	108	40	0	-	-	0
Durham	1	1	1	42	42*	-	0	0	0	0	0	0	-	-	0
Essex	9	16	1	724	202*	48.27	2	3	3	128	74	3	24.67	3-58	0
Glamorgan	5	8	2	672	213*	112.00	2	1	6	154	40	2	20.00	1-0	0
Gloucestershire	5	7	0	270	143	38.57	1	0	4	306	150	7	21.43	3-25	0
Hampshire	4	7	0	276	63	39.43	0	4	5	444	180	5	36.00	3-82	0
Kent	5	7	1	123	31	20.50	0	0	1	102	69	0	-	-	0
Lancashire	9	15	3	810	204*	67.50	2	3	6	636	312	6	52.00	4-52	0
Leicestershire	10	16	3	651	135**	50.08	3	2	4	132	64	1	64.00	1-13	0
Middlesex	5	8	1	348	92	49.71	0	2	2	390	142	5	28.40	4-44	0
Northamptonshire	11	19	3	825	209*	51.56	2	4	6	486	236	4	59.00	1-19	0
Nottinghamshire	8	15	2	464	75	35.69	0	4	6	90	70	4	17.50	4-51	0
Somerset	4	7	2	374	228	74.80	2	0	3	126	62	1	62.00	1-18	0
Surrey	4	8	5	556	164*	185.33	3	2	2	150	67	1	67.00	1-7	0
Sussex	6	9	1	635	130	79.38	3	2	2	120	76	2	38.00	1-32	0
Warwickshire	5	10	1	265	91	29.44	0	2	3	114	73	0	-	-	0
Worcestershire	5	10	1	213	66	23.67	0	1	6	232	92	2	46.00	2-30	0

First-class Career Record – Against Each Team (continued)

Team	M	Inns	NO	Runs	HS	Ave	100	50	Ct	Balls	Runs	Wkts	Ave	BB	5I
Yorkshire	10	16	1	596	140*	39.73	1	3	9	272	136	3	45.33	2-38	0
Minor Counties	1	2	1	29	15	29.00	0	0	0	0	0	0	-	-	0
President's XI	1	1	0	32	32	32.00	0	0	0	42	44	1	44.00	1-44	0
AROSA Sri Lankans	3	3	1	100	70*	50.00	0	1	1	201	99	3	33.00	1-5	0
Australia	6	10	0	381	79	38.10	0	3	5	60	33	1	33.00	1-16	0
Australian XI	7	13	1	512	173	42.67	2	1	6	676	288	8	36.00	3-61	0
DH Robins	1	2	0	80	55	40.00	0	1	0	0	0	0	-	-	0
England	3	6	1	179	104	35.80	1	0	0	0	0	0	-	-	0
English XI	1	2	1	21	17*	21.00	0	0	2	0	0	0	-	-	0
India	5	8	1	90	26	12.86	0	0	1	30	13	0	-	-	0
International Wanderers	1	2	0	13	11	6.50	0	0	0	0	0	0	-	-	0
Pakistan	1	2	0	60	58	30.00	0	1	3	66	26	3	8.67	3-7	0
SAB English XI	4	7	2	324	114	64.80	1	2	1	42	17	1	17.00	1-7	0
Sri Lanka	2	4	1	103	48	34.33	0	0	1	102	49	0	-	-	0
West Indian XI	7	12	1	455	88	41.36	0	6	4	162	66	1	66.00	1-14	0
West Indies	2	4	0	67	52	16.75	0	1	4	0	0	0	-	-	0

First-class Career Record – At each Venue

Venue	M	Inns	NO	Runs	HS	Ave	100	50	Ct	Balls	Runs	Wkts	Ave	BB	5I
In South Africa															
Bloemfontein (Ramblers)	1	1	0	25	25	25.00	0	0	1	129	48	6	8.00	6-48	1
Bloemfontein (Schoeman Park)	1	1	0	107	107	107.00	1	0	1	0	0	0	-	-	0
Bloemfontein (Springbok Park)	2	4	0	141	47	35.25	0	0	0	12	17	0	-	-	0
Bloemfontein (UOFS)	2	3	0	94	82	31.33	0	1	1	42	14	0	-	-	0
Bredasdorp	1	2	0	33	17	16.50	0	0	1	222	91	4	22.75	2-21	0
Bulawayo (Queens)	2	3	0	70	40	23.33	0	0	4	0	0	0	-	-	0
Cape Town	77	135	16	5769	204*	48.48	16	32	52	2815	1243	26	47.81	3-61	0
Durban	22	40	1	1048	133	26.87	2	5	12	514	208	8	26.00	2-24	0
East London (Buffalo Park)	15	23	3	1109	271	55.45	3	5	6	435	181	3	60.33	1-24	0
Johannesburg	25	47	2	1711	168	38.02	2	12	3	257	160	1	160.00	1-5	0
Kimberley	1	2	1	33	30	33.00	0	0	0	209	74	7	10.57	5-40	1
Paarl	1	1	0	15	15	15.00	0	0	1	0	0	0	-	-	0
Pietermaritzburg (Jan Smuts)	1	2	0	79	66	39.50	0	1	0	12	14	0	-	-	0
Port Elizabeth	23	39	2	1417	181	38.30	4	5	21	897	372	2	186.00	1-11	0
Pretoria	6	11	1	208	86	20.80	0	1	4	258	158	3	52.67	2-78	0
Salisbury (Police)	5	9	1	367	123	45.88	1	1	2	174	83	1	83.00	1-70	0
Stellenbosch (Coetzenburg)	1	2	1	200	197	200.00	1	0	0	108	40	0	-	-	0
Stellenbosch (Oude Libertas)	1	2	0	113	105	56.50	1	0	2	93	7	5	1.40	4-7	0
Verwoerdburg	3	6	0	245	92	40.83	0	2	0	24	10	0	-	-	0
Totals	190	333	28	12784	271	41.91	31	65	111	6201	2720	66	658.53	0	2

First-class Career Record – At each Venue (continued)

Venue	M	Inns	NO	Runs	HS	Ave	100	50	Ct	Balls	Runs	Wkts	Ave	BB	5I
In England															
Basingstoke	1	2	0	101	51	50.50	0	2	3	300	131	3	43.67	3-82	0
Birmingham	3	6	0	209	91	34.83	0	2	1	36	17	0	-	-	0
Blackpool	1	1	1	204	204*	-	1	0	0	48	17	0	-	-	0
Bristol	1	1	0	31	31	31.00	0	0	2	54	24	1	24.00	1-23	0
Burton-on-Trent	2	3	0	23	15	7.67	0	0	2	54	25	0	-	-	0
Canterbury	1	1	0	16	16	16.00	0	0	0	0	0	0	-	-	0
Chelmsford	1	2	0	14	11	7.00	0	0	0	110	58	3	19.33	3-58	0
Chesterfield	21	35	5	1327	206*	44.23	4	5	16	562	269	8	33.63	4-52	0
Chester-le-Street	1	1	1	42	42*	-	0	0	0	0	0	0	-	-	0
Coalville	1	2	0	186	102	93.00	1	1	0	78	38	0	-	-	0
Colchester	1	2	0	89	58	44.50	0	1	0	0	0	0	-	-	0
Dartford	1	0	0	0	0	-	0	0	0	0	0	0	-	-	0
Derby	30	50	11	2598	213*	66.62	7	11	20	1411	630	19	33.16	4-44	0
Eastbourne	1	2	0	153	85	76.50	0	2	0	0	0	0	-	-	0
Gloucester	2	4	0	200	143	50.00	1	0	1	234	121	6	20.17	3-25	0
Hove	3	4	0	241	130	60.25	1	0	2	60	32	1	32.00	1-32	0
Ilkeston	1	1	0	0	0	0.00	0	0	2	0	0	0	-	-	0
Leeds	2	3	1	198	104	99.00	1	1	3	24	13	1	13.00	1-13	0
Leicester	4	7	2	264	135*	52.80	1	1	1	12	13	0	-	-	0
Liverpool	1	2	0	21	14	10.50	0	0	1	222	116	1	116.00	1-69	0
Lord's	4	8	1	315	92	45.00	0	2	1	107	54	0	-	-	0
Maidstone	1	2	0	20	20	10.00	0	0	0	42	20	0	-	-	0
Manchester	3	6	2	301	162*	75.25	1	1	1	30	16	0	-	-	0
Northampton	6	9	1	230	67	28.75	0	1	1	138	84	1	84.00	1-76	0
Nottingham	4	8	1	267	75	38.14	0	2	3	0	0	0	-	-	0
Portsmouth	1	2	0	48	36	24.00	0	0	0	0	0	0	-	-	0
Scarborough	3	5	1	240	140*	60.00	1	0	0	42	44	1	44.00	1-44	0

First-class Career Record – At each Venue (continued)

Venue	M	Inns	NO	Runs	HS	Ave	100	50	Ct	Balls	Runs	Wkts	Ave	BB	5I
In England (continued)															
Sheffield	2	3	0	38	31	12.67	0	0	3	122	77	2	38.50	2-38	0
Southend	2	4	0	171	113	42.75	1	0	1	0	0	0	-	-	0
Swansea	2	3	0	121	47	40.33	0	0	2	24	9	1	9.00	1-1	0
Taunton	2	3	0	231	228	77.00	1	0	0	90	44	0	-	-	0
The Oval	3	6	2	134	103*	33.50	1	0	0	48	16	1	16.00	1-7	0
Torquay	1	2	1	29	15	29.00	0	0	0	0	0	0	-	-	0
Worcester	3	6	0	163	66	27.17	0	1	3	214	77	2	38.50	2-30	0
Worksop	1	2	0	77	75	38.50	0	1	1	0	0	0	-	-	0
Totals	**117**	**198**	**30**	**8302**	**228**	**49.42**	**22**	**34**	**72**	**4062**	**1945**	**51**	**38.14**	**4-44**	**0**
In West Indies															
Bridgetown	1	2	0	63	52	31.50	0	1	2	0	0	0	-	-	0
In Australia															
Adelaide	1	2	0	121	79	60.50	0	1	0	24	17	0	-	-	0

First-class Career Record – Record as captain and as player

	M	Inns	NO	Runs	HS	Ave	100	50	Ct	Balls	Runs	Wkts	Ave	BB	5I
Captain	65	109	12	4589	271	47.31	11	27	42	1836	861	16	53.81	3-82	0
Player	244	426	46	16681	228	43.90	42	74	143	8451	3821	101	37.83	6-48	2

First-class Career Record – Captaincy Record

Team	P	W	L	D
Border	23	6	9	8
Derbyshire	8	0	2	6
South Africa	6	4	1	1
SA Universities	1	0	0	1
Western Province	27	14	3	10
Totals	**65**	**24**	**15**	**26**

First-class centuries (53)

Season	Score	For	Against	Venue
1975/76	128 *	Western Province	Rhodesia	Cape Town
	123	Western Province	Rhodesia	Salisbury
1976/77	173 *	Western Province	Eastern Province	Cape Town
	103			
	107	SA Universities	Orange Free State	Bloemfontein
	165	Western Province	Transvaal	Johannesburg
	111	Western Province	Natal	Durban
	128	Western Province	Transvaal	Cape Town
1977/78	102 *	SA Universities	Eastern Province	Port Elizabeth
	106	Western Province	Transvaal	Cape Town
	106	Western Province	Natal	Cape Town
1978	206 *	Derbyshire	Glamorgan	Chesterfield
1978/79	197	Western Province	SA Universities	Stellenbosch
	105	Western Province	Transvaal	Cape Town
1979	103 *	Derbyshire	Surrey	The Oval
	135 *	Derbyshire	Leicestershire	Leicester
1980	162 *	Derbyshire	Lancashire	Manchester
	209 *	Derbyshire	Northamptonshire	Derby
	213 *	Derbyshire	Glamorgan	Derby
	202 *	Derbyshire	Essex	Chesterfield
	101	Derbyshire	Somerset	Chesterfield
	116	Derbyshire	Sussex	Derby
1981	114	Derbyshire	Northamptonshire	Derby
	228	Derbyshire	Somerset	Taunton
	204 *	Derbyshire	Lancashire	Blackpool
1981/82	114	Western Province	Eastern Province	Cape Town
	130	Western Province	Northern Transvaal	Cape Town
	114	South Africa	SAB English XI	Cape Town
	151	Western Province	Eastern Province	Port Elizabeth
1982	143	Derbyshire	Gloucestershire	Gloucester
	121 *	Derbyshire	Leicestershire	Derby
	102	Derbyshire	Leicestershire	Coalville
	113	Derbyshire	Essex	Southend
	164 *	Derbyshire	Surrey	Derby
	123 *			
	105 *	Derbyshire	Sussex	Chesterfield
	140 *	Derbyshire	Yorkshire	Scarborough
1982/83	168	Western Province	Transvaal	Johannesburg
1983/84	100	Western Province	Transvaal	Cape Town
1984/85	126 *	Western Province	Northern Transvaal	Cape Town
	133	Western Province	Natal	Durban
1986/87	204 *	Western Province	Natal	Cape Town
	173	South Africa	Australian XI	Cape Town
	105 *			
1989/90	185	Western Province	Orange Free State	Cape Town
	128	Western Province	Eastern Province	Port Elizabeth
1990/91	105	Border	Boland	Stellenbosch
1991/92	107	Border	Northern Transvaal	East London
1992/93	158	Border	Eastern Province	East London
1993/94	181	Border	Eastern Province	Port Elizabeth
	271	Border	Northern Transvaal	East London
1994	130	South Africa	Sussex	Hove
	104	South Africa	England	Leeds

Limited Overs Career Record

Limited Overs Internationals

Season	Series	M	Inns	NO	Runs	HS	Ave	100	50	Ct	Balls	Runs	Wkts	Ave	RpO	BB	4I
1991/92	India in India	3	3	1	95	86*	47.50	0	1	1	18	23	1	23.00	7.67	1-23	0
1991/92	World Cup in Aus & NZ	8	8	2	410	90	68.33	0	4	2	108	87	5	17.40	4.83	3-31	0
1991/92	West Indies in West Indies	3	3	0	52	28	17.33	0	0	0	54	38	0	-	4.22	-	0
1992/93	India in India	7	7	1	210	56	35.00	0	1	3	0	0	0	-	-	-	0
1992/93	Total Triangular Series in SA	6	6	1	139	45*	27.80	0	0	1	3	4	0	-	8.00	-	0
1993/94	B & H World Series in Aus	6	6	1	205	97	41.00	0	2	3	0	0	0	-	-	-	0
1993/94	Australia in South Africa	6	6	0	174	53	29.00	0	1	1	0	0	0	-	-	-	0
1994	England in England	1	1	0	8	8	8.00	0	0	0	0	0	0	-	-	-	0
Totals		**40**	**40**	**6**	**1293**	**97**	**38.03**	**0**	**9**	**11**	**183**	**152**	**6**	**25.33**	**4.98**	**3-31**	**0**

Limited Overs Internationals: Record against each country

Against	M	Inns	NO	Runs	HS	Ave	100	50	Ct	Balls	Runs	Wkts	Ave	RpO	BB	4I
Australia	11	11	2	281	53	31.22	0	1	3	0	0	0	-	-	-	0
England	3	3	0	30	11	10.00	0	0	0	6	9	0	-	9.00	-	0
India	11	11	2	389	86*	43.22	0	3	5	18	23	1	23.00	7.67	1-23	0
New Zealand	3	3	0	237	97	79.00	0	3	2	42	22	1	22.00	3.14	1-22	0
Pakistan	3	3	0	54	35	18.00	0	0	1	0	0	0	-	-	-	0
Sri Lanka	1	1	0	47	47	47.00	0	0	0	30	25	1	25.00	5.00	1-25	0
West Indies	7	7	1	193	56	32.17	0	1	0	57	42	0	-	4.42	-	0
Zimbabwe	1	1	1	62	62*	-	0	1	0	30	31	3	10.33	6.20	3-31	0

Limited Overs Career Record (*Continued*)

In South Africa:

Gillette Cup/Datsun Shield/Nissan Shield/Total Power Series

Season	Team	M	Inns	NO	Runs	HS	Ave	100	50	Ct	Balls	Runs	Wkts	Ave	RpO	BB	4I
1973/74	Western Province	1	1	0	10	10	10.00	0	0	1	0	0	0	-	-	-	0
1974/75	Western Province	3	3	1	55	26	27.50	0	0	2	0	0	0	-	-	-	0
1975/76	Western Province	3	3	0	54	41	18.00	0	0	0	0	0	0	-	-	-	0
1976/77	Western Province	2	2	1	45	23	45.00	0	0	0	0	0	0	-	-	-	0
1977/78	Western Province	1	1	0	2	2	2.00	0	0	0	0	0	0	-	-	-	0
1978/79	Western Province	1	1	0	18	18	18.00	0	0	0	18	11	0	-	3.67	-	0
1979/80	Western Province	3	3	0	91	60	30.33	0	1	1	132	79	1	79.00	3.59	1-29	0
1980/81	Western Province	4	4	0	26	17	6.50	0	0	3	12	13	0	-	6.50	-	0
1981/82	Western Province	4	4	1	128	57*	42.67	0	1	1	24	16	0	-	4.00	-	0
1982/83	Western Province	4	4	1	274	119	91.33	1	2	3	0	0	0	-	-	-	0
1983/84	Western Province	5	5	0	84	40	16.80	0	0	2	107	48	8	6.00	2.69	6-17	1
1984/85	Western Province	4	4	0	124	105	31.00	1	0	1	180	86	2	43.00	2.87	2-30	0
1985/86	Western Province	5	5	0	232	72	46.40	0	2	2	264	140	2	70.00	3.18	1-24	0
1986/87	Western Province	5	5	1	215	117*	53.75	1	0	0	168	149	2	74.50	5.32	1-22	0
1987/88	Western Province	5	5	0	192	72	38.40	0	3	0	108	84	2	42.00	4.67	2-55	0
1988/89	Western Province	6	6	0	352	108	58.67	1	3	0	120	83	1	83.00	4.15	1-34	0
1989/90	Western Province	6	6	0	327	126	54.50	1	3	2	84	72	5	14.40	5.14	3-39	0
1990/91	Border	3	3	0	33	20	11.00	0	0	0	66	48	0	-	4.36	-	0
1991/92	Border	5	5	0	127	43	25.40	0	0	0	174	141	2	70.50	4.86	1-25	0
1992/93	Border	2	2	0	18	17	9.00	0	0	1	46	31	2	15.50	4.04	1-15	0
Totals		**72**	**72**	**5**	**2407**	**126**	**35.93**	**5**	**15**	**19**	**1503**	**1001**	**27**	**37.07**	**4.00**	**6-17**	**1**

Limited Overs Career Record (*Continued*)

Benson & Hedges Night Series

Season	Team	M	Inns	NO	Runs	HS	Ave	100	50	Ct	Balls	Runs	Wkts	Ave	RpO	BB	4I
1981/82	Western Province	2	2	0	40	28	20.00	0	0	1	12	16	0	-	8.00	-	0
1982/83	Western Province	6	6	0	227	94	37.83	0	2	1	0	0	0	-	-	-	0
1983/84	Western Province	5	5	0	231	70	46.20	0	3	3	30	21	3	7.00	4.20	3-7	0
1984/85	Western Province	4	4	0	132	52	33.00	0	2	2	94	41	4	10.25	2.62	3-8	0
1985/86	Western Province	6	6	1	184	52	36.80	0	1	2	216	155	3	51.67	4.31	1-37	0
1986/87	Western Province	7	7	0	189	54	27.00	0	1	4	174	94	5	18.80	3.24	3-26	0
1987/88	Western Province	9	9	0	361	93	40.11	0	4	7	30	25	0	-	5.00	-	0
1988/89	Western Province	9	9	0	328	86	36.44	0	4	8	84	63	0	-	4.50	-	0
1989/90	Western Province	9	9	1	329	104*	41.13	1	1	3	144	96	3	32.00	4.00	3-21	0
1990/91	Border	7	6	1	265	98*	53.00	0	2	0	102	83	1	83.00	4.88	1-21	0
1991/92	Border	5	5	1	157	71*	39.25	0	2	1	48	30	1	30.00	3.75	1-7	0
1992/93	Border	1	1	0	39	39	39.00	0	0	0	54	35	1	35.00	3.89	1-35	0
1993/94	Border	8	8	1	395	134*	56.43	1	2	3	234	161	2	80.50	4.13	1-27	0
1994/95	Border	10	9	2	229	81	32.71	0	2	3	6	7	0	-	7.00	-	0
Totals		**88**	**86**	**7**	**3106**	**134***	**39.32**	**2**	**26**	**38**	**1228**	**827**	**23**	**35.96**	**4.04**	**3-7**	**0**

Unofficial Limited Overs Internationals

Season	Against	M	Inns	NO	Runs	HS	Ave	100	50	Ct	Balls	Runs	Wkts	Ave	RpO	BB	4I
1981/82	SAB English XI	3	3	0	50	32	16.67	0	0	0	8	3	1	3.00	2.25	1-3	0
1982/83	AROSA Sri Lankans	4	4	1	214	100	71.33	1	1	1	150	80	0	-	3.20	-	0
1982/83	West Indian XI	6	6	0	82	50	13.67	0	1	0	52	54	0	-	6.23	-	0
1983/84	West Indian XI	5	5	0	141	55	28.20	0	1	0	78	41	1	41.00	3.15	1-12	0
1985/86	Australian XI	3	3	0	73	26	24.33	0	0	1	18	13	0	-	4.33	-	0
1986/87	Australian XI	6	6	2	282	87	70.50	0	2	2	0	0	0	-	-	-	0
1989/90	English XI	3	3	0	52	40	17.33	0	0	1	84	48	0	-	3.43	-	0
Totals		**30**	**30**	**3**	**894**	**100**	**33.11**	**1**	**5**	**5**	**390**	**239**	**2**	**119.50**	**3.68**	**1-3**	**0**

Limited Overs Career Record (*Continued*)

In England:

Gillette Cup/NatWest Trophy

Season	Team	M	Inns	NO	Runs	HS	Ave	100	50	Ct	Balls	Runs	Wkts	Ave	RpO	BB	4I
1978	Derbyshire	2	2	0	6	6	3.00	0	0	0	108	61	4	15.25	3.39	2-15	0
1979	Derbyshire	1	1	0	0	0	0.00	0	0	0	30	14	0	-	2.80	-	0
1980	Derbyshire	1	1	0	29	29	29.00	0	0	1	0	0	0	-	-	-	0
1981	Derbyshire	5	5	1	229	84	57.25	0	2	2	12	8	0	-	4.00	-	0
1982	Derbyshire	1	1	1	110	110*	-	1	0	1	18	21	0	-	7.00	-	0
Totals		**10**	**10**	**2**	**374**	**110***	**46.75**	**1**	**2**	**4**	**168**	**104**	**4**	**26.00**	**3.71**	**2-15**	**0**

Benson & Hedges Cup

Season	Team	M	Inns	NO	Runs	HS	Ave	100	50	Ct	Balls	Runs	Wkts	Ave	RpO	BB	4I
1978	Derbyshire	5	5	0	100	41	20.00	0	0	2	36	30	1	30.00	5.00	1-16	0
1979	Derbyshire	6	5	1	207	70	51.75	0	2	3	114	94	3	31.33	4.95	1-6	0
1980	Derbyshire	4	3	0	89	52	29.67	0	1	3	84	70	1	70.00	5.00	1-14	0
1981	Derbyshire	4	4	1	76	65	25.33	0	1	2	36	18	0	-	3.00	-	0
1982	Derbyshire	5	5	1	296	77*	74.00	0	4	1	42	39	1	39.00	5.57	1-10	0
Totals		**24**	**22**	**3**	**768**	**77***	**40.42**	**0**	**8**	**11**	**312**	**251**	**6**	**41.83**	**4.83**	**1-6**	**0**

John Player Sunday League

Season	Team	M	Inns	NO	Runs	HS	Ave	100	50	Ct	Balls	Runs	Wkts	Ave	RpO	BB	4I
1978	Derbyshire	11	11	0	216	88	19.64	0	1	0	183	146	8	18.25	4.79	4-13	1
1979	Derbyshire	13	13	2	388	102	35.27	1	2	6	186	149	8	18.63	4.81	5-34	1
1980	Derbyshire	15	15	0	395	89	26.33	0	3	11	179	161	6	26.83	5.40	2-31	0
1981	Derbyshire	15	15	1	425	63	30.36	0	4	4	78	54	3	18.00	4.15	2-15	0
1982	Derbyshire	15	15	1	404	72	28.86	0	2	5	96	72	1	72.00	4.50	1-6	0
Totals		**69**	**69**	**4**	**1828**	**102**	**28.12**	**1**	**12**	**26**	**722**	**582**	**26**	**22.38**	**4.84**	**5-34**	**2**

Selected Index